The Messenger

The Void Runners Book 1

The Messenger

Michael J. Kearey

The Void Runners Trilogy

The Messenger

The Journey

The Signal

For those that believed

First Edition 2016

© Michael J. Kearey 2015

Cover art: Robert Batt

Editing: Amy Kearey, Margret Horwood

I walked across and empty land
I knew the pathway like the back of my hand
I felt the earth beneath my feet
Sat by the river and it made me complete

Oh simple thing where have you gone
I'm getting old and I need something to rely on
So tell me when you're gonna let me in
I'm getting tired and I need somewhere to begin

I came across a fallen tree
I felt the branches of it looking at me
Is this the place we used to love?
Is this the place that I've been dreaming of?

Oh simple thing where have you gone
I'm getting old and I need something to rely on
So tell me when you're gonna let me in
I'm getting tired and I need somewhere to begin

And if you have a minute why don't we go
Talk about it somewhere only we know?
This could be the end of everything
So why don't we go
Somewhere only we know?
Somewhere only we know?

Keane – Somewhere only we know

Preface

Can you imagine a world other than this one? Another universe just as huge as our own and occurring at all times and places all at once. One that is right around us even now.

A place where dreamers go on their night-time adventures only to awake in the morning with little or no memory of where they have been, or what they saw, or what they did.

Imagine a place where the souls of the dead go and where time is endless and meaningless. Somewhere you can go and exist in your own little dream world, but more likely your nightmares.

Imagine having no real body but being able to be hurt all the same. Imagine having no memory of where you came from or where you are going. Imagine your thoughts, memories and the very essence of your soul creating everything around you and those things becoming your reality.

Perhaps you should start to prepare yourself - that other world is real.

The cruel and wicked of heart will wander for countless years in misery. Of course they will find the exit eventually to one of the realms beyond, but that may be even worse unless they have changed their ways.

The goodly souls of this world, well they don't stay there for long. They soon find the way into the place of light on the other side, to forever forget their troubles and worries of their all too brief lives here on Earth.

It's not too late to change your ways. An act of kindness every day keeps the nightmares away, or so they say.

Those who choose the path of selfishness and greed just remember my warning; I am only trying to help. It's my act of kindness for the day.

So for you reading this now, I hope you spend less time wanting in this world and start making your plans for the next, because like it or not you will be going to the Void. You may be in for a long stay, but some of you may get lucky - we might find you first. We are the Void Runners, and I'm Squire Fox.

I.

The night was still in the small village of Shillyford in the heart of England. The last of the pub patrons had shambled home and left the empty streets to the roaming cats and the occasional fox. The eerie orange glow of the street lamps cast its light into a damp fog that gently swirled through the silent alleyways of the now sleeping huddle of brown stone houses.

It was from one of these alleyways that a ghostly figure moved with some purpose. Pausing to glance both ways up the empty street Squire Fox moved without a sound save for the occasional gentle crunch of his black boots on the pavement. An unseen silent wraith in the night he turned in the direction that led out of the village.

He was nothing out of the ordinary being a standard tall, blonde and blue eyed man in his late forties. His skin was weathered and dry from more than just his age. The challenges of his life would be hard for anyone to even imagine. It was true that in reality he had seen better days. His short, spiky hair was thinning and the blonde colour was fading slightly to grey. His body was slowly failing him but his fitness and agility would come as a surprise to many. Those that knew him best also knew his true strength was hidden away from view and was beating in his chest.

He passed lines of houses; their dark windows like unseen eyes watching him and deliberating where he might be heading at this hour of the night. Squire pulled his lapels in closer as a brief chill ran through him. The fog dew stuck to his coat like someone had sprinkled him with a layer of tiny diamonds and his hair glinted with moisture under the glow of the lights overhead.

A tabby cat ran briskly across the road but stopped in its tracks to view the oncoming threat. After a pause to consider whether the newcomer was friend or foe the cat decided it didn't care and carried on its search for some mischief elsewhere. It jumped over a low wall and vanished into the garden beyond.

Some distance behind now a second figure slipped from the alleyway like a ghost in the darkness. Like Squire had before, the second figure checked the street in both directions watching for the slightest thing that was out of place.

Keeping to the shadows and hiding places it moved off in pursuit of Squire Fox who was just out of sight and heading up the road.

As Squire reached the end of the village the pavement ended and gave way to a grass verge by the roadside. Now the last streetlight in Shillyford cast its lazy glow on the figure below who paused and stopped to take a slow steady look over his shoulder. He saw the village street laid out before him damp and shiny, but nothing moved and all was quiet. Once more he turned and continued on his way.

The streetlights slowly withdrew behind him as he strode into the gloom with his head down. Tonight he had important things on his mind and butterflies started to stir in his stomach. The emotional and physical roller coaster ride he was heading on was going to test his spirit once more.

A thousand times or more he had run the Void and his time was running out quickly. Life gives everyone a certain amount of luck and Squire was heavily in debt and knew it well.

A little way behind him a second figure slipped over a low garden wall and followed in the same direction, but now used the edge of the field that bordered the road. It moved like liquid black ink in the gloom with eyes scanning in all directions, but mainly on the dark shape of the retreating figure it shadowed.

Squire's journey now took him beyond the range of the street lights behind him, but he walked without concern into the damp darkness. This walk was a very familiar one to him; one he had walked many times before, and failing any trouble tonight would be walking again all too soon.

With his long black coat gently flapping beside him, he soon took a turning to his right which led away from the small road and into an even smaller gravel lane. Hemmed in on both sides by dense vegetation almost no light at all reached him save for the dim orange glow in the sky somewhere off to his right where the streetlights tried in vain to follow him. His boots crunched on the gravel with every step and there was the occasional snapping sound as a small twig cracked underfoot. It was as if they had been dropped carelessly by the trees overhead in an effort to make his silent approach almost impossible.

Some way behind him the second shadow arrived at the end of the gravel lane and stopped. Looking hard into the darkness down the lane and up the road in both directions the silent watcher slipped into the undergrowth and vanished from sight.

Further up the lane Squire still moved as silently as he could, although his thoughts were far away from this place. In the distance up ahead a dim bulb flickered against the foggy night like a lighthouse on a silent sea. Its wan, pale light cast a halo around itself in the drifting grey fog. Squire walked straight towards it and in minutes the dim shape of a darkened barn started to take shape around it. Giving a muffled cough he quickened his pace and headed for the weathered wooden door.

He paused in front of the dark building and slowly turned to the left and the right and gave the dark on both sides of him a good inspection. Not a sound reached out to him; as if the damp air had taken away even the small sounds of scampering tiny feet, and the rustlings of leaves that Squire knew had to be there. Satisfied he was totally alone and hadn't been followed he reached out and took the metal ring door handle in his right hand and gave it a quick twist. The metallic clink of the latch was the only sound as the door silently swung outwards. Gently closing the door behind him he headed into the open ground floor of the barn that was like a second home to him.

The large room he entered was a mixture of vintage farm and the latest in high technology. Old fashioned tools lined the walls along with the odd straw bale and every manner of the weird and wonderful components that make up a farm from the past. The faded wood plank floor was covered here and there in straw, but standing out from it was a painted white cross running from both sides of the barn and meeting roughly in the middle. On either side of that were two huge metal ring-like plates nearly as tall as a man. Wires ran from these and headed off to a jumble of electronic gadgets that were all piled up on top of each other on a bench that stood just off the centre of the floor.

To the average onlooker it was a barn full of junk and some machinery but the secrets were there if anyone chose to look harder. Behind the building two giant generators sat beneath their soundproofed bunkers. The cellar too was a little out of the ordinary; a computer mainframe and assorted electronics and the whole thing insulated and sound proofed in lead and concrete.

Stood in the middle of the barn busily huddled over the benches was the dark shape of Squire's brother Kass. His back was to the door where Squire had just entered but he didn't turn or pause in his work.

"If I had a gun," he began, his voice deep and slow, "and wanted to shoot you, I could have put a bullet between your eyes just from the sound of that cough." There was a gentle clink sound as something he was busy working on popped into place. Kass was taller and slimmer than Squire and was also a lot younger. He had long black hair which hung well beyond his shoulders and his complexion was pale as if it had forgotten what the sun was. In the dim light of the barn his pigment appeared almost grey and sickly. He chose simple solutions whenever possible so he wore black clothing which would be appropriate for any occasion. He wore a pair of black combat trousers littered with pockets, a black long sleeve T-shirt and a long black leather jacket accompanied by black boots.

"You don't have a gun," Squire replied while busily shoving his hands into the pockets of his coat and searching through them.

"I know I don't have a gun," Kass responded in a tone of quiet exasperation. "I was just saying that if I did." Sarcasm and the Fox family ran deeply together, and while it may have been considered the lowest form of wit, it came high on the entertainment level.

Squire had now begun one by one to search through the many pockets inside his coat. "If my memory serves me correctly," Squire retorted without looking up from his search, "the last time you fired a gun you failed to hit the target completely." With a satisfied sigh he

16

withdrew his cigarettes from a hidden pocket and quickly removed one.

Kass stopped what he was working on, gently laying the palms of his hands on the bench and turned his head slightly towards his brother. "Would this be the Fargle that was no bigger than a tennis ball?"

"That's the one," Squire responded from the side of his mouth that didn't hold the now lit cigarette.

"I recall I was falling at several hundred miles an hour at the time," Kass responded now slightly defensively.

"And you missed."

"Yes."

"And I hit." Squire blew out a long cloud of smoke and started walking towards his brother.

"Yes," Kass remembered gently nodding with a hint of a smile on his face. It had been a miracle of a shot Kass recalled, almost impossible, yet Squire had done it with calm nonchalance. The Master had always said Squire carried luck around like a jailor carried keys and in the past it had certainly been the case.

Fargles were the only natural predator in the Void, and together they had thankfully only ever run into a few on their travels. Almost shark like in appearance they patrolled the empty spaces and ate anything that wasn't supposed to be there. They could be very small or very big but they were always hellish fast.

"You should give those things up," Kass replied now turning and perching himself gently on the edge of the bench, "they make you cough."

"I know," Squire smiled, "but only because one day, if my head ever becomes as big as a barn door you might be able to shoot me in it."

They both laughed now, but it was a controlled gentle thing. Kass had a hawk like facial structure and a dark goatee which had run a little out of control of late. He didn't have time or energy for excessive grooming.

"I see Doris is working again?" Squire tipped his head gently in the direction of the bench.

Kass gave a gentle nod of affirmation and turned slowly to look down at his work once more. They both now looked at Doris: an ornate old fashioned clock set in a classical wooden box frame. The dark, weathered wood of the casing was damaged and broken in a few places, but the soft glow from the brass face was as it always had been. The classical timeless look was complemented by the slow and gentle 'tick-tock' that seemed to resonate through the old case. Two delicate hands reached out from the centre, each one having a different intricate shape cut into their thin black metal fingers. Instead of numbers the clock had large Roman numeral digits for every hour and small black segments marked out each minute.

The clock had only recently been returned from London, where it had been thoroughly inspected and checked over by a trusted and respected jeweller at considerable cost. Doris had to work faultlessly at all times so the price was well worth paying.

"I was thinking, maybe an hour will be enough?" Kass raised his eyebrows to emphasise the question to Squire. "We haven't been for some time so it will be good to get used to things again."

"A whole lot can happen in an hour, Kass." Squire took another long draw from his cigarette but didn't take his eyes off the hypnotic face of the clock. His eyes flickered back to his brother, "You sure you want to stay in that long?"

"It will be fine," Kass replied looking up at Squire. "Remember time flies when you're having fun."

"Yeah," Squire responded with a grunt, "and lots of the time we're not having fun. Change the settings to half an hour. I don't want to take any risks we don't have to."

"As you wish." Kass bent his face close to the clock and extended his long, elegant fingers to the hands to make some tiny adjustments. He moved them a small amount each and then paused for a long moment to ensure everything was right.

After he was satisfied that the minute and hour hands were lined up exactly right he started tapping in the time adjustments into one of the keyboards on the bench and watched his progress on a monitor in front of him. "Half an hour is set."

Reaching around the clock he withdrew a switch pack on a cable and laid it in front of the clock. There were three lights on the pack, red, amber and green.

The two men now started to mentally and physically prepare themselves for their journey from this world and into the next.

Glancing at the second of the monitors on the bench Kass studied a coloured display that showed the shifting magnetic fields that were happening naturally all around them. He was looking for a peak that would intersect the two ley lines that the barn was built upon and were marked by the painted white cross on the floor.

"We're going to have an opening in just over fifteen minutes," he said calmly with a brief glance at his brother. Stepping back from the clock Kass went to the right side of the bench and reached for a small brown cloth bag laying there. Opening it he removed the contents one by one and put them into several of the internal pockets of his leather coat.

When he had finished with the contents of the bag he checked it once again to ensure he hadn't missed anything. Finding the floppy bag totally empty he folded it and placed it back next to the clock.

Kass now moved to a large walnut box on the bench. Its smooth wood finish was dulled with age, but it was obvious it had been made by a real craftsman. Opening the box, he withdrew a heavy metallic bracelet and snapped it onto his right wrist. He then moved over to an object at the left end of the bench that looked like a microphone from the '70s which stood on its own small stand. He held his bracelet right up to it and momentarily small crystals within the metal of the bracelet lit up red.

A smooth female computerised voice rang from somewhere hidden in the barn.

"Target one, red locked in."

Kass looked over to Squire and saw that he had moved to a wooden trunk which had an orange fox tail painted on it. It was over to the left side of the barn and was generally referred to as the Fox Box. He was knelt down in front of it with the lid open and was removing various contents one by one and putting them into his coat pockets. At the bottom of the box lay a black and titanium Walther P99 handgun in its holster. He reached for it but then his hand flinched like it had been burned and he remembered the accident. He had shot an innocent soul by mistake and the memory still pained him badly. That must not happen again. He left the gun alone and closed the box.

Squire got up and also went to the walnut box on the bench and pulled out another bracelet and, like his brother had earlier, snapped it on to his right wrist. He held his bracelet in front of the scanner and watched the momentary flicker of blue around his wrist and once more the computer voice calmly spoke out.

"Target two, blue locked in."

Now Squire started clearing an area of the floor near the painted cross of any stray bits of straw or pieces of junk laying on the floor and Kass joined him to do the same. It wouldn't be the best of starts to get caught up on something when they dropped out.

Once they were both stood on a fairly clear patch of plank flooring on either side of the painted cross they looked around one more time to check for anything they might have missed, and then looked back at each other.

"You all set then?" Kass asked, looking straight at Squire with the slightest of smiles on his face.

"Yeah, I'm good I think." Squire's blue eyes had begun darting about faster now. This was the normal sign that his nerves were starting to kick in. Despite appearances the elder of the two was highly anxious about many things, but forced himself to cope with whatever came his way.

Both of them were now on edge and searched their minds for anything they might have forgotten, or any way of preparing for what was coming; even if they didn't actually know what that was.

Back in the lane the second figure crouched ever watchful in the undergrowth. A small mouse quietly rustled through the leaves and wandered past pausing only to sniff in the air and give its whiskers a quick rub.

Coming from the road came the almost silent sound of gentle footsteps and the second figure's eyes immediately went in that direction. There was nothing to see in the darkness, but the sound of the footsteps continued, and then paused at the entrance to the lane. From the undergrowth two eyes strained to see any movement in the gloom. This had never happened before. No one had ever broken the silent vigil in the lane even though the threat had been there for some time.

The moments of doubt were then instantly removed as the tell tale sound of footsteps gently crunching on the gravel of the lane started and came closer with every step. From a spot not far away a silent dark figure began to tense up like a cat ready to spring. All thoughts of who this intruder was, or whether they were armed and dangerous or just wandering lost in the night were lost in the focus bent upon the lane just in front. The steps came closer still without any pause, but whoever was there was doing everything possible to be as quiet as possible.

Right in front now the dark outline of a figure came into view, and aiming at the sound of the footsteps more than anything else the silent watcher sprang like a panther from the undergrowth.

The intruder had barely a second to react from the moment the undergrowth burst aside to the full force impact of Paige Fox. She led with her right fist which struck home at head height with a satisfying 'slap' sound. Then she let her momentum carry her forward into a body slam that threw them both to the ground in a heap. The intruder let out a small squeal as they hit the ground in a mass of arms and legs.

Paige Fox was immediately able to overpower the intruder and used all of her strength to pin her target down. "A little late for an evening stroll isn't it?" she said through clenched teeth while she struggled to stay on top of the writhing body underneath her.

Arms flayed and legs kicked on all sides. Paige already knew she was the stronger but this intruder was not giving in and was as lively as a snake. She fought as hard as she could, but in the dark it was impossible to see what was going on. The struggle wore on for a few more seconds but then, with an almighty burst of energy, Paige was pushed aside for just long enough for the intruder to get up and run.

Cursing under her breath Paige also got up and ran in the direction of the sound of rapidly retreating footsteps back towards the road. She reached full speed and heard, more than saw the intruder turn left at the road and towards the village. Slowing for the turn she followed, but could already hear the slap of feet going at speed down the road way faster than she was going to be able to match.

Paige slowed to a stop knowing that in this race she was beaten. Her breath came in quick, sharp gasps as she stared at the village down the road hoping to catch sight of her prey. She never did. Obviously the intruder had cut into the darkness around the village and was gone. No point going down there to look or she may well turn out to be the prey.

Turning around she reluctantly headed back down the lane and took up a new position on the other side this time. She settled down and reflected on the first time anyone had come even close to breaking through the watch.

Kass had moved to the bench once more and was watching a monitor which had the graph readout running on it. "The peak is now in seven minutes or so," he said carefully watching the gently rising line on the screen. "I've set the system for the first charge for then, and the second for half an hour after that." Squire just stood where he was gently swinging his hands backward and forward. He hated the waiting part and wished there was an easier way.

Kass looked at his wrist watch and compared exactly what it was saying to the face of the clock. Time didn't always work the same way where they were heading and he liked to have something as a reference point along the way. He also observed that Squire had forgotten his own watch again.

"Happy landings," Squire smiled over at Kass.

"Yeah," Kass responded, "happy landings." He turned and headed to his own spot on the other side of the painted cross and they both turned to face Doris.

The barn was now still except for the ticking of the clock on the bench. The monitors around it still continued to scroll information but they were not interested in that now.

Kass and Squire now stood totally expressionless and motionless looking intently at the face of the clock. Both pairs of eyes were trained intently on the minute hand which stood out as it was the longest, and had a gentle 'S' shape running from the centre to the outer edge.

They watched it for many minutes and gradually the comforting tick-tock of the clock appeared to have slowed and become a little louder to the two men who stood with almost unblinking eyes staring. Their breathing had become much slower and shallower now as everything in their bodies relaxed.

Still they fixed their eyes on the face of Doris but now the minute hand could also be seen to be moving. It wouldn't have appeared so to anyone else who might have walked in and looked at the clock, but to the two motionless brothers it was easy to see its smooth, slow movement. Their minds were now dropping out of normal time, slowed to such an extent that the minute hand could now clearly be seen to be tracing a path between the segments on the clock face.

They stood barely breathing now and still they stared. Their bodies were utterly still and quiet. The clocks rhythmic ticking had become even louder and was an all dominating noise in their minds. Even though they didn't know it both men were remembering the Master, and how he had shown them the way. They wondered too if they would ever be able to find him again.

The air around them felt like it was growing thicker and any movement they might have made would have been heavy and awkward due to their super slow mind rhythm. They stood almost in a sleep state while wide awake and still they stared at the slowly moving minute hand without breaking their concentration in any way.

The sound of Doris slowly seemed to get even louder. Nothing in the barn moved save for the clonking of the clock on the bench in front of them.

Fifteen seconds before the magnetic field peak went past them one of the monitors changed its display to read:

Magnetic Field: Alternating

Initiating Grab

A low hum started to resonate from the two metal panels that stood beside the two unmoving men and the sound grew louder by the second. It took only a matter of seconds for the huge electro-magnets to charge up to full power, by which point they were whistling loudly. The computer quietly displayed a countdown on the screen:

4, 3, 2, 1

There was a sudden burst of electro-static charge as the two giant electro magnets gave a split second of enormous power. The magnetic field fluctuation paused for just a moment; time also paused for a split second, but that was enough and Kass and Squire blinked out of the room and were swept into the Void.

Squire saw a bright white flash and the barn vanished out of existence and he was falling. In the very edge of his vision he had just caught a glimpse of Kass wink out of the room ahead of him. He too dropped out only a fraction of a second later, but in that brief moment of time his partner was already out of sight.

Within a second Squire was far away and his breathing and body burst into motion. The Void stood empty before him and he hurtled though it at freefall speed.

II.

As Squire fell through empty space every one of his senses burst into life. There was nothing around him to see except a dreary, shimmering grey nothingness in every direction, yet every sense of his being told him he was falling at a ridiculous speed. His coat flapped around him dragging like a parachute behind him and his hair felt like it was on fire. His stomach was now taking a trip on the rollercoaster called the Void.

He looked all around for Kass or any sign of anything that his mind could grip hold of as real, but there was nothing and he fell through the emptiness like a bullet without a single reference point to guide him.

After he had been falling for what he thought must have been several minutes with no sign of his brother his thoughts turned to the Master, and where it had all began all those years ago.

"Have you ever seen a ghost?" The old man's grey eyes looked closely at the younger, the question hanging in the air below the crackle of the open fire.

"Yes," the younger man responded after a time, "at least I think so."

"What was it that you saw?" The dancing flames flickered in the old man's eyes like bright stars in the night sky.

"Just a man walking a dog," the younger replied. "He was there one minute, but when I looked up again he was gone."

Not a flicker of emotion showed on the old man's face as he continued. "I didn't ask what you saw I asked what was it that you saw?"

"Oh," the younger paused to consider for a few seconds. "A trick of the moonlight perhaps or an overtired, overactive mind playing tricks on me." Neither spoke again for a few minutes, both men letting their thoughts wander to the dancing flames in the fireplace which gave an occasional crackle or pop.

"Do you think every sighting that has ever been reported can be explained as you have just done? Are all things we cannot fully explain a trick of our minds or a trick of the light?" The old man's voice was calm and measured. He was not testing the younger man's knowledge or feeling, and at this time there were no right or wrong answers.

"I don't know," the younger responded casting another glance in the old man's direction. "I have enough trouble telling myself it was a trick of the light." He still recalled clearly that journey home under the moonlight, and the sighting of the man walking his dog lit only by the moon's silver grey glow; the man that had vanished moments later. "Something didn't feel right about it."

The old man raised his eyebrows just a little. "How so?"

30

"Every hair on my body stood on end like a chill had gone through me. I still remember it clearly now."

"Did your hair stand up when you saw the man and the dog, or when you could no longer see him?" The old man's piecing gaze was fixed on the younger as if this was the question that mattered.

The other sat a moment longer and let his eyes settle once more on the heart of the fireplace while he considered the question. "After," he replied.

Before he could continue the old man prompted, "You mean when your mind realised something had just happened that it couldn't quite explain." It wasn't a question; it was a statement. "Your eyes had already told your mind there was someone there and moments later your eyes had lost sight of that same someone. Your mind was unable to account for the error and your reaction was to consider that you had experienced something supernatural, and hence the chill feeling."

"Yes, I guess so." The younger man absorbed everything the old man said and tried to assemble his thoughts. "Part of me really does believe I saw something though, and the educated part of me tells me I couldn't have."

"No," the old man replied gently but firmly. "That is the un-educated part of your mind that tells you that it can't be." The old man shifted forward closer and continued. "We are taught that anything that science is unable to explain can't really happen and we put too much faith in that fact. We are educated to think so from an

31

early age, but science doesn't know everything and that does not mean it cannot be true." The old man paused seeing that what he was saying was being accepted by the younger. "Do you believe in Heaven and Hell?"

"Yes I do," the younger replied without hesitation.

"But science would disagree with you," the old man jumped in. "Science cannot prove the existence of a Heaven or a Hell therefore it cannot be, yet millions still believe regardless."

Again there was silence as the two sat motionless, thinking. "Shall I tell you what you saw that night?" The old man settled himself back once more. "You really did see an old man walking his dog, but you saw him from a different time."

The younger man looked over again, now wanting the old man to continue. He knew his partner was wise and not easily fooled by common thinking, or what was considered to be acceptable by the public in general.

"Time, you see, can bend in on itself from time to time. The old man truly may have walked there many years ago. What you did was catch a glimpse of another time. What you saw was a small window into the Void."

"The Void?" The younger was all attention now.

"It's a place, if you can call it as such." The old man had produced his pipe and was now methodically filling it with tobacco. "It's as real as Heaven and Hell too. If you like, it's perhaps like a stop-off between this world and the next."

32

"You mean we go there when we die?"

"Yes," the old man responded still carefully packing his pipe. "For most it's only a journey they take briefly, but for others, well, they can get stuck there for a time."

The old man produced some matches and methodically shook the box to assure himself there was a point in opening it. Removing one match he paused and looked over once more at the calm, curious face of this evening's talking partner.

"What you saw was real my friend. The Void is real, time is real." He struck the match and put it to the end of his pipe and began drawing the orange flame in. After a satisfying cloud of grey smoke wafted up he continued once more.

"We can't see time, and we can't see any other plane other than the one we live in, but sometimes we catch a quick view of them both at the same time. If there are two gateways out of the Void, Heaven and Hell, it stands to reason there should be more than one way to get in too."

"How do you know all this?" the younger man's eyes were ablaze with curiosity now.

"Because I've been there."

"Yes," Squire said aloud, "and so have I."

He was still falling and there was still no sign of Kass. Squire would need to locate him soon or make the half an hour long journey alone.

From their understanding the Void could easily be as big as our own known universe and happening at all different times at once. It wasn't possible to bump into anything in a scale so huge but they did fall through people's memories and their souls as they searched for the way to the next plane. Squire relaxed into the fall and concentrated his senses as hard as he could manage on the things of the Void that couldn't be seen.

It wasn't much longer before he heard the whisperings of talking, or that's what it sounded like. In truth it was just vague whispered sounds in his head coming from the Void around him.

He focused on each sound he heard especially when he thought he could hear voices. One of the frustrations he and Kass both had was that most of the voices were in a language they didn't know or recognise so focusing in was even harder. Squire was falling through millions of dreams, millions of nightmares and millions of years of time all at once. Sooner or later he would pick up something.

A lost soul felt him and knew he was here again. She couldn't see him or hear him but still she sensed him there all the same, falling.

She reached out with all her emotions and stretched out her hand to the unseen presence, but he wouldn't find her like so many times before. She so longed and needed to be found but he always seemed totally unaware of her. He would travel on and she would be left alone again and would have to wait for the next time.

She tried to call out to him falling in the darkness but her voice didn't work. She was silent and lost in the Void, and he drifted by without ever knowing she was so close.

Kass had blinked out slightly ahead of Squire, which came as no real surprise to him. In recent years it was Squire dropping out fast and leaving the Master behind for a split second. It seemed that as people aged so the jump into the Void got that bit slower.

Now separated as usual Kass focused on everything around him and listened in to all the floating thoughts and voices that flashed through his mind. He hoped beyond all hopes that he would pick up something that would further their understanding, and take them closer to their goal, but most of all he hoped to hear from the Master.

It had been years since they lost him. That dreadful evening when Kass and Squire appeared back in the barn but the Master did not. Bracelet lavender was lost. They waited in the barn for a whole day for him, but there was no sign and no clue to what had happened.

To the normal reality of life on Earth he had simply vanished without trace. Kass though knew where he was. He was here, in the Void, and as he fell through nothingness he bent his entire mind on locating him.

Every now and then he picked up vague feelings or memories, but they were so fleeting and distant he couldn't follow them; just like trying to recall a dream that was fading fast. Kass knew his ability to focus on the voices of the Void was far below that of his brother and on most of their travels it was Squire who managed to locate something for them to investigate. He closed his eyes and concentrated.

Squire had picked up an echo of a voice he could only partly understand. It was a lady, quite old he suspected, and mumbling in French. He knew a little of the language and this allowed him to put bits and pieces together.

The more he focused on that one murmuring voice in his head the more he knew he was being pulled to it. That's how the Void worked. Any connection at all between the things going on there seemed to attract others in that same space and time.

Squire continued to struggle to hear what the voice was saying, something about a loss of a husband she couldn't find.

While he focused on the old woman's voice the second sound came, but this one was far more devastating than the first. Squire gave out an involuntary cry of pain, as the sound reached past him and right through him. He wasn't physically touched at all, but the emotional shock flayed his senses away and left him as limp as a wet tissue. The sound was just one word.

"Mummy!"

That one sobbing word carried with it enough pain and hurt to last a lifetime. Squire felt the full force of all the loss and hurt from that little voice in just that one word. There was a little girl lost in the Void. The fact that she had died was bad enough, but to Squire the additional pain that she was lost in this place was intolerable. Children almost always found the jump right past the Void, but some got stuck there for reasons they didn't understand. Maybe they didn't realise they had died, or couldn't come to terms with it for one reason or another. He and Kass had been trying to work out how the Void actually worked for years but they still only had scraps to go on. In general, the younger the person the rarer they were.

Kass thought that perhaps younger people's minds were less corrupted and they passed almost straight through to whatever came after the Void. As people got older their minds became bogged down in memories and feelings that kept them trapped somehow.

Squire focused on that one sorrowful sound, closed his eyes, and waited for the change to come.

A sound shot through the Void like a crack of a whip, one that should not have been there. Kass was shocked out of his thoughts in an instant. The small involuntary cry Squire had let out was a thousand times louder than the other voices in the Void. "Ah there you are," he whispered to himself. He faced in the direction he

37

thought the voice had come from and kept his mind focused on his older brother knowing that at some point they should come together. They did not belong in the Void and were too 'solid' for it. In time they would gravitate toward one another.

Void travel was so much easier to manage when there was something in the nothingness to focus on. It always seemed to draw you to that place just as someone dreaming can jump from one bizarre place to another just by thinking about it.

Kass once again focused himself knowing that if, as he suspected, Squire had found something he would soon be joining him there. He also hoped that his brother would follow the rules of the Void Runners and wait for him before engaging anything, but as he never had before he was unlikely to this time either.

The wind of the Void subsided slowly, and the grey area around Squire shimmered and began to change into a gloomy landscape with what looked to be sand dunes covering it. Patches of long wild grass stuck out from the tops of some of the dunes but everything had the same dull grey tone to it.

Squire stepped onto the sand just like he had walked out of one dream into another. The sand was real beneath his feet and everything around him had that dreamlike dreary look to it. He started walking in the direction he had landed already knowing he was heading the right way.

A solitary building came into view standing at the edge of the dunes like a lighthouse looking out over a sea of greyness. It was an old church Squire realised, complete with its own little graveyard. It didn't have any great grandeur to it at all though, just a little church from the coast somewhere.

To Squire the sandy beach seemed to slowly materialise around him, becoming something solid and real. If anyone had been watching it would have been the other way around and they would have seen Squire appearing like a ghost that gradually became solid.

His boots shifted and sunk a little as he walked in the grey sand which felt totally real but looked totally wrong. He looked up to where the sky should have been and saw that the total emptiness of the Void had gone, and been replaced by the most dismal of dreary skies.

As a child Squire had been lost on the beach in the sand dunes and had been totally disorientated with no idea how to find his family. He had wandered up and down for ages only managing to get himself even more confused and lost. He couldn't remember how scared he had been at the time but still remembered the helplessness he had felt. A little boy totally lost. Was this his memory he was standing in?

Again the sobbing cry reached him, "Mummy!" Squire spun his head to where he thought the sound had come from a little way off behind a cluster of dunes. He broke into a gentle run which was made more tiring and difficult as his boots struggled to make any headway in the slide of the sand.

He soon reached the ridge between two grassy dunes, and falling to his knees he looked into the area below. Down in the dunes in front of him was a little girl. Her curly blonde hair ringlets fell to her shoulders. She wore a plain white summer dress and little red sandals which flung out dull grey sand as she padded around from dune to dune. Squire also saw with horror that she wasn't alone. Three grey gargoyle like creatures were following her around. They poked and pinched at her continuously and seemed to delight in their game. The sobbing girl gave them no attention at all though and seemed oblivious to them, almost as though the pokes and pains were all just part of her hurt and desperation.

Squire realised the gargoyles would have been from the church he had seen. They looked like stone but moved just like they were alive. He saw their joy as they teased and tormented the girl and wished he had brought along his gun to teach them a lesson or two of his own.

The little girl looked up saw him kneeling there in the dunes above her and turned immediately that way and started padding towards him. Any thoughts she may have had about approaching a stranger seemed very distant. Perhaps in that state of loss anyone would do, even a total stranger. Squire briefly remembered he had done exactly the same as a small boy and had approached a man he hadn't known and asked for help.

Jumping to his feet he headed down the dune towards the little girl as quickly as he could manage. She looked to be only about four or five years old. Her face was tear stained and her bottom lip quivered in her gentle sobbing. The little look of distant hope on the girl's face was not lost on Squire either as he rushed to her.

As soon as he reached her he dropped to his knees in the sand and she shuffled to a halt in front of him. She looked straight into his face and uttered a tearful plea, "Have you seen my mummy?"

A second later Squire was sent crashing down to the sand behind him. One of the gargoyle creatures had run past the girl and punched him in the chest. He couldn't believe something even smaller than the little girl could hit with such force, but he now understood, they really were made of stone. Pain roared through his chest and left shoulder hurt but he shoved the feelings aside.

He started to lift himself onto his elbows but the three of them were on him all at once. Their gleeful expressions before had now been replaced by hateful faces, as if this new impostor would take away their play thing. Looking past them just before they struck he noticed the little girl was watching him and appeared not to be taking any notice of the gargoyles.

Squire immediately rolled to his right barely avoiding the oncoming attack. He used his right hand to push himself up and the second he had his feet under him he turned to the girl. His left arm didn't seem to work, but in one smooth movement he picked her up under her arms with his right arm and ran.

41

The gargoyles shrieked in outrage right behind him and gave chase. Running on sand in boots was hardly ideal, but Squire looked for the easiest path he could find to the church. The little girl didn't protest and just hung under his arm and her hands were gripping his coat.

Squire knew he wouldn't make it to the church. He was tiring fast in the sand despite his best efforts to run smoothly. His long legs gained him some distance from his pursuers that he knew were close behind him, but his breathing was soon ragged and he was slowing.

He could see the church quite close now but his legs were spent and he stumbled forward. As he crumpled to the sound he twisted so he would land on his left side and then roll onto his back. As he hit the sand his already injured left side howled in pain and Squire knew he was in trouble.

He lay on his back with the girl under his right arm. The gargoyles were on them in seconds but before the first arrived Squire lifted his right leg to take a kick at the nearest. He swung and connected and pain shot through his foot and calf as if he had kicked a concrete football.

He lay still for a moment, gazing at the faces of the furious creatures approaching him. His mind raced for any way of escaping the assault but he didn't think there was any way he was going to be able to get up again. He barely had the energy to move let alone flee. He hurt all over and his right foot was throbbing in pain, but he did all he could to move himself between the gargoyles and the girl.

Sweat and sand mixed together on his face and as he waited for the next strike the words of the Master came back to him.

"You cannot die in a dream. You will always awake before that happens. But should you die in the Void, you will die."

From somewhere just beyond the dunes behind him another sound came with a hollow crash. Bong. The sound of the church bell cut through the chaos like a shot. Squire tilted his eyes to just beyond the dune bank in the direction of the church. It stood not far away and was the only solid thing in the landscape of grey. Before he could consider the fact that there was also someone else around, he was pulled back to his present company.

The gargoyle-like creatures screeched as one and looked terrified. They rushed around in a small circle and then turned away and fled over the dunes as fast as they could run.

Squire watched them disappear from sight and gave a quiet sigh. The little girl had got up and was hovering close by and was looking down at him. Perhaps she was considering whether the man was going to help her, or was she supposed to do something to help him?

Squire pushed himself up to a sitting position with his right arm and winced at the pain from his chest and shoulder. He started to brush sand out of his hair with his fingers and tried to think what he could do. The escape from the gargoyles had left him a little dazed and confused.

The small girl inched closer, never taking her eyes off him. Her sobbing had stopped now but she still needed his help. He was the first person she had seen for longer than she could remember.

From the dune on the right another figure appeared and both Squire and the girl looked in that direction. Kass was sliding down the dune with as much grace as he could muster.

"Right," he said plodding towards them. "That's them taken care of for now, but they may be back." He looked straight at Squire with sad eyes, "You need to use the Catching, and then we need to get you out of here."

Squire gave his brother a small nod of acceptance and pushed himself up to squat in front of the little girl. He looked straight into that tear stained puffy face and tried to put on his calmest, most re-assuring voice.

"Hello little one," he said and gave her a smile. "What's your name?"

"I'm Alice," she responded in a rush, "and I can't find my mummy." The tears started to fall once more and her mouth started to quiver as she tried to keep from crying again.

Squire held his right hand toward her in an upward position in a motion of calm. "Shhh little one," he said quietly. "My friend and I have been out looking for a little girl called Alice, wearing a pretty white dress." Squire hid the lie as smoothly as he could but saw the effect on Alice was immediate. "Your mummy asked us to help her find you."

"Do you know where my mummy is?" The tears were in freefall now, but Squire suspected these were a release of relief as much as anything.

"Yes," he responded with another smile, "and we can take you straight to her."

Kass stood by watching calmly and tried hard not to blink in case his own emotions overtook him. The Void had its ways of shattering emotions rather more than he liked.

"Can we go now?" Alice's tiny voice told the brothers that her hurt was now being replaced by a hope she had all but given up on.

"Yes we can," Squire replied and tried to get to his feet. He couldn't quite do it, but Kass was there in an instant to pull him upright and steadied him while he found his balance. "We are going to send you to her in just a moment, but first I need to get my magical teleporter ready." Squire used the first term that came into his head. He knew explaining what he was really doing was going to make no sense at all to Alice, so for now magical teleporter would have to do.

Both Kass and Squire looked at Alice as kindly as they could to keep her spirits up and hoped she wouldn't start to panic.

She just looked up them again, "Okay then," she said simply as she wrung her chubby fingers together.

Squire reached into one of his inner coat pockets and withdrew a slender chrome tube which was about eight inches long. "I don't want you to worry anymore," he spoke kindly to Alice, "all your suffering will soon be over and you will be with your mummy again."

Gently nodding to her and motioning with one hand he said "Could you take a few steps back for me Alice? I need a little more room for this to work."

Very slowly Alice started to step backward, but she kept a close eye on Kass and Squire in fear that they would turn and run away. After a few steps Squire motioned that was far enough and gave her a happy smile.

Alice gave the smallest of little smiles back at him. She clearly didn't understand what was going on, but they had told her they were taking her to her mummy and that, for now, was all that mattered.

Squire held out the Catching at arms-length and the top half of the tube split into four sections which then opened out like a flower connected to the side he was holding. Two slim shiny rods stood out from the handle, and hanging between them was a small, clear gemstone that appeared to be almost totally flat. Squire then whispered quietly, almost just to himself.

"For judgement's here and judgement's me,
Take you to where you ought to be."

A flicker of light sprang up in the gem window and lit up the gloom of the day with its brilliance.

"Safe journey Alice," Squire whispered as rays of argent white light spread out toward her from the gem. In moments she was cloaked in white radiance and stood like a tiny beacon of light on the sand in front of them.

The light continued to spread and a high pitched noise came from the Catching. Kass and Squire stood waiting and could see the little girl starting to fade. Before she faded completely another figure also seemed to be in the light. The little girl seemed to reach up her arms and the other figure reached down to her like a dance of white light shadows. A moment later they were gone and the Catching shut down like switching off a light. The open four pieces gently raised up to once again form the solid tube.

"Happy landings Alice," Squire whispered. "Happy landings." He slumped down to the sand mentally exhausted and was joined moments later by Kass. They sat together side by side deep in their thoughts just staring at the horizon in the distance. They didn't speak, they didn't need to. The physical beatings they often had to endure in the Void were nothing compared to the emotional and mental hammering they received with every visit.

Kass was also pondering the return of the gargoyle creatures. If, as he suspected, they were part of her nightmare perhaps they snuffed out of the Void when she departed. He didn't really know but sincerely hoped they would not be back.

They had been lucky this trip for sure. Kass had also appeared in the dunes like his brother, and seeing Squire in difficulty he had gone instinctively to the church and sounded the bell. It was only now that the drama had stopped that he realised the gargoyles were probably part of her nightmare, and the church was part of theirs. Even so, they had been lucky.

Time rolled past as they pondered on. The church had vanished and even as they watched the whole place was starting to fade. Soon they would be once again falling through the Void as if this part of the dream had been washed away. Squire still had his mind full of the little face of Alice. She was so upset. He tried to focus on the pain that was spreading all around his chest and body to keep his emotions under control. The sand slowly vanished and Squire was falling through nothing again. Pain filled his mind now.

"You need to hang on," Kass called from close to him, but sounded far away. "Another three minutes should do it."

Gently Squire allowed his eyes to close. He started to drift to sleep but was nudged out every few seconds by Kass who just wouldn't let him rest.

"Stay with me a bit longer," he called. "Don't go to sleep."

The air around him suddenly seemed to change and even with his eyes closed he saw the bright flash of light. His eyes flicked back open and looked straight at Doris sitting on the bench in the barn.

The clock tick-tocked just like normal but was accompanied by the gently slowing noise of the generators for the electro magnets. As the half an hour had counted down to zero they had emitted another enormous pulse of energy which was just enough to pause the Void and return the visitors once more to reality.

Other than the clock the room was falling silent and .still. Moments later Kass was in front of him looking down at his brother slumped on the floor. "Do you think you can get up?" he asked softly. Kass squatted down in front of Squire with a look of real concern on his face.

"I'm not feeling too good," his brother responded in barely a whisper, then his eyes closed and he remained still.

After another brief check Kass walked over to the bench with the clock and the now silent computers. He found the electronic key pad with three buttons down its centre in traffic light formation and without hesitation Kass pressed the red button.

In the quite village of Shillyford, bedroom lights started to come on.

III.

The farmhouse living room was silent again despite the number of people crammed into it and the atmosphere was tense and oppressive. Kass had just finished recounting to the whole team exactly what had happened last night in as much detail as possible. Everyone had sat and listened to everything Kass had to say, and now several of them shifted a little in their chairs and waited for the group's chairman, George Brooker to continue the meeting.

Kass' wife, Anna busied herself moving in and out of the room delivering fresh cups of tea and coffee. Her long brown hair tumbled down her back in waves and her smile was a permanent resident on her face. She kept herself busy by serving refreshments, but at the same time listening into every detail.

George Brooker shuffled his bulk a little in his chair. His thick, grey eyebrows pulled down low over his tiny eyes were a clear sign that thunder was brewing. He showed no emotion at all, but it was clear before the meeting had even started that he was highly unimpressed. A set of thin, flat lips laid straight before speaking.

"It is clear," he began in his normal formal tone, "that another lost soul has been saved. Also, that Kass has been able to put together a few more pieces of the puzzle connecting dreams and nightmares. But," he patted the arm of his chair while looking around the room with a stern set to his face, "once again the cost has been higher than we would have wanted."

No one spoke; most just gave their drinks their full attention.

"Another red button jump," Brooker went on, "indeed, I don't know if I can recall the last time we had a green." His look was pure agitation and frustration. He changed the direction of the conversation and swung his attention on the team's medical officer. "Mr Dawes," he began, his voice full of authority. "Could we have your report please?"

Ted Dawes cleared his throat briefly from his comfortable wing back chair next to Kass. His usual Jamaican high spirits were, for this meeting, not on display. Ted had a bald head, brown skin, along with a pair of big shiny eyes of a very dark brown. He always carried a smile with him, baring his overly straight, white teeth whenever he got a chance. He was a jolly man to be around, although right now he looked uncomfortable as he shuffled some paper in a folder on his lap. "Yes, George," Ted began. "Three broken ribs; one of them quite serious but no lung damage. Left collar bone broken. Extensive chest muscle bruising, tendon strain in the right ankle and a stress fracture of the right fibula. No serious internal injuries other than bruising."

It read like a shopping list and having finished it Ted put down his papers and seriously hoped no one would ask him anything else. Being the director of the local private hospital in Mendip he had a great deal of experience with the Void Runners and their injuries. When his time wasn't taken up looking after the crew and whatever they had broken on the last run, it was taken up altering paperwork to cover it up.

"How long is he likely to be out of action for Mr Dawes?" George Brooker aimed the question firmly and without hesitation. The atmosphere in the room had grown uncomfortable to say the least.

"Hard to say exactly," Ted began. "Normally we would be looking at somewhere from six to ten weeks." Around the room there were a few sighs and a few groans. This was not good news. "Ah," Ted tried to sound positive, "we're doing lots to help though," he paused and looked at the gathered members trying his best to reduce the damage this news was causing. "Maybe less if he gets lots of rest." Nervous exchanges were once again cast around the room.

"I think we all know," George sat forward to emphasise the point, "that Mr Fox is not very reliable at getting lots of rest." His drooping cheeks were flushed red, a clear sign that the agitation levels were rising. "I don't like the red button being pressed after a run. We have lost too much and too many."

No one in the room would argue with that, the losses over the last couple of years had been devastating.

"Isn't it about time," Paige Fox began without looking up from her work, "that you gave him a break." Paige had typically straight brown hair which was tied up into a ponytail as this seemed fitting for the day. Her skin was fair and warm. Her face had a similar structure to her father's being both strong and long; a Fox family trait. Her stunning blue eyes certainly did catch her some attention, but this was never a problem as she could easily flatten anyone who troubled her. She had been scraping under her fingernails with the pointed edge of a military spec army hunting knife, but as she finished speaking she did look up and met the eyes of George Brooker. They both held that look for many seconds and everyone else in the room held their breath. Very few dared to risk getting on the wrong side of Paige. Squire's eldest daughter was also held in high regard at the nearby army barracks which she had joined as a cadet in her early teens. She had learned fast and was soon a good match for any of the full time soldiers based there.

Finally, the tension broke. "I will give him a break Miss Paige, when he stops making mistakes." George let out a long breath and gently sat back in the single armchair. "He is reckless all of the time and it's getting worse. The report is clear," he went on, but more calmly now, "he went off alone, again. He went off without his partner, again. I don't doubt he has the best of intentions but he is impulsive and jumps into every situation without thought. He is going to get himself or you killed Kass, and you know it."

"He is also the best at what he does." Daisy Fox spoke for the first time in the meeting. It wasn't the first time her father had been in trouble and it wouldn't be the last. Her golden blonde hair shone brightly from the back light of the large window behind her. She had shiny blues eyes the same as the rest of the family, and had bright rosy cheeks and a shy smile. As a quiet girl, she did lots of thinking and not much talking, but she had an eye for things as her father did. Even at her age she could spot minor details and string pieces together to complete puzzles that others wouldn't even consider. Clever and young: a good combination.

"My dear," George looked over to her with a renewed kindness in his voice. "I have been looking after the Master's estate since all this began." He paused to recollect, and one by one addressed everyone else in the room. "For thirty years we have searched the Void. The Master, Squire and Kass," he looked over to Kass last. "We lost the Master and I don't want to lose Squire next. He is too old for this."

The tension in the room grew once again. Everyone already knew Squire was on borrowed time. Even Kass, some fifteen years younger was at the edge of what was considered acceptable for Void running.

"Before it's too late," George addressed the room, "I want new people trained and working the Void." He looked at each face one by one almost daring anyone to challenge him. "We need fresh people and we need them right now."

Everyone in the room looked uncomfortable. Finding new people who could be trusted was difficult and the entry test was another matter entirely.

"On top of that," George went on, "Squire was tailed in last night only to be thwarted by Miss Paige. This has never happened before and the identity and purpose of the intruder remains unknown. These are dangerous times and we must all be on our guard and uncover what is going on."

"The tail was a she," Paige spoke up.

"Are you certain of that?" Kass responded, even though he did not doubt Paige for a second. The comment was more for the other members in the room.

"Yes I'm certain," Paige went on. "Probably in her twenties I should think. She was fit, strong and very fast. It was only pure surprise that gave me the edge for a few moments." No matter how casually she was trying to sit in her chair there was no mistaking the strength in her. She was toned and a formidable opponent and perfect for the position she had looking after security.

Paige was secretly and deeply concerned about last night's visitor to the barn. She had landed a thunderous right hand that would have laid out most people, and yet her opponent had reacted like lightening and spun away from the punch. On top of that Paige had been pushed away and then out-sprinted. Whoever had traced them to the barn was needed to be respected more in future.

"Um," Daisy started, but then stopped again looking nervously around.

"What is it Daisy?" George encouraged while shifting to face her in his chair.

"Well," Daisy went on, "it's more complicated than it looks. If someone tailed us to the barn they already suspect, or know something is going on there. No point in following someone for no reason, surely?"

"She's right," Kass cut in. He was curling his long fingers through each other almost as if he was re-enacting the knot the group now found themselves in. "Someone is on to us. That much is clear. How they know or what they know or who they are will all need answering before too much time goes by."

George Brooker looked even more concerned. He rubbed at his temples and sighed. "This is all getting very difficult," he began. "Things were never this complicated in the past and things just keep getting worse." He waved his hand in the air as if dismissing all the possible objections that anyone could have had to his comment. "I think we will leave it there for the time being."

He got to his feet and buttoned the jacket of his stiff brown suit. "I want a plan set out by the time we meet next Sunday." He slowly looked at all the faces in the room, one by one. "I wish you all a good afternoon."

Having said all he was going to say on the matter he turned and strode from the room. No one spoke until they heard the front door close on the way out.

"Hey, that was fun," Anna chirped up. Her American accent mixed with a dose of sarcasm brought a little relief to the tension in the room. "Who wants tea?" Every hand in the room was raised.

"Okay," Justin spoke up for the first time, "let's take a moment to calm ourselves then we can perhaps continue without getting ourselves in a stew." Justin Naylor had a long face and a wide jaw. His lips weren't symmetrical but he smiled a lot, a comforting and reassuring smile that could sooth anyone's mind. Justin was tall, average in build and had dark deep set eyes and broad shoulders. He was the pastor of the local church and had been with the project since finding out about it by pure chance several years ago. He was the voice of reason within the group and always saw the best in people, and dealing with everyone with kindness and care, even George Brooker.

"I think," he began, pushing his black plastic glasses up his nose with his index finger, "we all understand that George has a deep set resentment of Squire and nothing is going to change that." It was true. George held Squire personally responsible for losing the Master in the Void all those years ago, but only because he had to blame someone and there was no one else. He had looked after the Master's financial estate ever since and was the primary source of funding.

"Shall we put those feelings aside and work with what we have?" Justin cast a look around the room and it was clear everyone was waiting for him to take the lead and continue.

He chose his next words carefully to ensure the meeting stayed on a positive note. "There is an element of truth in what George is saying, and deep down we may hate to admit it but we all know it. Squire is making mistakes and has become more and more unpredictable both in the Void and outside of it."

It seemed like everyone glanced at the floor at once so as not to meet the eyes of anyone else. Justin held the silence long enough for anyone to jump in with a comment of their own. No one did.

Anna had arrived with a tray of steaming cups of tea and was once again flitting through the room passing out cups to everyone in turn. Once there was only one left she took it and settled on the arm of the chair with Kass.

"There is something else you guys should know." Justin lowered his voice even more than his normal gentle tone. "Something we have kept from you for some time now. I think the time is right to share it with you."

The room had grown totally still now. No one wanted to hear whatever was coming. They knew that if Justin had withheld something it must be of great importance, but also had to be kept from George Brooker.

"Ted." Justin cast a sideways glance at the Jamaican. It seemed only right that Ted delivered the news. It had been him that had brought the information to Justin one stormy night. Information that from that point on they had kept to themselves.

Ted rubbed his temples and waited until the right words came to him. "This won't be easy for you all to hear." He looked up to the circle of faces looking straight at him. He looked especially at Daisy who sat motionless with wide, unblinking eyes. Then he looked straight at Kass. "Squire failed the testing."

"What!" Daisy exclaimed sitting forward suddenly. Her reaction was repeated several times around the room.

"When?" Kass calmly responded. It didn't appear that he was even the slightest bit surprised by the news. His reaction set him apart from the rest of the gathered members.

"Last test," Ted responded, "three months ago." Ted paused while the news settled in. "And every test before that for the last couple of years."

The news was horrific. There were genuine looks of shock around the room. Kass closed his eyes slowly and kept them closed until he could absorb what this meant. Anna reached down and took Kass' hand and gave it a gentle squeeze.

"I'm sure you will understand why we couldn't make this public before," Justin continued. "If George knew the truth Squire would be kicked off the project straight away."

"He's still the best." Kass addressed the room although his look was to Daisy, then to Paige. "Knowing what you know now, which of you would surf the Void with Squire?" Kass glanced at each person one by one, and one by one every single hand was raised.

59

"It's settled then," Justin jumped in. We continue as we are for now, but we must work on our plans for the very near future."

"Does he know?" Daisy cast a look at Ted.

"No," Ted returned the look. "He doesn't know. I told him it was fine. It's only the physical section he's fallen behind with, and that is just down to age and cigarettes."

There was a silence as everyone acknowledged the risk Ted had taken in keeping this quiet.

"Well I think it is clear," Justin went on, giving his glasses another push, "we do need fresh people in the project. Squire and Kass cannot keep doing it all themselves."

"Everyone we tried is either dead or already institutionalised." Ted spoke without lifting his head, his tone calm and relaxed. "Where are we going to find more people Justin? It's not like we can go public and advertise the position."

"You know I will go," Paige volunteered immediately.

"Perhaps you can," Kass responded, "but until you learn to control your anger you will not pass the testing. If your mind is not at peace you won't be able to make the jump."

Anna spoke up, "How about sending an email to every likely candidate we know of and ask them to come for testing for a special project? We could run a session on Friday evening and potentially have some new people by Sunday.

There were some nods of agreement from around the room and Justin started making notes on the pad that sat on his knee.

"Okay," he said in a more upbeat tone. "If no one has any objection I would like to ask everyone here to put some real thought into how we continue from here. There will be no Void runs for now so we all have time to have a really good think, and maybe things will look better by next Sunday and the meeting with George?"

Everyone agreed at once. Without exception they all wanted to be out of that room to have a quiet think about everything that was going on. One by one they all made their excuses and left the cottage to go about their business, leaving Kass and Anna alone with their feelings. Kass didn't think he was going to get a lot of sleep that night.

Mendip Private Hospital was familiar territory to Squire Fox. He and Kass had been regular visitors for many years, but the staff never asked any questions. Ted had seen to it that all the paperwork regarding their visits was always altered to something that wouldn't arouse suspicion. Whenever any of the staff asked, which was regularly, he just tapped the side of his nose with his finger and said "Shhhh, can't talk about it."

The pair had always been given the very highest standards of service and admiring looks from all the staff. They were the source of many whispered chats in the tea room with debates regarding what they might do that meant no one could talk about it. Ted had overheard one of the nurses whispering to one of the others that the

'MI5 man' was back again. This was better news than he could have hoped for. The staff would not discuss a possible British spy outside the hospital in case they breached national security. Right now the 'MI5 man' was recovering from a nasty hit and run incident last night. Although the Police hadn't been seen at all it just confirmed even more to them that the Mr F, as he was known was very important indeed.

As it was Mr F didn't feel very special at all. He was laid up in a single room feeling totally miserable. His chest hurt all the time and his breathing was painful and coughing was just; well he tried his hardest not to. He hated the fact that he was laid up and unable to do anything useful. He also hated the sterile cleanliness and the echo that bounced around the sparsely furnished room, but most of all he hated himself for not taking his gun last night. With it he would have blown a few gargoyles apart and not be laying in a hospital bed in pain.

Kass had brought Daisy over after lunch and they had all sat gently talking. Nice as it was to see people Squire really wasn't up to it. He was sure he had been able to shake off injuries so much better twenty years ago. Now he didn't bounce back so quickly and the last thing he wanted to do was just lay around doing nothing. He wondered how long it would be before he could discharge himself without Ted going insane at him for not resting up enough.

The mood must have been catching as Daisy also seemed quiet and not quite herself. Squire asked several times if she was alright, but she just hushed him up with "I'm just tired. If you remember we were all woken up at stupid o-clock when Kass pressed the red button."

It was true enough of course. Any red button used alerted the entire team and must have been pretty scary for them. Many times in the past it had been because someone was dead or seriously hurt. Now only Kass and Squire remained so any alarms got everyone jumping pretty quickly.

Daisy gave Squire a full account of the incident in the lane where Paige had laid in wait as usual and pounced on an unwelcome guest. Squire had looked concerned during all of it but Kass also detected some private pride in the way his eldest daughter had handled herself last night.

"She got one really good punch in," Daisy said smiling. "She was well happy that one landed. She said she felt the jolt of it go right up her arm."

Kass and Squire had then gone on to discuss who could possibly know about their work and track them down, but no matter how hard they tried they couldn't think of anything or anyone that might have put together any clues they might have left along the way.

Kass and Daisy had made their excuses and left shortly after 2pm leaving Squire to gaze at the ceiling and wait for evening visitors. Justin had brought him in a couple of magazines but he didn't have the energy or inclination to look at them yet.

He set his mind to considering the Void. There was so much they didn't understand and progress was always so slow. Kass was doing everything he could to unravel the mystery of the Void and all its many variations. After every run he carefully logged everything down that had happened on that trip in the hope of discovering any patterns there might be. So far they were almost as clueless as they had been when they lost the Master.

So many questions and so much to do, and he was just stuck here with nothing to do but think. Somewhere around 3pm that day the old lady walked into his room and everything changed.

Back at the farmhouse Kass was sitting with Paul McCoy, or Tinker as he was known to the team. Paul had neatly trimmed dark brown hair which covered the top of his head, pale skin and a rounded jaw, a large pointed nose and big ears that seemed just a little too large for his head. He had been born and raised in Ireland and his accent was strong and rich. The quiet Irishman was listening intently to some ideas Kass was running past him.

He had been with the team for years and was not only an extremely deep thinker, but also had remarkable skills when it came to making things, or 'toys' as the team called them.

Kass was now asking for more toys; lots of them. "The way I see it Tinker, there are going to be more of us in the team soon, and that means you're going to have your work cut out matching the toys to the team."

The most special of the toys Paul made were carefully matched to the member of the team that carried them. They didn't just work for anyone and hours of work and care went into creating every one.

"Ya, I guess so," Paul followed in his soft southern Irish accent. Words were few with him, and if he didn't have anything important to say he just didn't say it. "So you want me to put some weapons together then?"

"We are getting hammered too often Tinker. We tried normal guns for long enough but they didn't work on some things, and every now and then an innocent lost soul got hit by accident. We don't want any more of that."

Paul gently rubbed his rough hands together slowly. His eyebrows were pulled down low over his dark eyes as he considered his options. For sure he could make anything given the time and knowledge, but the most amazing of all his gadgets had to be given that extra special treatment.

"I suppose to start with I should go and see Sasha and see what she can come up with, and her sister of course." Only one of Paul's eyebrows was now up which always meant it was a question waiting to happen.

"Yes please Tinker, as soon as you can." Kass was always careful about pushing him more than he wanted to be pushed. It was good that it was Paul's idea to approach Sasha as Kass really didn't want to be the one to suggest it.

If Squire was armed once again he could defend himself and with any luck not keep getting hurt. Kass needed George off his case as soon as he could, and keeping Squire in one piece during Void runs would help to keep the peace.

"So you're thinking of weapons but not guns," Paul probed. He wanted to know as much as he could if he was going to create the right thing.

"It's not the guns that are the problem Tinker, just the bullets." Kass hadn't considered what he was saying at the time, he was just stating a fact. The comment was not lost on Paul though and in no time at all he was forming some ideas.

"Oh, and Tinker," Kass added as a new thought came to him. "Could you see if there is a faster way of locating each other in the Void? Maybe run that one past Sasha and Steph too."

Paul did a reflex rubbing of his chin, a sure sign he was considering something important. "Ya mean a little like Void sat-nav then?"

"Yeah," Kass responded with a dry smile. "Void sat-nav – I like that."

Squire was still busy thinking later that afternoon. He was laying flat on his back propped up on pillows to try and keep any weight off his chest and shoulder. He felt every single breath like a bruise in his chest and a steady supply of painkillers was not enough to take it away more than a continual dull ache. His left arm was in a long sling to ensure the weight of it was supported and not pulling on his broken collar bone.

The door to his room opened slowly and he looked over expecting to see a nurse or doctor coming to check on him. He was wrong once again.

An old lady had walked in. Squire guessed she was in her sixties or seventies judging by the short grey afro hair which was the colour of freshly burnt coal ash. She wore a simple light green dress covered in small flowers and a grey woollen shawl covered her shoulders.

Something was wrong about her though. He could see it straight away, but couldn't figure out what it was. She just looked like a kind old West Indian lady, but his senses were overwhelmed with the 'something' he couldn't see.

"I hope I didn't wake you," she said. Her smooth deep voice was quiet and calm and a hint of a smile touched her eyes.

Squire tried to reply but found nothing at all happened. He thought the words in his head but his voice did nothing. He tried to get a grip of himself but he was too relaxed to fight. Without knowing or caring why he just accepted that he couldn't speak.

The old lady came over to the chair next to his bed and slowly sat down. That gentle reassuring smile still on her face.

She looked bigger to Squire than she should be. It was impossible to explain but she had far more life force in her than her appearance suggested. He momentarily thought of pulling away from her, but almost immediately he found that he didn't have the energy to move even the smallest amount.

She perched on the edge of the bedside chair like a queen sitting on top of a horse. "Yes," she started gently, "I know you got questions. Your head is full of them."

It was, but Squire didn't know which questions she was talking about or how she knew. The most immediate ones he was thinking were about her, but maybe she was referring to the questions he had been busy with since lunchtime.

She tilted her head a little and her smile grew for a moment as if she had read his thoughts. "Questions Mister, always more questions. They are going to have to wait for now though because you are not ready yet."

She spoke with all the wisdom of the world with her soft voice full of care and patience. She seemed so unrushed and at peace. Squire found that his breathing had slowed and he felt warm and relaxed without knowing why. Her voice seemed to be coming from further away than sitting right next to him like she was talking to him in his sleep.

"Funny thing is though," she smiled to herself, her voice now almost a whisper, "you already know all the answers. You just don't know which questions you want to ask yet that's all."

Squire looked back at her with leaden heavy eyes. He was so calm he wondered if he was awake or already dreaming.

She reached her hand out to lay it on his chest. Squire instinctively felt alarm at the thought of anything going near that most tender of areas. He needn't have worried at all though, her hand landed on his chest like a tiny feather landing on a still pool.

Now her voice was coming from miles away, Squire was slowly sinking and he couldn't stop himself. "For what you done Mister. For what you do."

His eyes drifted shut but Squire was asleep before they did.

IV.

Kass arrived in the evening with Daisy but Squire slept through the whole visit. He was so deeply asleep that Kass had asked a nurse to check that everything was okay. The nurse busily went about the obvious checks, but seemed rather flustered having two of those MI5 men in the same room. Not wanting to make any mistakes the nurse took the option of paging for a doctor.

A few minutes later a doctor arrived and gave Squire a careful check over suspecting it was more than his job was worth to miss anything on one of these 'special forces guys.'

"I think he's just sleeping very deeply," he said in his best reassuring but slightly nervous voice. "There is a possibility he is in some kind of delayed shock from the incident last night." He meant to say hit and run but for some reason incident had popped out instead.

"It's quite common," he rambled on quickly trying to recover. "We often see this kind of thing and it's really nothing to concern yourselves with."

The doctor waited for the ground to open up and swallow him whole but Kass just nodded calmly. "Well, thanks for checking anyway," he offered and sat back down at his brother's side.

A few minutes later the discussion in the staff canteen had turned to post battle stress disorder, and the general buzz was of the two heroes who were so modest they never spoke of what they did. And what of the girl? She was definitely a decoy or something to make it look more normal.

When Ted left for the day he was quietly confident that all within the hospital was well. He was also pretty sure that the more times Squire and Kass checked in the bigger their stories of heroics were going to grow. He allowed himself a big smile once he was behind the wheel of his car in the hospital car park. Now his native joy caught up and he drove away laughing like he had just picked the six winning numbers.

Squire had no idea that visitors came and went, or that hospital staff came and checked on him from time to time. He was in a deep sleep, and nothing short of someone firing a gun in his room was going to wake him. He surfed the Void in his dreams without fear and without consideration for anything else. The old lady was talking to him while he floated from one bizarre place to the next. A strange mixture of dream stuff that had no meaning and no obvious direction.

"You already know all the answers," her smooth voice would interrupt his sleep, and Squire would dream on.

When morning came he opened his eyes slowly and came back to the world again in his sterile little room. Nearly all his dreams evaporated from his mind in an instant, but he clung to the parts that were fresh. A haze of images, faces and strange places was all he could remember. The old lady was forgotten totally.

Parts of the puzzle he and Kass had been working on for so long seemed to be so close but at the same time evading him. He tried to grasp more of the dream but it was already floating away. He was sure there had been clues in there but what had she been saying to him?

"Some things that cannot be broken can be repaired." Her voice came out of his dream back to him once more.

"That doesn't make sense," Squire said only to himself. "If it can't be broken how can it need repairing?"

Frustrated again he rolled over and reached out with his left arm and pressed the nurse call button. The bandage sling his arm had been resting in fell harmlessly on the bed.

It was only after he had pressed the button that his mind finally woke up and considered what he had just done. He looked numbly at his arm reached out above him next to the button. "That's not possible."

He carefully lowered his arm again and placed it by his side. He remembered very clearly that his left arm hadn't wanted to work

72

at all yesterday. His broken collar bone had stabbed him with angry pain every time he tried to move, and his chest had been equally fragile. He had just reached behind him for the call button and had felt no pain at all. A good sleep didn't mend bones, but from the feel of it they had indeed mended.

Squire was still laying there in wonderment when a nurse came in. "Good morning," she said in an upbeat and cheerful tone. How are you feeling today?" She bustled her way around the room and picked up his check board from the end of the bed and started studying it for no apparent reason.

"Could you call a doctor please," Squire responded quietly. "Oh, and good morning to you too."

"Are you in a lot of pain again?" the nurse continued. Her short brown bob haircut wiggled as she shifted from the end of the bed to his side, and the sunlight from the window sparkled off her round wire framed glasses. "I'm afraid it's a little early for the doctor's rounds but I can get you some more painkillers. I'm sure that will help until the doctor comes in."

"Thank you, but no." Squire's response was not what the nurse was expecting and she stopped on the spot trying to think what else she could offer. "Could you call Ted for me please?"

All the staff knew the golden rule with the "special guests" that came in from time to time. If they needed anything Ted was to be called at once, day or night.

73

"Yes, of course," the nurse responded immediately. "Is everything okay? Can I get you anything? I will go and do it right now." Without waiting for a reply to any of her questions she headed out of the room and Squire heard her footsteps withdraw quickly down the corridor.

"The foolish man can find a path the wisest of men can never see."

Again a fragment of dream came back to him leaving him more confused than before. "Who are you lady, and where are you from?" Squire said it to the ceiling but didn't expect a reply. He was not disappointed.

A thought suddenly occurred to him and he sat up in bed and pulled back the covers on the right side. His foot and shin were heavily strapped in stiff, clean bandages. Bringing his knee up he reached for the safety pin and promptly began unwinding the bandage.

The previous day the pain had been pretty bad but now there was none. As the bandages came off it was also clear there was no bruising of any kind, and now his ankle only showed squeeze marks from the bandage.

He swung his leg out and rested it on the cool vinyl floor and then slowly put some of his weight on it. No pain. Another thought came to him then; "How long have I been asleep?"

Daisy was rushing. Late for school again but they seemed to be quite used to that idea. Squire had been called to the school no end of times to explain the repeated late arrivals but he simply stated that his work went on late into the night and was disturbing Daisy.

Eventually the school had relented after a visit from one of the school's major benefactors, George Brooker. Now the random lateness was just ignored by the school.

She had left her research on the kitchen table ready to take to the hospital for her dad to look though. Now, two late nights in a row was starting to impact on the seven-hour compulsory education club she was forced to attend.

She threw her homework in her school bag and raided the fridge for her lunch and headed for the door. Paige was not even up yet but would eventually stir and then, hopefully tidy the house before she got home later.

A little over half an hour had passed and the door to his private room opened and a slightly dishevelled and concerned looking Ted came into the room. Squire was sitting in the visitor's chair fully dressed but did not turn around to see his visitor. He sat staring past the bed at nothing in particular.

"What in the name?" Ted began while slowly turning to close the door. He paced to the other side of the bed so he could look back at Squire who still sat where he was, motionless.

"What are you doing up?" he started with surprise written all over his face. "No wait. How did you get up?"

"Some things that cannot be broken can be repaired." Squire responded without looking up.

"What?" Ted had the feeling he was still sleeping and hadn't really got a phone call asking him to come straight in.

"Does that mean anything to you?" Squire replied now focusing on his friend and looking straight at him.

"No," Ted looked totally bewildered. "Squire, please tell me what is going on. I don't get this. Why are you up?"

Squire stood up and walked around the bed to Ted, who now had utter disbelief written all over his face. "You keep accurate records of everyone who comes and goes in this place, yes?"

"Well, yes you know we do. Everyone has to check in and check out as always. How," Ted had to step back and stare again at his friend; the one who should not be able to stand let alone walk. "How is this possible?"

"I will tell you what I can, when I can. In the meantime, I need you to go and check the visitor record for yesterday." Squire stepped back and sat down on the bed. "While you do that I need to make a call." As Ted started to turn away Squire was pulling his mobile from his coat pocket and switching it on.

"Oh, and Ted," he continued. "Please don't look so worried." He tried to emphasise this with a brief smile. "Everything is fine, so relax."

Ted gave the briefest of nods back then headed for the door. "Someone with a list of injuries like that does not get up and walk around a day later," he mumbled to himself. "There's no way that happens."

Kass pushed the report papers on his desk out of the way to find the ringing phone. Finding it he picked it up and seeing "Squire" in the call window he answered straight away.

"What can I do for you, one who should be resting?" he started with his usual dry humour tone. Strange as it was for his brother to be ringing, Kass was delighted for the chance to have a break from things that were not making much sense.

"Kass," Squire started. "Did Daisy find anything out about our last run?"

"Yes," Kass pushed his chair back and dropped his feet on the desk. "We told you all about it last night but you were busy in the land of nod."

"Tell me again." Squire sounded in rather a hurry, and that was highly unusual.

"She pulled a news report from a couple of years back from somewhere on the south coast, I can't remember the place. Mother and small child caught out by the tide and both lost. Mother's body washed up next day several miles away, kid never found."

"Her name was Alice, yes?" Squire had slowed a little.

"Yes, it was Alice." Kass concluded but his eyes had glazed over. The pieces of the puzzle coming together made it all more personal. He had met the person that had died and had seen her nightmares. She wasn't lost anymore though he thought. "Justin is heading over to the coast to check out the church where the mother was laid to rest. We suspect there will be gargoyles on it."

"That's good, and yes, I suspect there will be."

For a few moments there was silence at both ends of the phone as both were lost in their memories of Alice in the sand dunes.

"Kass," Squire broke the silence. "Something a little weird has happened. I can't talk about it right now but I will as soon as I can." Another pause, "Kass, I need to."

"Why does something a little weird not surprise me at all," Kass responded while acknowledging Anna who had entered his cluttered office with tea. "Maybe we can talk when I visit this afternoon?"

"No, don't do that," Squire went on. "I won't be here."

With that the line went dead. Kass took the phone from his ear and stared at the display to convince himself the call was over. With a question written all over his face he put his feet back down and slid the phone on to the desk.

"Squire?" Anna questioned although she already knew the answer.

"Yeah," Kass' reply was more of a sigh that anything else.

"How is he?" she asked as she perched on the corner of the desk and took a sip of slightly too hot tea blowing steam that fogged her glasses.

"I can't be sure," Kass replied looking up at her, "but I have the feeling something is really bothering him."

Ted sat in Squire's room with the visitor log on his knees and was leaning on it with his arms. "There was no one else," he said gently, raising his eyebrows. "We both checked."

"It's okay Ted, don't worry," Squire paced the room. "I know you don't understand, and for that matter neither do I, but I'm telling you she was here and she did," he stopped pacing and waved an arm in his own general direction, "this."

Squire had related all he could of his visitor the previous evening and was not surprised that she didn't show up on the visitor record. He knew something was strange about her at the time and now he was even more sure.

"On the one hand," Ted started, "she could not have just appeared in the room without anyone seeing her, so I would say you must have been dreaming." Ted paused for effect while both men considered the words. "But on the other hand you didn't just dream broken ribs better."

Squire just looked back at Ted knowing there was every chance he had dreamed the old lady. He could see the questions all over his friend's face but at the moment he didn't have any answers either.

"*You already know all the answers.*"

"None of these things matter anyway," Ted sat back holding his hands up. "Whether she was here or wasn't here is beside the point." Ted pointed a lazy finger all around Squire. "How did she do this anyway?"

"I don't know Ted," Squire shrugged. "Right now I have other things I need to do. Can you get me out of here?" He looked desperate. Ted knew his friend was as lost as he was, and still had many questions he needed answering about the last Void run. He needed Kass.

Ted slapped his hands down on the visitor log then stood up. "Oh yeah, sure I can. I can just walk outta here with the busted up guy and no one will think anything of it." Ted gave the reassuring 'of course I can buddy' smile.

Squire started to laugh in spite of the situation and Ted's worries seemed to float away. They were both smiling now.

"Can you give me a bit of time," Ted went on pointing a finger at his friend. "I need to arrange an immediate wheelchair transfer for that 'special forces' guy." He started to head for the door then paused and turned to Squire. They both did a spontaneous high five and he mumbled "I should be getting myself a medal for all the paperwork I do covering up for you boys." Ted did his best to look a little grumpy and hard done by, but everyone knew Ted couldn't manage grumpy if he tried.

Squire didn't disagree but just smiled at Ted as he left the room. He couldn't help thinking how lots of people needed medals for what they did for this team, but he was sure they would settle for some answers instead.

V.

"You sure you're gonna be okay?" Ted called from the driver's seat of his car through the open door on the passenger side.

"I'm sure Ted," Squire responded with his hand on the top of the door. "Thanks for the lift." With that he swung the door closed, and turning he headed off into the car park of the mental wing of Highgate Hospital.

Ted didn't like it as he couldn't remember his friend ever looking so full of thought. There was nothing else for it though so he pulled away and headed out of the car park. Just before pulling back onto the main road he looked in his mirror and saw his friend lighting a cigarette and staring up at the building.

Squire stood where he was for several minutes enjoying every bit of his first cigarette since before the last jump two days earlier. His head swam a little but he puffed all the harder as he wanted his nerves as calm as possible for this bit. Highgate Hospital Mental Institution had a way of sapping all of his energy and another couple of minutes wouldn't hurt.

Justin had arrived in West Lulmouth on the south coast after a long drive down in his battered Vauxhall Omega. The place he needed to find was not far away, just a couple of miles out towards Swanage. Daisy had done a thorough check of the area and found a nice little cove which was an infamous spot where people got caught out by the tide.

With the location of the local church set in his sat-nav he had headed down and was already pretty sure what he was likely to find, a village church and three gargoyles. He stopped at a local fuel station and after filling the Omega to the brim again he brought some flowers and a pack of sandwiches.

He was only a few miles away from the church when the call came through to his phone mounted on the hands free holder on his dashboard.

Justin keyed the answer button straight away seeing it was Ted ringing him. "Ted," he called out in a rather over-loud voice, "how are things with the patient today?"

"Just dropped him off at Highgate," was the reply from his speakers.

"What?" Justin was thrown off balance by the response and was looking in his mirror. "Ted, can you hold on one minute please?"

Looking for a spot Justin spotted a lay-by just ahead and indicated in. Once he had pulled over he stopped the car and switched it off, then grabbed the phone from the hands free. "Ted, did you just say what I thought you said?" Justin knew Ted was not one for jokes, sarcasm or humour regarding serious matters so he was pretty sure he had heard the last thing he had expected to hear.

"He's all better man," Ted sounded like a man discarding a great weight off his shoulders. "I kid you not Justin, he was up this morning walking and talking and wanting to leave."

Justin slumped back in his seat and put his left hand on top of his head and rubbed his hair. "How is that possible?"

Ted went on pleased to be able to share the information he didn't understand and was having trouble believing. "He said some old lady turned up last night talking all kinds of strange stuff. She put him to sleep just by talking to him. He woke up this morning all mended and is as confused as we are."

Justin just sat there trying to take it all in, or at least come up with some kind of plausible explanation. As a church pastor he had seen and taken part in healings of kinds but nothing ever approaching fixing broken bones and trauma.

"Before you ask," Ted continued, "we checked the log. Nothing. No one saw her come in or go out. I don't know if he had dropped off and dreamed the whole thing, but he's better regardless."

"Ted," Justin tried to gather his thoughts, "who knows about this?"

"You, me, Squire and probably Kass by now. He was going to head home so the girls will be in on it soon enough."

"Okay Ted," Justin said, "I really don't think George needs to be in on this yet. I will give you a call on the drive back and we'll see how things are going then."

"No problem," Ted said sounding relieved. "Is George going to flip out or is he just going to flip out? I'm saying nothing."

They said their farewells and then Justin sat motionless for several minutes just thinking and watching the world go by. He had no answers but badly wanted to be back at base and involved rather than being stuck on the south coast. Starting the car again he pulled out and went off in search of the church.

The church of West Lulmouth was small compared to many but Justin thought it matched the small town rather well. Hundreds of years old it had probably been here before most of the town. As he opened the weathered wooden gate to the inner graveyard his eyes were scanning the roof line of the church, but for now he could only see the tower and the clock which looked like it hadn't turned for many years.

He was halfway up the path to the church when a voice stopped him. "Good morning, can I help you?"

Justin looked down and registered the smiling vicar in front of him. He was wearing a black shirt and white dog collar, and his silver hair fluttered in the light breeze. He had a kindly face and was slightly stooped with age.

"Good morning," Justin replied, "beautiful day."

The vicar's smile seemed to broaden a little more and now it also reached his eyes. "Yes indeed," he said, "but I think every day has its own beauty, don't you?"

Given the time Justin knew he would enjoy the company of this vicar but this was not the right time. He simply smiled back but there wasn't much cheer in his face.

The vicar's eyes fell to the bunch of flowers Justin was holding and his expression changed to one of compassion. "I mustn't delay you further, unless there is anything I can help you with?"

"Actually," Justin replied, "I am here on behalf of a friend who couldn't make the journey." He brought up the flowers a little and looked down at them, "I would like to pay my respects if you could point me in the right direction."

The vicar held his arm out wide in invitation, "of course I can my friend. Who is it you are looking for?"

Justin stepped forward and the vicar swung in beside him. "Hannah Clover," he started, and then added for good measure, "and Alice."

"Ah yes," the vicar's tone deepened as he recalled carrying out the service himself. "A terrible loss to the town, and poor Adam, he never really recovered from it."

"No," Justin said, "I can quite image, bless him."

Hearing the clear religious reference, the vicar steered Justin to the right and across the graveyard. "It's this way, just around the side here," he said pointing with a lazy prod of his finger. "My manners are slow I'm afraid, I am Father Peters."

"Thank you for showing me the way Father," Justin replied. "If you hadn't been here I would have spent some time searching. I'm Justin Naylor and I'm here to represent the Fox family."

The vicar slowed and looked up to the slightly taller figure of Justin, "then I am delighted I was here at the right time. I don't recall the Foxes, but then I am old and have forgotten too much that I should like to have remembered. He looked to his right and down at the marble headstone laying there. "Well here we are." He gave Justin another of those compassionate smiles. "I will leave you to your thoughts now."

"No, Father, "Justin gave a quick look to the turning vicar, "please wait with me."

The vicar stopped and offered a brief smile then bowed his head and stood silently. Justin looked at the mottled white and grey marble headstone and read the inscription.

HANNAH MARY CLOVER

1985 - 2011

BELOVED DAUGHTER WIFE AND MOTHER

TAKEN FROM US TOO SOON

AND

ALICE JASMINE CLOVER

2006 – 2011

SUNSHINE OF OUR LIVES

TOGETHER IN HEAVEN AND OUR HEARTS ETERNALLY

Kneeling at the side of the grave Justin laid the flowers gently against the headstone, and then closed his eyes for his own heartfelt prayer.

Several minutes passed and Justin became aware of the birds singing and the peace of the place. He opened his eyes and looked around, it really was a beautiful day.

He re-joined Father Peters and together they walked though the graveyard. When they reached the east side of the church Justin spotted what he was looking for jutting from the corner of the rooftop. It was a stone creature, almost childlike in appearance but with a grotesque face.

"Don't worry my friend, it can't see her," the vicar said as if he had read his thoughts.

"I'm pleased," Justin stopped while gazing up. "Alice didn't like them, did she?"

"Yes, your friends really are friends of the family I see. Indeed, little Alice was very frightened of them for some reason. She would cry in misery if she had to go past them." The vicar followed Justin's gaze, "we found a special place in the graveyard where she wouldn't have them above her, even in her rest." Both men looked at each other and Justin thought how pleased his friends would be to hear this news.

"How many are there?" Justin went back to scanning the roofline as far as he could see. "Oh, the gargoyles I mean."

The vicar once more started to walk slowly on and Justin stepped in beside him. "There were four added to the church a century or more ago."

"I see," Justin replied slightly surprised.

The vicar continued, "then one night, oh, it must be forty years ago or more, there was a terrible storm and the following morning there was one smashed on the ground below." He looked to his side at Justin, "it was a fearful mess I'm afraid and no chance of repairing it."

Justin smiled to himself and they wandered around the church and eventually arrived back at the front gate.

Justin thanked Father Peters for his company and they shook hands and said their parting words. As the pastor of Shillyford got back into his car he couldn't help thinking that his day had been a success, and that perhaps Kass and Squire would take some comfort and be able to find some closure and peace.

The smell was the first thing to hit Squire as he stepped into the front foyer of Highgate Hospital; sanitised and deathly. He knew why of course, but how could people exist and work with this overpowering stench of chemical in the air.

He walked past the reception desk where a middle aged nurse tapped away on a computer keyboard. She looked up as he approached and knowing who he was immediately reached for a door release button that would let him pass in to the corridors. Squire nodded his thanks and continued through the security doors and in to the corridor beyond. His boots squeaked quietly on the highly polished, highly bleached tiled floor. The first of the cries reminded him where he was, Highgate Hospital, a place where they locked the mental patients away from the world and kept things that should not be seen out of sight.

Having passed through two corridors he found the stairs to level two. The occasional deranged howl or cry was getting louder as he passed into the 'patient' area, or as he liked to call them, 'the prisoners.'

He headed through the doors for the stairs and climbed with his head down and mind thinking.

Once on level two he turned right and headed down the corridor which had the echo of a tunnel. Coming towards him was a porter pushing a wheelchair. Its occupant hung out of one side twitching and flinching at the air. Squire wanted to say hello or good morning, or something, but his eyes betrayed him and found a spot to look at so no eye contact would be made. The rubber wheels of the wheelchair squeaked against the floor as it sailed past with its slightly groaning occupant still shuffling about.

Squire had a sudden fear that as they went past a hand would reach out and grab his arm, a hand that had no mind behind it and he would turn to face a vacant face with mad, lolling eyes. The moment passed without event and a few moments later, with the squeak of the wheelchair still echoing down the corridor Squire arrived at room 220.

He paused and gathered his thoughts for a moment before pushing the door and heading into the best room in the hospital.

The smell of bleach was less in here and the sudden change in environment was strange. The floor had a nice warm green carpet for a start, and on one side there was a comfortable sofa and a coffee table. A television sat silently by, and vases with flowers stood in sterile defiance on the table. Such a shame that none of these things had, or would be used.

This was one room in Highgate that didn't feel like a hospital, but that was only because George Brooker saw to it that everything was made available and no care was missed.

The owner of the room lay on her bed as always. She was slim and olive skinned and was gently tripping and twitching. Her brown eyes gazed at nothing at all and her hands would occasionally flick up, like a conductor controlling an orchestra for just one note at a time.

"Hey little one," Squire said gently.

Sasha's eyes seemed to focus just for a second and her mouth seemed to make a small smile. Both these things were fleeting though and hard to tell if it was a reaction or just an involuntary movement.

"Let's get you some air," he said and moved to the window. He would be in trouble for it but he didn't care. He reached out and pushed the window open as wide as it could go and breathed in the fresh burst of clean air that flowed into the room.

Turning slowly, he sat down on the side of the bed next to Sasha. He could feel the cooler air gently wafting down and over her and he hoped it might be nice for her to breathe something clean and less stuffy.

She was only young still, not yet sixteen. Perhaps not the most dominant feature, but certainly an eye catcher was her thick yet feminine eyebrows which arched naturally complimenting her oval face shape. Sasha's eyes were narrow but not squinted. Her mahogany brown eyes were clear, but it was immediately apparent that they stared right past everything, as if they were blind. Her hair was wrapped around her like a silky veil and Squire gently pushed it aside so it wasn't in her face. He then took her small and limp left hand in his and gave it a gentle, reassuring squeeze.

It was never easy starting up the one sided conversation but he had plenty of practice, "Say hello to Steph for me."

Whether it was his voice or what he said he never knew, but once again her eyes pulled more into focus and wandered around the room as if she was searching for him. Her mouth opened and worked as if trying to speak words that her mind hadn't thought of yet. To Squire it was pure magic, it was life where the doctors said there was none. Sasha was there, somewhere. She might not be fully around but he knew some part of her knew he was there, and that made the visits so important.

For nearly two years he had come, partly out of guilt and duty but mostly because he didn't want her to be forgotten or left alone. Every two or three days he had sat talking to her about things going on in the world and their trips to the Void, and every small sign that she was in there was like a beacon to him.

"I used the Catching again Sasha," he went on. "I'm so pleased you and Steph were able to make it for me. I use it whenever we get the chance." Again Sasha seemed to be trying to smile in amongst the twitches and spasms.

The day they had lost her sister Steph was engraved on many hearts. It was supposed to be a day of celebration, but had turned into a nightmare that no one there would ever wake up from. Squire held her hand and remembered the pain that had brought them to where they were now.

There was joyful laughter in the air on that glorious summer day. The home and garden of George Brooker had never seen so many guests. Friends, family and friends of friends all mingled around the pool and the barbeque of the estate as they celebrated George's 70th birthday.

Nothing was left to chance and George had laid on everything. Caterers cooked food and there was music, singing and games on the lawns. As the day had turned out so warm many were clustered in and around the huge swimming pool where people jumped and dived and played.

Steph had brought some of her friends and they were busy throwing a ball at each other in the pool while various boys looked on and laughed. She was grinning from ear to ear and shouting at everyone in a joyful tone.

Her younger sister Sasha was also in the pool with a couple of her friends and they splashed and schemed plans for games for later.

Kass and Squire were chatting with Ted over in the cooking area and were eagerly awaiting the food. The smell of the barbeque going at full tilt wafted around the garden making everyone hungry.

Ted was laughing loud enough to be heard all over the garden as Kass did his famous impressions. Squire joined in while puffing on a smoke even though he had heard most of them a thousand times already.

A few minutes later George was calling everyone to attention and announced that the food was now ready, and that an orderly bundle could begin. Kass turned immediately and headed for the food and was forced to barge past Justin who had tried to cut in front of him. They jostled light-heartedly for position all the way like a couple of hungry schoolboys. The whole gathering started to move towards the food area where chairs and tables had been laid out piled high with salads and drinks.

Sasha and her friends had joined everyone else in the pool swimming towards the edge to get out. There was some friendly pushing and shoving at the ladders as everyone scrambled to find towels and head to the tables for a good seat with their friends. When her turn came on the ladder Sasha had turned to look for her sister and saw her swimming in the pool still.

"Come on slow coach," she called. "All the good bits will be gone if you don't get a move on."

"In a minute," Steph called back, "I just want to get in a few more lengths while it's empty."

Sasha continued on her way knowing Steph loved to swim. Now that she had the pool all to herself she could do some of her famous power laps. During her school years Steph had been asked by the school plenty of times to try out in the nationals. She could swim like a fish, but she had no interest in it. Her time was taken up with football and cross country running and she didn't have the time to swim as well.

Now she had her head down and was doing the front crawl at a speed no one else there could have matched.

Sasha had left her to it and after grabbing her towel had headed for the tables. People were now in eating mode and there was plenty to keep them busy. The catering crew turned out burgers, hot dogs and minted lamb steaks and all manner of fine food. People queued at the barbeques and loaded their plates with anything they wanted, and quite often more than they could eat. Sasha took her place and looked down the line at the sizzling food and chatted with Tom in front of her. He ran the local church youth club and was always smiling and chatting. He was tall and athletic in build with a strong and wide set jaw which honed his familiar boyish grin. Tom's hair was a colour that was not really a colour at all, but was closest to a mousy blond more than anything else. A dull colour though somewhat illuminated by a pair of glassy blue eyes. As a selfless man, he always turned the conversation away from himself and was a natural leader.

Once her plate was bulging Sasha cast a look around for a seat and spotted some room with Daisy and the Foxes. There seemed to be a lot of noise coming from that table and that was a good sign.

Heading over she plopped herself in a chair next to Daisy and smiled at everyone in turn.

"Hey Sasha," Daisy piped up. "How's it going?"

Sasha had interrupted some usual humour around the table, which seemed to be Kass talking like Sméagol.

"Yeah all good," she smiled. "Your uncle is such a loony."

Daisy looked over at Kass and laughed, "Yes, I'm worried it might run in the family."

"It does," Squire butted in. "Hello little one," he added with a smile at Sasha and got one back. "Speaking of family, where have you left Steph?"

"Oh, she's swimming still," Sasha added while bearing down on the salad bowl.

There were a few rumblings of "she's missing the food," around the table before Paige got up and said "I'll go," and started walking towards the pool.

The conversation struck up once more, talk of school, work and other things but was abruptly stopped by a loud shout from the pool, "Steph!"

Everyone turned to follow the call and witnessed Paige fully dressed dive in. The table holding the Fox family was the first to react but was closely followed by everyone else. Kass and Squire were running for the pool as fast as they could go with Justin closing in fast. As they reached the edge Paige was hauling Steph to the side and Squire's heart lurched in his chest. She was limp in Paige's arms.

Both he and Kass also jumped into the pool and helped pull Steph to the side. Now Justin and a crowd of others were reaching down to pull her out.

They carried her a little to the side and laid her gently down and made way for Ted who was calling out instructions. Justin was now on his phone calling for the ambulance that would arrive too late. By the time a puffing George Brooker had arrived Ted had already checked for a pulse and found none, and then turned Steph over and was pumping her arms up trying to empty her lungs.

The younger people were crying already and the joy of the day was gone in an instant. Squire was at Steph's head calling to her "Come on Steph! Come back."

When he was happy that the water was mostly gone Ted had turned her back over and was doing cardio pumps and was calling for others to take over from him in a minute or two.

There was a feeling of total helplessness now as Ted and others did all they could to revive her. Heads turned looking for the ambulance which they could hear in the distance.

Anna and some of the ladies were ushering the younger ones away and trying to clear some space and a certain amount of dignity for the stricken Steph laying on the grass in her black swimsuit.

A second panic started around them then as Sasha had been found collapsed on the grass nearby and people were trying to bring her round. At the time it all seemed so obvious, just a natural reaction to the situation with her sister, she had probably just fainted.

The ambulance crew arrived after what seemed too long. They were guided to the garden and came armed with their bags of lifesavers, but it was soon evident that they were too late. They tried everything they could and didn't stop until they had called for back-up, and she was in an ambulance heading away.

The second ambulance took Sasha, who they thought had collapsed from the shock and would come around soon. She never did. To those closest Sasha had fled this realm with her sister and had stayed with her, unable to return. George and Justin went to see their parents after the party had been called off. They wouldn't know it yet, but they had lost two of their daughters that day.

A seizure of some kind was given as the reason for Steph's drowning. Not all that uncommon in reality, and is just as able to strike someone in full health as one who may already have other problems. The funeral was a desperate affair and the whole village had turned up to show their support. Sasha remained in hospital for another two weeks before being transferred to Highgate Hospital Mental Institution. George Brooker had funded everything from the start; the room, the funeral, the care and just about everything else that needed taking care of. He spent his money on his feelings of guilt but for others it wasn't so easy.

Sasha's hand still lay limp and loose in Squire's but he held it like he had a tiny living bird in his grip. "Sasha, tell Steph we miss her," he whispered. "We miss you too."

He closed the window up again and made his promises to be back in a few days to see her again. As he backed away to the door he kept his eyes on her for any sign that she knew he was going but there was no movement at all and her eyes simply went back to their normal vacant stare. "See you soon little one," he whispered and left the room.

Sasha would have answered if she could. She knew he was there, but she was so far away and could do little to control her own body. Her mind was interlocked with Steph's and they communicated with their minds as easily as if they had spoken out loud.

As he walked back through the corridors he encountered more staff than on the way in. A porter pushed an empty wheelchair past and a janitor was mopping a section of corridor with long, slow swishing movements, and a yellow plastic sign warned of a slippery floor. The occasional cry broke the antiseptic rich silence and eventually Squire was back at the security doors leading to the way out and freedom.

He pressed the door button on the side and waited for the nurse to look up and spot him. She released the door and he nodded his thanks once more before heading out of the building and back into clean air.

Once in the car park again Squire reached inside his coat and withdrew his cigarettes and his phone. He turned the phone on and lit a smoke while it powered up.

He started walking across the car park with his phone in his hand and felt its familiar buzzing. Looking at it he saw messages had arrived from Kass, Paige and Daisy. News of his sudden and swift recovery had spread thanks to Ted, so Squire replied with quick responses and walked into town and found a sandwich shop to refuel in.

Half an hour later he was in a taxi and heading for home. He called Paige and Daisy telling them he was fine and would tell them all about it later. He also called Kass and said he would ring him when he got home as he had a lot to tell him.

After that he sat back and enjoyed the fifteen-minute journey back to Shillyford, and home.

VI.

Highgate Upper School was super modern when it was built, but times had changed. Now it looked like an out of place dinosaur sitting in the suburbs of Highgate Town. Every lunch time the volume at the school always increased ten fold from the general goings on of lots of people milling around, and playing on the hard courts and field.

Even through the noise and clamour of hustling teenagers going about their lunch break free time, Elle Naylor was determined now was the right time and tried to find a quiet spot for a phone call.

In the corridor leading out she saw Daisy trying to pack her whole school bag into a locker and called out, "Hey Daisy," and topped it off with a big smile.

Daisy looked up and shot back a shy smile but didn't reply. She looked half asleep so Elle walked on.

Elle was pretty high on the popularity charts at school which made trying to be alone for a change something of a challenge. She was constantly approached by flocks of friends, but smiled quickly before explaining she had to dash.

She decided there was nothing else for it but to head to the back of the field and try to stay clear of the boys playing football, and the usual suspect crowd of smokers.

Once she reached the grass and was marching towards the fence at the back of the field she reached for her phone and switched it on, and waited for the usual barrage of text messages to subside.

Today's messages were pretty typical and in large consisted of boys trying to hook up on a date, potentially finding the pastor's daughter something of a challenge, but one she was not the faintest bit interested in. She thought there should be a qualification in deleting text and was sure she would pass that one at least.

She had to avoid a gang of lads who thought she was coming to join them for a puff and endured the taunts as she ignored them and walked on. Whilst not being on the top shelf for beauty according to that year's potential suitors, she did have a naturally pretty face, and her subtle dress sense was getting her a lot of attention from the testosterone loaded boys from her year.

Finally, once she was as alone as she was likely to get she ran through the contacts on her phone, and after taking a deep breath to steady her nerves she pressed the call button.

After three rings the line at the other end was answered by Anna, who was covering for Kass who was also on the phone to Squire.

"Hi Anna, it's Elle here."

"Um, Elle?" Anna sounded confused.

This was half expected so Elle continued, "Justin's daughter."

"Ah of course!" Anna caught on suddenly, "how are you?"

"I'm good thanks." The lump in Elle's throat was growing so she pushed on before she could doubt herself. "Dad says you guys need people to try out?"

There was a moments silence before Anna continued. "That is right Elle, but you are too young and there is no way your dad is going to allow it."

"I know, but I want to do the tests anyway." She knew she still had six months to go before the critical age of sixteen, and she also knew her dad would have a fit. Even though this project was important to him she was also pretty sure he would not want his own daughter joining the list of people lost in the Void.

Anna went on, "Elle, I've put your name down for Friday evening but your dad will be there, and I think you need to have a discussion with him before you turn up."

"I will, I promise." Elle felt the first tingle of excitement. There was no certainty that she would pass the testing anyway but it was a start. "It's at the Manor House, 7.00pm. Don't wear a skirt."

"Okay thanks Anna. Will Kass be there too?"

"I don't know that yet but I expect so."

Once the call had ended Elle headed back past the gaggle of smokers towards the main building to see if she could find Daisy. If anyone could give any clues about the testing and what to expect it would be her.

Friday was only a day away so Elle started planning how to tackle her father that evening.

The taxi dropped Squire at the small parade of shops in the centre of Shillyford just after 2pm. From there he headed into the newsagent to stock up on cigarettes and a paper. Ellie was on the till and smiled her usual greeting and swapped pleasantries in her smooth northern accent. Squire Fox was well known in the village and was considered polite, caring and eccentric. He usually had a kind word for everyone but today he seemed a little lost in his thoughts and was uncharacteristically quiet.

The short walk home was easy enough and to top it all the sun had put in an appearance. He walked with his head down, deep in thought. He had so much to do and so little time to do it in.

He had thought he was going to be laid up for weeks, or months, but instead here he was back on the street, and he wanted to make good use of this unexpected bonus time he now found himself with.

He was in his own road now, a peaceful place with lots of established trees and hardly any traffic to speak of. It was as good a place as any for all the thinking he needed to do.

"Mr Fox." The female voice came from some way behind him. He didn't pause or slow in any way and just kept walking like he hadn't heard anything. He was half expecting the caller to announce she was doing a local survey or something equally trivial along those lines.

"Mr Fox." Once again the voice came from a lot closer and with more urgency to it this time and Squire had that almost certain feeling that whoever was calling him was closing in fast. Again he didn't pause; he was only a couple of houses from home and his sanctuary.

A third time the call came but was now right behind him, "Mr Fox, please."

Squire stopped and turned on his heel and was suddenly face to face with a beautiful young lady. Some may even call her a girl as she appeared to be in her early twenties. She had high and wide set cheek bones and overly large brown eyes. Her skin was pale and looked soft under her mass of shoulder length mousy brown hair which hung in her face a little, as the gentle breeze from earlier had turned into rather abrupt gusts. She had painted a colour onto her lips which appeared to be too bright for this dull and gloomy day. It was a warm shade of coral that could be said to be red, if it had been applied thicker.

She stopped suddenly, almost walking straight into him and had a mixture of nerves and alarm showing in her eyes. "Mr Fox, I'm sorry." She would have gone on but Squire was quicker.

"Lady," he started, "I don't know you, and I don't have time to talk to you, and I am late for something more important."

She looked at her feet for a moment as if scolded and then looked back into his eyes. "Please, this is very important to me," she continued and looked genuinely sincere.

Squire was taking in details fast but processing them slow. The mousy blonde hair, the smart but casual attire, the athletic build and the dark brown bruise covering most of her left cheek. The penny dropped for Squire but he didn't hesitate before continuing.

"And you are?"

"Moreton," she responded. "Bailey Moreton."

Her voice told Squire she was well educated and that she had spent most of her time in the wealthier parts of London.

"Well, Miss Moreton," he went on in a gentle but firm manner. "Please don't think me rude or impolite, but I don't know anyone of that name and time for me is a precious thing." She had started to chew on one side of her bottom lip in her desperation to speak but Squire went on. "If you want I can meet with you another time, but for now I really must be getting on."

With that he turned on his heel and continued on his way. He could see his front path and was determined to get there.

"Please Mr Fox, please wait," she was following but slowly now, hardly able to keep going after him. Despite the obvious passion in her plea he did not flinch and continued to walk on.

"Some things that cannot be broken can be repaired," she called at his back.

Squire stopped on the spot and remained totally still for a few moments as the words hit home like a lightening strike. Slowly he turned around with a face that was rapidly losing its colour and walked the few steps back to her.

He reached forward and gently took hold of her shoulders. "What did you say?" he implored in a calm and gentle voice.

Bailey was staring at the ground but looked up into his face just long enough for a single tear to drop from each eyelash and then looked back down again.

Squire was the one pleading now and his voice was slow and kind, "Who told you that?"

Once again she looked up and her eyes filled with tears, "You did."

Justin arrived home tired from the long drive from the south coast. Dropping his things down on one of the chairs in the living room he headed straight for the kitchen to put the kettle on as a cup of tea was urgently needed.

The kitchen was where he spent a lot of his time preparing his sermons and dealing with the other business of the day, and he had his small wooden desk against the wall just outside the main kitchen.

On his way to the kettle he noticed the message light blinking on the answer phone perched on his desk. Ignoring it for a minute he walked straight past and filled the kettle. Once that was switched on he went back to the phone and played the messages.

There was one from George asking if they could have a quick catch up before the testing on Friday evening, and another from his wife Sarah to say she hoped he had a safe trip and to let her know he was home safe. The last one was the most interesting one though and caused him to sit up in the hard wooden chair at his desk.

"Hello Justin, it's Ashley. Thanks for the email about finding people to help with your special project and the meeting tomorrow evening. Could you put my name down please and I will see you there? Bye."

Justin was still sitting there thinking when the kettle clicked off and woke him from his musings. He got up and made tea while still deep in thought. Ashley was a good candidate, a really good one, and he was surprised and pleased she had agreed and was going to be at the testing. She was both highly spiritual and had a warm personality that would be good for the team. All she had to do was pass the tests.

His email had gone out after the meeting at the barn and he was dubious at the time about getting any response at all. The message had gone to everyone in the critical age group of the sixteen to twenty-five year olds from his church and the surrounding ones.

They had been invited to a testing to select the strongest and most intelligent candidates for a special top secret project the church was sponsoring. They would need to be ready for severe physical and mental challenges. Details had been kept vague as a matter of course, with no mention of what the special project was or what it would demand from people. In the past few years many had been lost and with every one the emotional pain was enormous.

The missing persons list would have been worrying had it not been for all the covering up that the team did, with excuses of emigrated, went off to get married, joined the navy and the like. The parents of the lost were a different matter and they naturally wanted answers, something Justin was rather good at.

Armed with his tea and already feeling the relief to be home he called Sarah at work and let her know he was back, and that everything had gone better than he could have asked for, and that he would treat her to dinner tonight. Elle would be home from school soon and they could have a quiet evening in together.

Sometimes you can just be so wrong.

Highgate Hospital Room 220 received a second visitor that afternoon, another one of its regulars. He was one of few words but the staff were always pleased to see him. He always had a kind word to say to everyone.

Paul McCoy sat at the side of Sasha's bed talking business. His job was to make the gadgets for the team, gadgets that were beyond his or anyone else's understanding.

At his feet lay a case holding the pieces he had made or purchased through secret hidden contacts. In truth if anyone had stopped him and checked everything over they would have found nothing of interest as nothing actually did anything. Well, not here anyway. Today would have been different however. A search of his bag would have landed him in jail pretty quickly.

His greatest joy was Squire's Catching. He had made it one afternoon and while he made it he poured all of his memories of its new owner into it. There were no distractions that day so he could think and work. While he cut and shaped the metal he remembered Squire's character traits and his emotional strengths, and had tuned the new gadget to the person who would own it.

He had built something totally useless that did nothing at all, except open and close at the touch of a tiny button on the stem. The second part of the process was where the impossible had started to happen.

He had laid the new tool in Sasha's hand and told her all about Squire and his need for an incredible weapon for good. He believed those thoughts and messages had also reached Steph, who was not part of this plane of existence, and together they had added something of the Void to it.

The last part had been down to Squire himself, something that would make it unique to him, and him alone. As it turned out it was something he said over it, but the words carried enough of himself to make it come to life.

The work he had for Sasha today would be easier as there was no real personal tuning required as he just needed them to work for anyone entering the Void that was carrying them.

One by one he selected pieces and laid them in Sasha's hand, and then spoke to her about what they were and what he needed from them.

Each time Sasha gave no response at all that she was aware of anything, but Paul trusted that somewhere far away she and her sister were working their magic over them. He wouldn't know for sure until they were tried out in the Void for real, something that was potentially very dangerous, but Paul McCoy had something few would understand or be able to quantify.

His faith was real, and it was massive.

Squire sat at the natural wood table in his kitchen holding the steaming cup of tea Bailey had made him. She sat opposite him but was quiet and still and observed his still gently shaking hands.

"I'm sorry," was the only way she could start the conversation.

She hadn't realised the impact those words would have on him outside the house, but she had known they were important. She didn't even want to have to use them but he was walking away and it was the only way of really reaching him.

Those words had done something to him though. When she had met him in the street just minutes earlier he had shone out like a hero from her imagination and now he just looked devastated.

He lifted the trembling cup and took another sip with his eyes still cast down on the table between them. Finally, he replied. "I'm not a clever man," he said very slowly while lifting his eyes to meet hers. "We have to take this very slowly," he paused and raised the cup once again seeming to take comfort in the tea. "You need to explain to me carefully, like you are talking to a child. I don't understand what is happening or why, so you must be slow and allow me time to think."

There was still barely any colour in his face but he was starting to recover himself. Bailey agreed immediately. It had taken her the best part of two years to find him and he had been in her dreams since then. She was sitting with the man she had met while she slept, someone she couldn't believe was real.

"How about if you ask me questions and I will answer," she started. "That way you can put things in the right order for yourself." She also sipped at her tea and considered the slogan marked on the mug.

FEEL THE FEAR AND THEN DO IT ANYWAY

She was sure that meant something in this household. Her quick scan of the place on the way in told her that more than one

113

person lived here, and none of them spent too much time making it look tidy.

Everywhere had that comfy 'lived in' look to it although everything was clean. Books were piled up all over the place and there was something she guessed was school work spread out all over the table in the dining room.

The shelf over the fireplace in the front room was covered in a clutter of photo frames of different sizes and faces she didn't recognise smiled out of them from memories past.

There was peace in the house though - she hadn't missed that bit. She had felt at ease the second she walked through the door, like the house itself radiated something soothing in to the air.

"I only heard those words a day ago," Squire had begun again. "I had never heard them before and I don't understand them even now. You say I said them to you but I don't know how that is possible. When did I say them?"

Once he had spoken he went back to his tea as if it would hold him up for the bad news he was waiting for.

"I don't understand the words either," she began, "but I don't think you told me those words so that I would understand." She let the statement sink in for a moment before continuing. "I think you said them to me so that when we met you would believe me."

Squire was nodding slowly. Yes, he believed her alright but there was still one major problem - he had never met her.

"I can't tell you the exact date, but give or take a bit I've been looking for you for two years."

Squire's head came up and his forehead was grooved with wrinkles, or as he liked to call them, 'care lines.' "I said those words to you two years ago? That's not possible."

Now it was Bailey's turn to look at the table while turning her tea cup from side to side.

"This one is harder," he went on. "Where did I say them?"

"Oh," Bailey seemed relieved the question was easier than she thought, "in my dream. You had already told me your name but before you left my dream you told me the other bit."

"A dream?" Squire's eyebrows were at full salute, "I told you that stuff in a dream?"

Bailey smiled for the first time, just a small one. "Of course in a dream, where did you think it would have been? We met in a dream and you told me your name and that other stuff and then I spent the next couple of years trying to find you."

Squire didn't know if he felt better about things or worse. His understanding of the situation wasn't getting any better though - that much he knew.

"That's what you do isn't it?" She pushed on now hoping she was nearing some answers herself, "up in that barn place that is kept so secret."

"You think we go there to dream?" His question was straightforward and was giving him a chance to think. He realised

115

she didn't know what the Void was and more questions were forming in his mind quicker than he could cope with.

"I don't know what you do Mr Fox," she continued. "I only know I followed you there and was jumped by someone in the dark to stop me getting too close." It was said without any malice, as if she had taken the beating as a penalty for arriving at a party without an invite.

"So it was you," he said confirming what he had expected about the brown bruise she was sporting. Paige really did land a good one. "Please call me Squire from now on; after all, it appears we are old friends already."

There was a small laugh from Bailey this time and her smile reached her eyes. "I don't think you go to dream there, but I do think you have found a way to enter people's dreams or something. I don't know how you said stuff in the past that you only heard recently though; that's a bit strange."

Squire had already considered this fact more than anything else, and if he was right, suspected he was going to die sometime soon. Why and how he travelled back two years to give a message to Bailey was just a mystery that would keep him guessing.

The sound of the front door closing stopped their conversation and a moment later Paige entered the kitchen. She looked at her father first and her eyes told her the same thing Ted had called about. He was better in body but his eyes were full of thought.

She wandered in to the kitchen, "So Ted wasn't kidding then? You really are all mended."

"Hey honey," Squire responded with only a half hearted effort to sound cheerful. "I would like to introduce you to Bailey." He cast his eyes at Bailey, and Paige did the same while stepping forward to offer her hand.

They shook hands and said hello politely while they measured each other up mentally and physically.

"Have we met before," Paige said having spotted the fresh bruise on the cheek of the visitor.

"Yes you have," Squire added which caused Bailey to blush as she realised who she was now being introduced to.

"Oh, how awkward," she offered to fill the sudden silence.

Paige didn't seem fazed at all - if her dad was sitting down with a cup of tea with the intruder from last night that was fine with her. "I'm sorry about your face," Paige now headed to the fridge to see what could be raided from there.

Bailey touched her face without thinking, "It's fine, I guess I knew I was being sneaky and probably deserved it."

Paige abandoned the fridge and turned to the table again. "I wouldn't mind learning to run like you though," she said taking in Bailey with her eyes. "You run like a gazelle."

Bailey's response was just a smile. Yes, she could run when the need arose. Four years in her athletics team had its uses even though she had never taken it very seriously at the time.

117

"Do you have plans tomorrow Paige?" Squire was looking straight at her and she looked brighter than when she had walked in.

"Nothing that can't be changed easily enough," she replied. "What do you need?"

Squire looked over at Bailey and took a moment to let his mind settle down. He had the strangest feeling about all of this and words from the Master repeated in his head.

"When clouds of doubt hide your goal it is best to follow your heart."

Bailey also waited for what was coming and hoped it would not be to frog march her out of the county or something equally bad.

"Would you take Bailey into town and find her some new clothes?" Squire asked.

The two ladies looked at each other. Paige seemed to have guessed what Squire had planned straight away, but the poor visitor looked confused. She looked down at her dress and wondered what was wrong with it as it was one of her favourites.

"Is this what I think it is?" Paige put in.

"Yes honey," Squire leaned back in his chair having made his choice. "We go in tomorrow evening."

VII.

Paul McCoy stood in the entrance hall of the barn having been greeted and told to come in by Anna. His normal habit was not to come in though, at least not at the first request. He stood there quietly and slightly awkwardly until Kass wandered out.

"How goes things Tinker?" Kass began and immediately turned and headed for the living room.

This time Paul followed with his brown case held firmly in front of him. "Oh, I think things are going okay," he replied as he entered the living room. He selected his usual chair and sat down stiffly and perched on the edge of the seat.

Anna called from the kitchen, "Tinker, can I get you anything?"

He looked up to where the kitchen entrance was and called back, "Ah maybe a little coffee would be nice, thanks."

Kass was lounging in his wingback with his feet on the coffee table in front of him and trying to not sound too eager. "Did you go to Highgate as planned?"

"Ah yes," Paul responded and laid the case on the floor and clicked the latches.

"How are Sasha and Steph?" Kass knew it was a stupid question the moment he uttered it, but past experience with the team's equipment specialist meant that he knew the best approach was to keep him talking.

Paul opened the case and was casting around inside with his eyes trying to work out what to produce first. "Ah, you know."

Kass did know unfortunately and wished things were better. The arrival of Anna lightened the atmosphere as she bustled in with a tray of cups. She handed them out and then took a chair herself and settled down with her tea.

Paul had produced one of the bracelets from his case and was holding it up for inspection proudly. "Void Sat-nav," he announced.

Kass and Anna stared back but couldn't see what had changed, although something was definitely out of place.

Paul passed his new work over to Kass who took it and spun it around in his fingers. It looked just the same as before, "What is that smell Tinker?" The slightly musty smell was neither too strong nor unpleasant, but was gently wafting around the room.

Now was the time that Paul liked the best when he could do something really useful for the team. "Well, I heard there was this butterfly. It gives out a scent that can attract the same species from miles away."

Kass could see where this was heading straight away and liked it a lot. Smiling was not something he did very often, but he allowed himself just a small one before passing the bracelet to his wife beside him.

Paul was happy with the response, "I asked the girls if maybe they could boost the power and draw them together."

Anna was on her feet and heading for Paul at once, "Tinker, you are a genius and we love you for it." She bent down and gave his neck a big hug. Heading back to her seat again she threw Kass a great big smile. This was the sort of thing that would really help them on the other side.

Kass was also really pleased and he was slightly more animated than his normal dead pan expression. "What can I say," he began. "If this works it will be brilliant." It would also mean he could stay a lot closer to Squire, and hopefully keep a close eye on him.

Paul had proceeded to remove all the bracelets from the case and the musty smell in the room grew stronger.

Reaching for another Kass held two of them in his hands and moved them closer together until he heard the faint click as they touched. He had been wondering if there was going to be something like a magnetic pull toward each other. There was nothing. He made a mental note to test that again in the Void and suspected there would be a different response.

"What else have you got in there Tinker?" Anna called over excited.

Paul then removed his second project of the week. In his hand he held what was obviously a gun. He turned it over and looked at it closely to make sure everything was up to standard.

"I've got a bunch of these," he said and passed one to Kass.

As soon as he held it Kass knew what it was. Squire already had one shut away in the Fox Box in the barn.

"You said it wasn't the guns that were the problem," Paul offered. "It's a Walther P99 Titanium but I modified the bullets to be non-lethal."

Kass looked it over and was impressed. Tinker had a list of very handy friends, and to have gotten all this together so quickly he must have had some help. He pressed the magazine release button and ejected the sleeve.

Looking closely at it he saw that the frame was the same, but where the bullets would normally go, was filled with something different.

"Please don't ask me too many questions about how this is going to work," Paul predicted the next question. "The bullets are basically a compressed gas shell that fires a gel ball containing a tiny fragment of the same quartz that Squire has in the Catching. I figured if it hit any of the team nothing would happen, other than it would sting like crazy. If it hits an innocent target the worst that could happen would be to send them on like the Catching does. If it hits anything else, I think it will banish it and that's why I called it a Banisher."

Kass reloaded the magazine and pointed the gun across the room and pulled the trigger. There was a loud bang, very much like a normal gun and one of the pictures on the wall jolted as the gel ball hit it and broke apart.

"This is excellent Tinker," Kass was delighted. "Squire will be really pleased. I expect he will want to try them out as soon as possible."

Once again Paul seemed quietly pleased with the response. He now turned the case to face Kass and tipped it up. There was a heavy clump as the contents emptied onto the living room floor. "I've got ten so far," Paul began, "and holsters too and some for right hand and some for left."

Anna was beaming again. The thought of Squire armed once more was a massive relief to her. "This is so much better than we could possibly have hoped for," she said full of emotion. "Thank you so much Tinker, you are amazing."

Paul may have blushed slightly but did his best to brush the praise aside. He looked at Kass, "You boys risk your lives every time you go into that place. This is the least I can do to help."

After their drinks were all gone and they had caught up with all the other news, the pair took the bracelets and the Banishers to the barn. The bracelets once more went into their wooden box on the bench and they stashed the guns in the Fox Box, until they could find somewhere better. Kass removed the P99 with real bullets so they wouldn't get confused and found a secure place to hide it away in the farmhouse.

"I can't believe you took a case full of guns into the hospital Tinker," Kass said. "That was some risk you took."

Paul didn't look overly concerned. "Well they haven't searched me yet so I figured it would be safe."

When everything had been put away Kass walked Paul to his car and thanked him once again for getting everything together so quickly.

"Is there anything else you need Kass?" Paul said. As always he was keen to help with anything he could.

Kass gave it a moments thought, "Perhaps an auto-hit function on the guns would be handy for me." They both gave a gentle laugh and Kass was soon watching Paul drive off down the lane.

His mind turned to his brother and how much he was looking forward to telling him about the new equipment, but remembered Squire had told him he was going to ring that afternoon. So far that bit hadn't happened. No doubt he was busy getting side-tracked as usual. Kass headed back into the house and he and Anna started to check through the paperwork they would need for the testing evening tomorrow.

When Daisy arrived home from school she had found her dad, sister and Bailey gathered in the living room chatting. She dumped her school things and was introduced to Bailey, and given a speedy run through of how they had come to meet.

She sat herself down and announced her only bit of exciting news of the day. Elle had applied for testing and was going to break the news to her family this evening. There was a sudden rush of opinions given by Paige and Squire on how that was likely to go, probably not well.

"How about," Squire cut in, "we do a carpet picnic and a film tonight?"

Paige and Daisy both approved in unison and started offering suggestions for food. While that was going on Squire excused himself to go and phone his brother but promised to be back quickly to get dinner ordered.

"Paige," Bailey asked. "Maybe I should just go now and let you guys be alone to have a nice evening with just the family?"

Both Paige and Daisy gave each other a knowing look then turned and smiled at their visitor.

"You can stop thinking like that right now," Paige began. "You are part of something bigger now, and that makes you part of a different family."

Bailey was so happy she could have cried. She had followed her heart and her instincts, even though for most of those two years she was convinced she was on a wild goose chase. It was only recently that she had discovered someone called Squire Fox actually existed, and then things had begun to move much faster.

Her instincts had brought her here even if she didn't know why. Now a family had accepted her for no better reason than she had remembered some words from a dream that meant a great deal to the dream walker. It was early days still but Bailey Moreton was telling herself she was not going to let anyone down.

The one thing Kass really needed right now was a good long chat with his brother. He had already heard from Ted about an old lady that had arrived at the hospital but hadn't shown up on any visitor records. She had then gone on about a miracle cure as well as inflicting immediate sleep and dreams that she had haunted with strange riddles.

Now that he had actually got Squire on the phone he was informed that this had to be a quicky as he was treating the girls to a carpet picnic.

"I'll tell you about the old lady another time," Squire had promised.

Kass found that highly doubtful the way things were going, but had news of his own. He relayed the news about Justin's visit to the church, the gargoyles and the grave, and then gave a brief account of Tinker's visit with more toys.

The whole conversation couldn't have been longer than five minutes and left him thinking events were going like a runaway train. The trouble was Squire was on the train and Kass was running along behind it.

Just when things seemed to be calming down slightly the next bombshell arrived. "Oh Kass, we need to jump tomorrow evening. I'm going to be bringing someone. Keep it to yourself."

"But tomorrow evening is testing," Kass said as quickly as he could but the line was already dead.

When Squire returned to the living room he found a gathering around the photos above the fireplace.

Bailey had put a lot of the names to faces as most of the photos included the family she was going to be spending the evening with.

"This one," Daisy said pointing at another photo, "is our Uncle Kass and Auntie Anna." She waited a moment for Bailey to take in the new faces smiling out of the frame. "They are both barking mad though. You will meet them soon enough I'm sure."

"Is this your mum?" Bailey had noticed that there were photos with four people in and the slender blonde lady in the pictures seemed to have features she could see in the girls.

"What do we want to order then ladies?" Squire said from the doorway as he entered.

Bailey knew at once she was on slippery ground from the way the conversation stopped in its tracks and she dropped the subject. "I think Pizza is top of the list," she said with a hopeful smile. "Why don't you choose though?"

Squire headed over to the phone on the side and handed it to Paige. "Do the honours please honey." The phone was taken from his hand and an order placed that would feed more than the four of them.

While food was being taken care of Daisy had gazed through the shelves of dvds and pulled a candidate out for their entertainment.

"Pick us something sensible won't you?" Squire gave her a knowing look.

Daisy just smiled and her face was full of peace. "Why would you doubt me?" She threw a wink at Bailey who smiled in return.

Squire was dragging the coffee table away so that the floor was clear and they could all sit down to their picnic in front of the television.

"Job done," Paige called as she put the phone back on its charger. "We won't be able to move afterwards so I'm off to find some comfy clothes instead."

She and Daisy both left the room to change leaving Bailey and Squire alone for a few minutes.

"I'm sorry if I was being nosey," she said watching him, "about your wife."

Squire looked at one of the photos. It was a larger portrait of the woman in the group pictures. "It's okay," he replied, but his eyes rested on the photo just a little bit too long and he seemed to drift off in thought. Bailey knew it wasn't okay and didn't press the subject.

"Will you tell me what it is that you do Mr, sorry, Squire?"

The haze vanished and he looked back at her, and then went to settle himself in his favourite chair. "Sure," he offered, "but after the film." He looked calm again and whatever ghost had arisen moments before was gone again.

The carpet picnic started in earnest half an hour later. Paige and Daisy had both changed into joggers and sweatshirts and the four of them huddled around a feast spread out in the centre of the living room floor.

"I've never had a carpet picnic before," Bailey said while balancing a slice of southern spicy pizza in her hand. "Just a shame I'm overdressed for the occasion." Her patterned summer dress now felt a little too formal for her dinner engagement, but she was having a fabulous time.

There were pizzas, spicy chicken wings and garlic bread spread in front of them, and Daisy was loading four glasses with Coke in a manner that suggested these picnics happened regularly.

The talk was casual and had a ring of humour about it all the time, something Bailey was having trouble keeping up with. So many things were said that were obviously close to the three of them and she liked the way they laughed together as they fought over the food.

Fifteen minutes later, with only half the food gone she caved in and leant back against the sofa groaning. "Oh I can't eat another thing."

"Lightweight," Paige said without taking her eyes off the chicken wing she was busily dipping in the barbeque sauce.

"Pathetic," Daisy joined in.

"Useless," Squire added last.

Bailey was concerned; they all seemed to be so serious, but then the three of them burst out laughing. The Fox family humour once again left her at a loss but she joined in the laughing. Part of her didn't want the evening to end. She hadn't laughed so much or felt so comfortable around people for a long time.

Justin sat downstairs alone and his anger festered just below the surface. There had been serious words in the house over dinner. His wife Sarah had gone out to visit her mother and Elle was upstairs in her room with her headphones on, and in no mood to talk further.

Everything had started well with Justin filling them in on his visit to the south coast. Sarah and Elle were family and knew most of the goings on with his work, even if they were not allowed to discuss them outside the house.

Sarah had also had an eventful day at work. The charity she worked for had been donated a substantial amount of money, which meant they could plan in earnest for at least another year of operations.

Both Justin and Sarah had replied at the same time when Elle had announced she wanted to try out in the testing, "No, you're too young."

Elle had seen a shadow of fear pass briefly past her father's eyes at the same time. Too many lives had been lost already and this was not one he was prepared to risk.

She wasn't about to give up that easily though and the debate had soon turned rather heated when she asked a second time.

"I said no, and that's the end of it," Justin said firmly.

Sarah had tried to be the peacekeeper and added, "Why don't you wait until next year honey? Your exams will be done and you will be sixteen then."

"No," Elle was adamant. "I want to enter now. The team needs people and I think I'm ready."

Justin and Sarah had exchanged a look between each other and the meaning was clear. He was becoming annoyed, something that rarely happened. Sarah was trying to keep the peace for all parties, and already knew that whatever came out of this evening was going to leave hurt feelings on both sides.

Justin went on, "Elle, we have said no, and while you live under our roof you will listen to what we say."

It was an argument that had been put to her a dozen times at least. She was considered a child and therefore had to obey her elders. She understood the principle and had always backed down in the past, but not this time.

"Do I have to move out then dad? Is that what you are going to make me do?"

Sarah reached for Justin's hand on the table to offer her support, and also to urge some reasoned thinking.

"Why would you want to join the team," Justin fired back, now clearly getting angry. "People die in there, or hadn't you noticed. Do you think that's what I want for my own daughter?"

Elle was ready, "So it's fine for other people to gamble their lives for you but not me? You think another year is going to make a difference?"

There was no comeback this time, Justin was cornered and had nowhere to go. Elle was right and he knew it. "Go to your room," he ordered.

The discussion was over. She saw the look in her mother's eyes and got up and left the table. In her room on her own she sat and stewed, but resolved not to turn childish and do anything stupid.

Before going out her mother had come in and told her she was proud that Elle wanted to join the team and hoped it was for the right reasons. She left her with simple advice, "Why don't you sleep on it for tonight? I will support you whatever you decide, but I'm sure you know how much this is hurting your dad."

Of course Elle did and she knew if things were the other way around, and it was her dad thinking of entering the Void she would be equally against it. Her mind was already made up though. Tomorrow she would take the tests and allow them to make the choice for her.

They sat together watching the movie and Bailey was introduced to Monty Python during her twenty fourth year of life. Both Paige and Daisy had retired to bed shortly afterwards, but before they turned in they brought down a spare quilt and pillows.

"I wasn't expecting to stay," Bailey announced. "I can go back to the hotel. I don't want to put you guys to any trouble."

"I think by the time I have explained what I do it's going to be stupid o'clock so you may as well just accept that tonight you have a couch." Squire had made coffee for them both and now sat opposite her.

Only the lamp on the desk was on and the room was quite dark. They sipped their coffees and they began a long evening of talking.

Bailey gave a brief rundown on her life. The father she hadn't known and the mother who preferred dating than looking after her child. At an early age she had decided not to grow up the same, and had worked hard at school and graduated with an honours degree in history from Oxford University. She had left her job at the Natural

133

History Museum in London three months earlier to pursue something different, and had done a bit of support teaching in the time between.

Squire made more coffee then settled down for her induction into a new world. "Imagine the Earth and everything you know of in this universe to be an island. Also try and picture Heaven and Hell as other islands." He paused and watched her eyes to make sure she was making the connection. "Those islands float, if you can call it that, in a sea that keeps them apart. We call that sea the Void. It is as real as this planet of ours, although it is highly unpredictable."

"And you go there?" She said it more as a statement than a question. "You go to the Void." She held her coffee cup in both hands while perching on the edge of the couch eager not to miss a single word.

Squire recounted the basics and described how he and Kass jumped in and out of the Void. He gave examples of the things they had encountered, and how they had been able to send lost souls from there to somewhere else.

"What are you looking for in there?" Her mind was filling with things she couldn't quite imagine and wondered what she had got herself involved with.

"Heaven." Squire's response was simple and final. "To find out if it really is there. So far we are pretty sure something else is there, but if we could prove the existence of Heaven it would change a whole lot of things back here."

They talked into the early hours of Friday morning but there always seemed so much more they needed to talk about. Bailey spoke of her dream in as much detail as she could remember, which wasn't really very much. Most of it had faded away by the morning as dreams do, but she had clung to the words of Squire Fox, and they had not left her.

"Did I dream a premonition, or déjà vu or something?"

Squire put out the cigarette he had been worrying over in the ashtray on the coffee table. "Perhaps. I don't know right now." He got slowly to his feet and headed for the hallway. "Get some sleep. It's going to be a long day tomorrow." He offered a tired smile. "Goodnight."

Bailey's mind was too full of things to rest so she made another cup of coffee and then put the quilt and pillows over the couch, and eventually drifted off. In her dreams she was falling.

Squire Fox was standing like a statue against a tide of evil. He held a gun in each hand and was firing in all directions but his face was haunted with a mixture of determination and resignation. He knew he was not going to survive.

Bailey tried to reach him but her movements were slow and clumsy and panic rose like a flood in her, but still she moved so slowly.

A hand grabbed her shoulder and pulled her backwards and she turned to see who it was. A man she vaguely recognised with black hair and beard yelled at her, "Come on!"

He was dragging her away. She tried to resist but he was hauling her now. She turned back to join the fight with Squire. He was totally outnumbered but still firing all around himself.

"COME ON!" His hand still held her shoulder and his face was a mess of concern.

Suddenly everything went white.

"Bailey." A new voice called from far away. A hand was shaking her shoulder. "Come on wake up."

She opened her eyes to find Daisy staring down at her. She was on the couch and her thrashing had turned the quilt into a piled up wreck on top of her. Her breathing was hard but settling quickly.

Daisy held her shoulder softly. "It's only a dream," she said in her calm and soothing voice. "I have to go now but I will see you later."

She turned to go and Bailey noticed her school blazer and skirt, and the scruffy book bag slung over her shoulder. Daisy gave her a wave on the way out and soon enough there was the sound of the front door closing.

The dream was fresh in her head still and she immediately concentrated on it again trying to stop it evaporating. She replayed it over and over until she was sure it was going to stay and then slowly she allowed herself to start the day in earnest.

The house was quiet so she guessed no one else was up yet. She shoved the quilt off of herself and onto the floor and swung her legs down. She stood and walked over to the fireplace in just her underwear, and once again scanned the photos lined up there. Almost immediately her eyes found the face of the one with dark hair and beard looking back at her: Squire's brother.

Looking at herself in the mirror over the fireplace she stuck a hand into her hair and tried to make it look a little less like she had slept in a ditch. She gave up almost as quickly and shrugged. She turned and trampled over the quilt and picked up her dress from the floor and then headed for the bathroom. She hoped the shower wouldn't wake the others.

VIII.

The day was bright and fresh and Daisy arrived a few minutes early for the bus to school. Climbing on she went to her normal seat and threw her bag onto the rail above her row and slid in up to the window.

A few seconds later Elle dumped herself down next to her. "Hey Daisy," she said with tired eyes.

"Hey," came the reply. "So how did your evening go then?"

Elle rolled her eyes but managed a small smile with just one side of her mouth. "Like gulping down cold sick really." There was smiling from both girls now.

She had used one of Daisy's own expressions on her and it seemed to fit the situation perfectly. "Oh joy. That good?"

"But I expect I will be seeing you tonight," the smile now reached her ears. "Be nice won't you?"

Daisy was both happy and surprised in equal measures, and smiled as she turned to watch the village of Shillyford slide past the window outside. "I'm always nice."

Bailey walked into the kitchen forty minutes later with her hair still damp and she had that hot, clean smell. She was back in her dress again and once again felt out of place.

"Morning," Paige said looking up from her toast. "Sleep okay?" She was in jeans and a sweat shirt today and looked like most eighteen year olds who didn't dress to impress.

"Um, not too bad," her hesitation was the only clue that she didn't feel like she had really slept much at all. She set herself down at the table and realised she was looking at the same features as yesterday but on a much younger face.

She saw the same determination on the face of Paige as she had her father. The pitch of the eyebrows and the slender mouth were both the same. "Help yourself to breakfast."

Bailey was momentarily taken aback that she was no longer being treated like a guest, but soon realised it was a compliment. Already she was part of the house.

Getting up she opened cupboards and searched around. She found breakfast cereals and a bowl without any trouble and also flicked the kettle on as she headed for the fridge.

On the door there was a note jotted down on yellow paper and held in place by a magnet. It was simple and to the point.

Paige
Bailey can have anything and everything she needs. You have good judgement so have fun with George's money. Put it all on the card.

Dad x

"Wow," Bailey said smiling. "Anything and everything I need. I can think of quite a few things to keep me going." She turned and beamed at Paige who had got up and was making tea for them.

"As long as it's for a Void jump that is, but don't worry. We are going to have some fun with this," she finished with a wink.

Half an hour later they were both in Paige's Fiat 500 heading for the shopping centre in Milton Keynes for a few hours of retail therapy.

Squire awoke to an empty house and was pleased to find he had some time to himself. He wasted half an hour in the bathroom having a shower and a shave, and thought he looked less haggard afterwards. His breakfast was eaten while at his desk checking through the post, most of which consisted of offers and junk which he then stored in special file b.1.n.

Seeing that the day was bright and clear he resorted to go for a walk and hoped the cobwebs would get blown away. Twenty minutes later he was strolling through the village park with his hands stuck firmly in his pockets and his head down. He didn't notice the flock of mums heading home after various school drop offs, talking passionately about last night's meaningless soap operas, or the sudden outbreak of nits at the junior school. The small huddle of boys on their bikes hovering around the climbing frame eyed him carefully in case he turned out to be an undercover cop. Squire didn't even notice them.

There was a small lake in the park complete with a rustic and totally out of place wooden bridge, and its own compliment of ducks that looked a little too well fed. Skirting the lake Squire kept walking and noticed nobody. His ability to zone out was pretty well known, and in the past he had totally ignored people talking straight at him. It was this element of total detachment that made him so able to sink out of reality and into the Void.

At the furthest point from the entrance there was a copse of trees with the odd bench thrown in for good measure. During the hot summer days' people would retreat to the relative shade and peace of this area, and it was to this small island of tranquillity that he now headed.

There was a wooden bench facing the park which had a plaque on it, informing any who took the time to read it, that it had been donated in remembrance of the fallen in the Great War.

Squire settled down on one side and rummaged for his cigarettes. Lighting one he slid as far forward as he could and leaned back and gazed above him at the slowly swaying branches of the trees against the background of a clear blue sky. The sun was out but the day was not overly warm and the breeze was fresh and cool on his face.

As the cigarette burned down he felt some of the tension drift away and slowly he relaxed completely. Only half way down his smoke he cast it away from himself and crossed his arms, almost like giving himself a hug against the coolness of the day.

As he watched the hypnotic dance of the trees he allowed his eyes to glaze and his blinking slowed. He didn't know how long he sat there motionless and peaceful but the voice next to him brought him straight to his senses.

"It's good to see you looking better." The voice was smooth and calm.

Squire looked to his left and gazed at the West Indian lady on the other side of the bench. He sat up and turned to face her unsure of how she had got there or how long she had been watching him.

"You're not from here are you?" Squire's question was unhurried and quiet.

The old lady gave a brief smile then considered her lap while she spoke. "I told you before, you already know all the answers."

Squire looked closely at her face and thought he could have read a book in the wrinkles and wisdom held there. "I don't though; at least not the ones that matter."

She turned her face to look at him and her eyebrows rose. "You didn't ask me if I'm from here, you told me, and I said you already know all the answers."

Squire just sat there looking at her with his mind racing trying to bring the conversation back under his control, but she was twisting him around and he knew it.

She smiled at him kindly. "So you knew the answer but asked me the question anyway."

"Maybe I hoped you would answer the question yourself," he replied hopefully.

The old lady didn't look in the slightest bit troubled. "If I had it would only have given you more questions to worry about."

There was silence between them for a while as Squire realised she was right. She sat in complete peace while he struggled to find a way forward that was not going to confuse him even further. A thought sprang in his mind and he followed it blindly. "Do you know what I seek?" His eyes remained fixed on her, searching for any hesitation or falseness in her answer.

"Oh yes Mister, I do," and she looked into his eyes, "but do you?"

"Yes," he responded straight away thinking now he was on firmer ground. "I'm searching for Heaven."

The old lady looked out at the park and breathed in the clear air. She was totally unhurried and Squire couldn't help thinking he wished he had that level of peace in his life.

"Why do you seek out something you're already convinced is real?"

Squire once again was caught out by her answer. She was right again of course. "Being convinced isn't the same as knowing," he said.

"No, it isn't." she replied looking at him again, "but does convincing yourself change anything?" Again there was silence for a minute or more. This time it was her turn to ask a question. "Tell me Mister, do you have faith that Heaven exists?"

"Of course," he responded at once.

"And have you read the Bible?"

"Yes, well, most of it."

She clutched her hands together in her lap and gazed once more at the park. "Tell me how it begins."

Squire didn't think she was testing him so began, "In the beginning God created the Heavens and the Earth."

The old lady next to him nodded slowly to herself and smiled gently. "Did you say Heavens; plural, and Earth singular?" Squire's face became a picture of thought but he didn't have any words to answer her. She continued in the same calm tone that she always had. "So there is more than one Heaven, but only one Earth. That is what you said isn't it?"

"I suppose I did," he responded. His eyebrows had gathered for a meeting at the top of his nose in an effort to concentrate harder.

"Best thing is," she responded with a smile, "nobody told you the answer but you already knew it, deep down where your mind didn't bother to look."

Squire was nodding to himself. Of course, more than one Heaven. This realm and the Void he already knew about. He also knew lost souls were being sent to yet another place.

His train of thought was then broken as the old lady began once more, "Before you ask your next question let me tell you that, for now, you are not ready."

He listened to what she said but asked anyway. "What can't be broken but can be repaired?" He looked up at her now with his head dipped down.

The old lady simply gave a quiet chuckle. "You already know, but you are not ready to realise it for yourself or do anything about it." Seeing the troubled look on his face she added, "Mister, I can explain things to you and that might make you feel better for a while, but it wouldn't help you." She looked at him now wearing her serious face. "You walk a dangerous road. No one can tell you the way, you have to find it."

"Will a foolish man find the path that the wise cannot see I wonder," he spoke, perhaps as much to himself as to the woman beside him.

The old lady looked at him and held his eyes. "There is no way of knowing for sure, but you have more chance than most I think."

"Because I'm a fool?"

"If you prove the wise ones wrong they will become the fools. Then what does that make you Mister?" She reached out and patted his hand kindly. "Don't fret so. You know everything you need to know so you are the only one holding yourself back."

Squire was still trying to absorb everything she said but was falling behind. "Finding Heaven - Is that the dangerous road?"

She looked back to him, her expression flat, "The greatest prize requires the greatest sacrifice."

Squire pondered once again. The prize was finding Heaven and the sacrifice was death. "You are saying I have to die to find Heaven?" He already knew it - The Bible said so many times.

"Dying is just part of life," she replied calmly while looking out at the park. "It's what you do with your life and how you are remembered that grants you access." Once again Squire sat silently pondering what she was saying but was still itching to ask more questions. She seemed to sense the inner unrest going on in him and spoke again to calm him. "You got time Mister so don't rush. You are going to see the things right under your nose soon enough."

The wind picked up then and the leaves above them rustled on their branches like the sea withdrawing over loose pebbles. Squire gazed up and watched the dance of the branches swaying in the breeze and felt his hair try to copy the dance. His eyes gently closed and he breathed out his worries, and sucked in the fresh new day.

He opened his eyes again suddenly and looked to his side. The empty bench greeted him in return and his stomach sank. How long he had closed his eyes for he didn't know but knew once again it was possible he had dreamed the whole thing.

"I didn't dream you lady," he said to the empty bench, "and I'm not going to worry because I know you are as real as I am." He got to his feet and walked stiffly back into the park with his head hung down and thoughts fighting for a chance to be heard, pouring through his mind.

The shopping trip had been a great success. They went shoe shopping first and everything Bailey picked up was rejected by Paige, who then went about selecting some items for her, and then stood with her arms crossed while they were all tried on and purchased.

The clothes selection was even more dynamic, and Bailey was wearing the smile of a lady who was being introduced to a side of herself she had never met before. They both carried bags in each hand by now and Paige directed them to various shops to sort out underwear and jackets and finally, nightwear.

Bailey couldn't believe how many items she had brought, or the ongoing cost. "Who is paying for all of this?"

Paige just shrugged the question away. "Don't worry about it," she said. "Not only can he afford it without blinking, I want to be there to see his face when he sees you in it." There was almost an evil glint in her eye as she said it.

They had as much as they could carry now and both agreed a Burger King would make a good reward for all their hard work. They wandered to the new section of the shopping centre and its spacious high ceilings and windows, and Bailey sat at a table outside with all the shopping while Paige went to order. She returned a few minutes later with a tray of food and drinks that would add more than their daily dose of calories.

"I'm confused," Bailey said between mouthfuls of her Whopper, "why did I have to get stuff to sleep in?"

Paige tried to stifle a Coke fuelled belch and failed. "If you are staying with us you are going to need it."

"I haven't been told I can stay though." Bailey replied. "I can just stay at the hotel. It would be wrong to just impose on you guys."

Paige started to pick up some of the many bags of shopping they had collected and waited for Bailey to do the same. "It would also be wrong to expect a member of the team to stay in a hotel. At least this way you're covered wherever you end up."

The day had been a great success and the two had become firm friends very quickly. A question had been burning a hole in Bailey all day, one which she had bitten back repeatedly. Now, after hours of shopping and laughing it just spilled out. "Paige," she waited for a response, then, "your mum?"

"Gone," the reply was quiet but firm. "Went into the Void but didn't come back. It would be best not to talk of this at home, if you know what I mean."

"I'm so sorry. I shouldn't have asked," Bailey went on, "but in a way it's better to know so I don't put my foot in it. I don't want to hurt your dad."

Paige turned to her as they walked and gave her a tight smile. "I know, and that's why it's okay."

Heading back to Shillyford with the back seat of the Fiat covered in shopping bags Paige reflected on a job well done. Bailey would still have to undergo the testing, but for now the team was up to three, and that would be better for everyone. Once things settled down her dad could step down and then he would be safe for a change.

The east wing of the Brooker Manor House was quiet and still. Justin paced around checking and re-checking that everything was ready.

He walked back through the main hall which had been converted years ago into an assault course. All manner of gym equipment was laid out and the route through the course was marked. For a fit person it was a challenge likely to leave them soaked in sweat before they got even half way around. For the unfit they would not get to the end and that would be the end of their selection. The Void was a physically tough place and they could not risk people entering if they didn't have the strength to survive.

The next room had the monitoring equipment and a nice couch to lie on while it happened. The computer equipment sat silently waiting to test the first candidate in a bombardment of mental agility tests. This would be made all the more difficult as the entrants would still be physically exhausted after the assault course.

After that the route would take them outside to the firing range. Pistols would be taken out of their locked boxes and the targets were already set up ready. This was no ordinary firing range though and the task was severe, although failure here was allowed if a candidate was strong enough in other areas.

The last room was the dark and quiet one where each candidate would be given differing situations and their answers to them monitored.

For years the tests had eliminated most who tried and the Void had removed the rest. Justin felt each loss as a personal blow and tested his resolve to continue each and every time. He had watched and allowed so many talented young people to vanish and it never got easier to deal with.

Last year he and Kass had devised a new and much tougher course feeling it was better to only put through the very best, and reduce the losses of such valuable life.

While he walked the route of the testing there was a knot in his stomach that wouldn't go away. Elle would be running the course later and that concerned him. She was so desperate to join the team and he was equally desperate for her to fail the testing. In truth he didn't expect she would complete the assault course; most didn't.

Squire was sound asleep when the girls returned with their arms full of bags of shopping. He had been reading the newspaper in his usual chair and had nodded off. Now he sat there quietly breathing and still.

They carried their stuff up the stairs as quietly as they could and Paige whispered back, "We'll go to my room." Once she reached the top of the stairs though she noticed the door to the spare room was open, and that it had been tidied out and the bed was made. She headed in for a better look and then turned to Bailey, "Dad's been busy." They put down their shopping and started to open bags and remove the new clothes and were getting excited to see it all together for the first time.

"I can't believe all this stuff," Bailey said looking at the growing pile of her new collection. "I would have never picked this stuff without you telling me what to get."

Paige thought it was funny. The posh London girl was going to be handing out a surprise tonight for sure.

When Squire finally woke up he could hear quiet voices from the kitchen and went to join them. Paige, Daisy and Bailey were sat around the table all playing games on their mobile phones. Seeing him walk in they all stopped and looked up.

"How are we all?" he began, and was greeted by three smiling faces. Each gave an account of their day and everyone was in a Friday mood for sure. Bailey was highly animated about her shopping trip and Squire noticed she was now wearing jeans and a T shirt.

Paige explained that after they had dropped their things off she and Bailey had headed to the Trusthouse where she had been staying and checked out. She had tried to pay the hotel bill with the account card but Bailey wouldn't allow it.

"It doesn't seem fair. You have all been too kind as it is," she spoke up.

Daisy asked if they could all eat as she needed to get over to the Manor House to get everything set up for the evening. There was a sudden flurry of action as everyone got involved in making food and getting the table ready.

While that went on Squire got a call from Kass asking what time to expect him. "I will see you early, maybe just after six. We need to discuss things before the jump."

"Good plan," Kass responded. See you then."

Forty minutes later they were sitting around the kitchen table eating bangers and mash and discussing their plans for the evening.

"We'll drive up tonight," Squire said. "We need to be there early and walking will just attract attention we don't really want. We can drop you off at the Manor on the way Daisy."

"Thanks," she replied. "I can get a lift back with Ted afterwards so don't go worrying that I'm walking on my own in the dark."

Once the dinner was dusted off they cleared everything away and fed the dishwasher. Now the four headed off to their respective rooms to get ready for the evening.

As always Squire was first back down and headed to the kitchen for a smoke. He was in his typical black jeans and a military style black jumper with elbow and shoulder pads. While he smoked he laced up his boots and awaited the arrival of the others.

Daisy appeared next and looked comfortable in her black ski pants and a hoody top. She sat down with her dad and they discussed the testing, especially Elle.

"Do you think she will show up?" Daisy knew she was keen to do the tests but was not so sure her family were going to allow it.

Squire blew smoke into the air and considered all he knew about the Naylors. "I don't think Justin is going to like the idea one little bit, but I also do not doubt that in the end he will do the right thing for everyone concerned."

They were joined shortly afterwards by Paige who wore her normal security outfit, black jeans and sweatshirt and a close fitting black combat jacket over the top. Her hair was tied up and back, and in her hand she carried her black woollen hat and her sheathed military knife.

Finally, Bailey came down having easily spent the longest time to get ready. As she walked into the room the three turned and

153

Squire's eyebrows went off to meet his forehead. "Good grief!" he said in a tone of quiet surprise.

Bailey was wearing mottled white and grey leggings with red canvas ankle boots. On the top she had a plain white vest top with a black stone washed denim jacket. She looked a different person from the one they had met the previous day and Paige looked quietly smug at the astonished faces looking at her fashion choices.

"Do I look okay?" Her question was really to Squire as the leader of the team.

"Okay?" He was smiling broadly, "more than bloody okay. You are going to shock Kass into smartening up his act and George is going to have heart failure."

"I'll drive," Paige offered as they stepped outside and reaching a hand towards her dad for the keys.

"Um, no," Squire replied and pressed the remote that popped open the doors on the black Mercedes which was parked next to her Fiat.

They dropped off Daisy at the Manor and saw that Justin's car was already outside along with Ted's Audi and Paul's pick-up truck.

"Stay safe you lot," Daisy smiled at them as she closed the door and headed for the house.

Squire drove back down the long gravel driveway and past all the neatly trimmed bushes, and once back on the main road he headed for the farmhouse.

Ted found Daisy setting up her part of the testing and checked to make sure they were alone. "Daisy," he started, "where are they?"

"Who?" She looked at him with the question written all over her face.

How could she not know who? "Squire, Kass and Paige obviously," he said.

"Oh, something important came up and they had to go out," she replied as if it didn't mean anything at all that the main members of the team were not even there.

Ted looked to the ceiling and counted to five before returning his gaze to Daisy. "Is going out what I think it is?"

"I wouldn't know what you might mean," she replied and the glint in her eyes told him all he needed to know.

Ted's smile returned and he let his concerns go. There was no point trying to change them as Squire and Kass had never been able to follow the rules or procedures. He only hoped he would not be getting a pager message from the hospital saying they had arrived there broken again.

Kass and Anna sat in their front room listening to the story of how Bailey had found Squire from her dream and had tracked the team after months of searching. When they had arrived Kass had been stunned to silence by Bailey's appearance.

"Suddenly I feel so scruffy," he said and looked down at his own humble outfit.

Now they sat listening while Paige clattered around in the kitchen making teas and coffees for everyone.

"This is highly irregular," Kass said to Squire who was lounging in his normal chair. "I'm not questioning your judgement, but she hasn't done the testing."

"No, it's true," Squire replied in an easy and relaxed tone. "I have done the testing, and I expect I have been failing, but I already know there is something about this one that means she needs to be on the team."

"Why do you think you failed the testing," Anna asked. Her American accent was soft and kind.

Squire just smiled back, "Just because I'm stupid does not mean I am 'that' stupid." The tension in Kass, Anna and Paige lifted. The secret they had been keeping from him had not been a secret at all.

Changing the subject Squire looked at Bailey, and then turned to Kass. "I've explained in quite a lot of detail what we know of the

Void, and some of what we have been doing there. Will you explain how we make the jump while I go for a smoke?"

Agreeing at once Kass began relating the history of the clock, the Master and the magnetic field theory that had led to the Void. For an hour he spoke in slow, measured words and checked regularly that Bailey was following.

Squire was outside walking up and down the driveway lost in his thoughts and a smoke trail followed where he walked. When he re-entered the farmhouse he left Kass talking and headed for the kitchen and talked quietly there with Paige.

The testing would be getting under way over at the Manor House and they wondered if they would have anyone new joining the team afterwards. George wanted a new team of younger, stronger people and Squire would be retired, followed closely by Kass. They had done their time and it was now the turn of some fresh faces to advance their knowledge.

Paige explained that there was a meeting on Sunday evening to discuss how to move forward with the team. At the rate they were going the meeting was likely to be a busy one. New toys, maybe new members and a suddenly recovered to full fitness Squire in strange circumstances. Yes, they would have plenty to discuss.

IX.

Justin faced those gathered in the entrance hall of the east wing. He noticed excited faces and worried ones, but most of all he was surprised at how many there were. For most of the testings there would only be two or three, and sometimes just one. Tonight he faced five new recruits.

"Welcome everyone," he raised his voice to everybody. The whispering in the room quietened. "I know most of you don't know what you are here applying for but you do know what you are here to do." He gazed at the faces now all paying attention.

"I can't tell you yet what the special project is that I mentioned in the email I sent you, but I will to all those who pass the tests. If you don't pass please do not be disappointed, they will be very challenging and it is only to ensure we have the ablest people."

He looked at the five new young hopefuls stood in front of him. "I need to be straight with you before we start," he said and his face was serious. "These tests are hard. They were designed that way for good reason. If you are hurting from everywhere and mentally and physically exhausted, we have done your part well." He looked at each candidate and saw their determination. "For you guys this will be tough and for the ladies even harder, but give it your all and we will see how you do."

He went on to explain the route through the testing and that they would have to go one at a time. Each test would have a monitor supervising and recording all the results. He then went on to introduce his team for the evening and the area they would be testing.

"I expect you all know Ted Dawes," he indicated to his left. "He will take you through the assault course." Justin now raised his arm and pointed. "Daisy Fox will be looking after you in the mental agility section and Paul McCoy will be your host for the firing range. Last but not least, Anna Fox will finish with emotional reaction testing."

Everyone seemed to be taking it all on board so Justin pressed on. "Please remember everyone, you are not in competition with each other. There is no pass limit so just do your best and have some fun along the way."

Ted Dawes now stepped forward. "Okay, listen up everyone," he called through his ivory smile. "First up is Tom." He found him with his eyes standing near the front in his grey tracksuit. "Follow me please."

He led Tom to the main hall and gave him a moment to remove his tracksuit top. "Follow the course and my instructions," he said while casting his eyes around the room. "If you cannot go on you can stop at any time. Are we clear?"

Tom was looking at the array of equipment spread out in front of him and none of it looked too difficult. "Sure Ted," he said in eager excitement. I'm ready when you are."

"Excellent," Ted said while writing on a pad on the clipboard he held. He asked Tom to approach the first part, a wooden climbing frame that went almost to the roof of the hall. It was surrounded by foam matting for any who let go. "When I say go I will start the timing," he went on. "You will start by climbing the frame in front of you with only your arms only please. You must not use your feet for this part. Are we clear?"

The testing had begun. Tom had great body strength and fitness and the course was going to be straightforward for him. He completed the frame easily and moved on to rotations of push-ups, dips and squats. Sweat ran from his forehead and his breathing was becoming harder, but he kept going as quickly as he could. The tests were not all aimed at strength though and he had to complete balance tests as well as agility sections. Finally, he found himself at one end of the hall and looking back he saw an obstacle course of benches and horses. At his feet was a bag of cement.

"Grab the bag Tom," Ted called. "Get it to the other end as quickly as you can."

Tom hefted the bag onto his shoulder and went off. He dumped it on top of the first horse and then climbed over himself before picking it up again on the other side. Now his shirt was damp and his eyes stung with sweat. The rest of the course went on before him, and he pushed on until finally Ted blew the whistle marking the end. Tom slumped to the floor on his back and his breathing was heavy and harsh.

"Not too bad, not too bad at all," Ted said taking the time from the stopwatch. His noted the time on his pad and went to check on Tom. "You okay?"

"Sure," he responded, still sucking in air harshly. "Was that fast?"

Ted gave him a smile, "Not as fast as Paige, but pretty good all the same." He offered Tom a hand and pulled him up. "Grab some water from the table there and head through to the next room."

Wandering off on unsteady legs he picked up a bottle and drained it, then dropped it in the bin and headed for room two.

Next into the assault course was Ryan Grey. He wasn't as physically powerful as Tom but was still fit and agile. His light brown hair was dripping wet by the time he got to the end and his brown eyes looked slightly sullen from exhaustion. Justin had said the course would be tough for the guys and he had been right. Their superior strength had made some parts easier for them but they were both worn out by the end.

Following him was Ashley Lord, a nineteen-year-old with long blonde hair and sparkling blue eyes. Her engaging smile at the beginning was gone as soon as she started the course. She barely managed the frame and was a puffing wreck by the time she reached the top. She did well on the agility sections but found the static wall

161

almost impossible. She managed it finally but was virtually exhausted. When she finally staggered to the cement bag challenge she was almost totally spent. Her legs were numb and heavy but she pushed on. She hauled the bag down the course and using hidden reserves she didn't know she had lofted it over the obstacles. With her teeth gritted and her hair matted and soaked in sweat she fought the bag with everything she had.

Halfway down the course she slumped to the floor and lay there with her chest pumping air in and out in short gasps.

Ted walked over to her and squatted down at her side. Gently he encouraged, "You're nearly there kid. Come on. Just a little way further."

Ashley looked at him through sweat filled eyes and slowly pushed herself up. Her arms shook as she tried to push her body up but eventually she was back on her feet. Reaching down she took a corner of the cement bag and dragged it to the remaining horse.

It took another five minutes and used every remaining ounce of her energy to get the bag over the top and finally the whistle blew. She slid to the floor completely spent. Ted was there in a moment offering her water.

"Sip this slowly," he said. He took her wrist and looked at his watch and counted her pulse. "Dammit girl, you gave that everything," he said in quiet admiration.

He left her there for a couple of minutes before helping her up to her feet. It was clear she was unstable and not able to get to the

162

next room on her own. Ted stuck an arm around her and half carried her to the next section.

Daisy had finished with Ryan some time ago and could hear the regular crack of gunfire from outside, when Ashley entered held up by the Medical Officer. He laid her on the couch and handed her another water bottle.

She was a wreck to look at. Her clothes were soaked through and her long hair was stuck to her face but her eyes burned with bright determination.

Ted looked at Daisy and nodded down at the heaving body in front of him. "Massive respect for this one."

He walked from the room and headed back to the main hall collecting his clipboard on the way. He didn't think anyone was going to match that one for sheer determination.

Now laying on the couch Ashley's body heat doubled and she ran with sweat and she felt like she was being cooked alive. This was all part of the testing. Now they would find if she could still concentrate with her body physically punished and under stress.

Daisy handed Ashley a clipboard with a pen. There was a piece of paper on the board with black dots marking out a shape of something that looked like a house. The board shook as Ashley's arms quivered with exhaustion.

"Join all the dots with a line please. You may only touch each dot once and must join them all."

Still blinking sweat out of her eyes Ashley looked at the diagram. She traced it out in her mind to make sure she could complete the task before putting pen to paper.

While she studied it Daisy went on, "A car travels at 60mph for four and a half hours. How far has it travelled?"

The mental agility test rolled on. The questions were not really difficult, but after the physical challenge that had gone before it was hard to concentrate. There were also two tasks at a time; a mental agility question and a paper puzzle. Doing both at once showed a great deal about their thought processes and which they excelled in. On top of that those doing the tests were also uncomfortable. They started out normally dripping wet and very hot from their exertions and by the time they were finishing they were starting to cool and chills set in.

Meanwhile, outside Ryan ran the firing range. Paul McCoy explained how everything worked before letting anyone loose with a gun.

"The course needs to be run," he began. "If you don't go fast enough the targets that pop up will be too far away and hard to hit. You need to balance your speed though with your ability to fire the gun straight. Targets will pop up all around the course so hit as many as you can."

Ryan was nodding with each part of the instructions and had been looking forward to this bit the most.

Paul showed him two guns sitting on a table along with more bottles of water. "These are very small calibre and won't do much damage, but they will hit the targets. There is very little kick-back so don't be afraid of them, but remember always that guns can kill so please be careful." He then offered Ryan the guns. "You may take one gun and an extra clip, or two guns and no extra clips but you have to consider that using your weaker hand may result in missing targets."

Like Tom had done before him, Ryan took one gun and the spare ammo. Paul showed him how to reload and asked him to remove the safety catch. When he nodded that he was ready Paul started the test.

A target popped up thirty metres in front of Ryan and he started running towards it. He wanted to get closer before firing, but before he got to it another popped up to his side fifteen metres away.

He reached out his right arm and fired. There was a sharp crack sound as the bullet whistled away and hit the grass well wide of its mark. Ryan didn't slow down but ran on firing at every target he saw.

He soon realised there were more targets than he had bullets for, and as many as three targets to choose from at any one time. They were also popping up further from him. As he slowed down to shoot they were outpacing him. This was a test to see how many he could hit, and he tried each time to choose the safest target that would count.

Less than halfway round he ejected the magazine and reloaded without breaking stride. The second set went better than the first and he started to enjoy this challenge. He hadn't finished the course when he ran out of bullets so he slowed to a walk and headed back to Paul McCoy knowing the test was over.

Ted turned to the page that said Emily Watts - an eighteen-year-old from Shillyford. She was easily the shortest of the candidates at barely five feet tall but was going to have an advantage in this test. The fair skinned local girl was also a highly trained and able gymnast and her small body was both light and powerful.

She listened to Ted as he explained the instructions, her cool blue eyes looking nervous but full of fire.

When the whistle blew she was off like a rabbit. Her small body was packed with power and many of the tests were easy for her as she bolted around. Ted raised an eyebrow and glanced at the time on the stopwatch, she really was flying. She did the rope climb in the fastest time he had seen anyone do it and jumped and hopped from one test to the next.

Finally, one test slowed her down, the cement bag. She didn't have the sheer power to lift it but was fighting it like a terrier. When Ted blew the final whistle he couldn't believe his eyes at the time.

Emily slumped down and sat on the floor leaning back on her arms with her knees up. Her breathing came in hard gasps but she had finished in the best shape of any so far.

Ted offered her water and checked her pulse while she drank. Everything was added to his notes.

Anna greeted each entrant to the final stage of the testing. They sat in a darkened room with two chairs. By this stage most were physically exhausted and they wanted nothing more than for it to be over. Their damp clothes were now chilled from being outside and they looked shattered.

She looked at Tom in front of her and explained the test. "I am going to give you a whole series of situations to think about. For many there is no right or wrong answer but your response is important."

"For the first batch of questions I will explain each part and you may ask two questions for every question I ask." Tom nodded that he understood and was ready to get underway.

"You are in a dream," Anna started. "There is a young girl and a man with a gun. Which one do you save?"

Tom considered for only long enough to hear the question, "The girl."

"That is the wrong answer," Anna looked up. "The girl is a psychopath and has already killed the man's wife and family. He has the gun for self defence."

Knowing he had blown it Tom rolled his eyes up and mentally berated himself for his foolishness.

"Please use the questions you are allowed to ask Tom, they will help."

The second series of tests were dilemma based and had no specific correct reply. This was to help understand the morality of the candidates and each answer was carefully marked down and would be assessed with the help of a computer later.

"A girl has requested an abortion," Anna began. "Do you approve?"

"Was the baby conceived by accident?" Tom replied with his forehead furrowed.

"No."

"Was the baby conceived against her will?"

"Yes, well done Tom," she encouraged.

He inwardly smiled, "Then yes."

Last, but not least came Elle Naylor to the assault course. Ted worried most about her. He already suspected that Justin would be outside praying for her to fail, but also knew Elle well enough to know she had enough guts and determination for two people.

By the time she had hauled herself up the first frame and was doing sit ups Emily had finished with mental agility and was outside on the firing range. The test wore on and Elle was soon staggering. She was well built and fit but not overly strong and the tests made no allowance for the differences in power between the males and females.

The natural balance challenges and body agility made up for these. Elle arrived at the snake and Ted guided her, "Crawl through the tunnel and come out the other side," he said. She bent down and went into the wooden structure in front of her. Inside was a zig-zag maze of walls that had her twisting and turning to squeeze through. Earlier, Emily had gone through like a trained dog at a show, whereas Tom and Ryan could barely fit around many of the turns and fought not to get totally wedged in.

Elle used it as a breather from some of the more physical tasks and completed this section easily enough. When she came out the far side she found she had an audience and her heart sank.

Tom and Ryan were now watching her and called out encouragement as she started the second half of the course. She was already soaked through and her arms and legs felt so weak she felt like a baby.

Next was the wall. Nearly the same height as she was, and nothing to help her get over it except her own technique and strength. She had little left of either. She ran in a slow and exhausted style and jumped at the wall. She hit it flat with her arms hooked over the top.

Her feet skidded on the front of the wall trying to get some grip to walk up it, but her arms had no energy left to haul her up.

There was a shout from the side of the hall, "Come on! Try again." It was Ashley who had arrived a few minutes earlier. The call was then echoed by Ryan and Tom. Elle heard the calls and allowed herself to slip down the wall and she backed up to have another go. Justin watched from the doorway in quiet admiration of the effort being put in. Elle ran again on legs too numb to control. At the last second she pushed into the ground and threw her arms to the top of the wall again. She was a few inches higher this time and she immediately pulled with every ounce of strength left in her arms.

The shouting from the side was non-stop now as the three hurled encouragement at her and willing her on. Watching from only a few feet away Ted whispered through clenched teeth, "Come on kid. Don't give in."

She moved inch by inch higher. Everyone could see from the slow motion assent how much energy was being burnt up and they called out harder.

Justin watched with watery eyes his daughter throw her soul into the task and finally, he cracked. "Come on!" he shouted from the side. He clapped his hands at her effort and called out with the others.

Slowly Elle hooked one leg over the top of the wall and used it to pull her body up and over. As she crashed down the other side the room erupted in cheering. She struggled to her feet and walked like a drunk to the cement bag.

Everyone knew this was going to be the breaking point but they kept calling from the sides.

"Get the bag to the other end of the course," Ted said with an air of resignation. She could hardly stand, let alone make it to the far side.

Elle looked back at him with sweat dripping from her nose and chin. "Does it have to go over the horses?"

Ted looked at his clipboard and checked, "It just says get it to the other side."

Elle bent down and grabbed two corners of the bag and hauled it. She walked backwards with the bag dragging along the ground. When she came to the first horse she didn't pause, she just bent down further and reversed straight under it to a mass of cheering from the side of the room.

"Smart kid," Ted muttered to himself.

When the test was over Tom, Ryan and Ashley were at her side offering her water and patting her shoulder as she sat slumped against the far wall. Ted was there too, and standing beside him was Justin.

He was grinning and trying to stop his eyes watering, not just in pride of his daughter's efforts, but in a new realisation. They didn't just have more people here, they had a real team. People who would work hard for each other and look out for them. Things were suddenly looking brighter.

Justin sat in front of the five young people who had finished their work for the evening. On four more chairs around him were Daisy, Anna, Ted and Paul.

Five exhausted faces looked back at him; their faces pale from exertion and effort and their bodies limp and still.

"I have the results here," Justin began. "Normally we discuss the results with you individually," he paused, "but tonight I want to share them all with you together. I think it will help if we do this as a team of people rather than as individuals.

Everyone was too tired to ague. Some nodded their approval while others just sat and waited.

"Tom," he started, "Assault course; pass. Mental agility; fail. Firing range; 50% targets hit. Morality; pass." Justin then continued without stopping to explain further.

"Ryan," he turned to the second page on his clipboard. "Assault course; pass. Mental agility; fail. Firing range; 65% targets hit. Morality; pass.

Once again he moved on and turned to page three. "Ashley, Assault course; pass," he looked up and found her eyes with his. "That was an incredible achievement; well done." Ashley smiled in return. "Mental agility; pass. Firing range; 35% targets hit. Morality; pass."

"Emily," he looked up again and made eye contact. "Assault course; pass. Mental agility; pass. Firing range; 60% targets hit. Morality; pass."

Finally, he turned to the last page on his pad. "Elle; assault course; amazing pass." There were rumblings of approval around the room. "Mental agility; pass. Firing range; 30% targets hit. Morality; pass."

Justin then looked at the five one by one; his expression relaxed and not giving anything away. "We have been honoured with some incredible performances this evening," he paused while still looking at the brave faces in front of him. "I really mean that, you made all the team here so proud tonight. I have to mention the performances of Ashley and Elle on the assault course which showed real grit and determination."

The five looked back at him and their spirits were lifting higher as the minutes went on. Not only were they happy to have just completed the testing, they had a pretty good feeling they had done well.

"There was one performance that was so impressive I have to mention it in isolation. Tonight, for the first time in a very long while a new record was set." Justin paused and looked up once more. "Paige Fox holds the time record for the assault course; but not anymore." He raised his arm and let it come to rest pointing at Emily, who sat squatted on the front edge of her chair. "Congratulations Emily."

Everyone responded and applause broke out and there were smiles from the whole room.

"Don't get too comfortable though," Justin added. "I have little doubt that Paige will be back to challenge you." There were knowing smiles from the team at his side as they agreed; yes - Paige would be back.

"Not only that," Justin went on raising his hands until the general noise calmed down. "Emily, your total points for the whole testing are equal to the best of all time." There were now a few gasps and cheers breaking out. Emily was smiling but also looked quietly embarrassed by the sudden attention.

"There is a kind of reward for you Emily," Justin went on, "and one that has only been handed out once before." He waited until he had everyone's attention.

"The holder of the record will now get to name you," he said. There were looks of puzzlement from in front of him so he continued. "You will be given a new name that will be used from now on. Your new name will be given to you by the current record holder; Squire Fox, who was given his name over twenty years ago."

The atmosphere in the room was getting better all the time and weariness was draining away to be replaced by new excitement.

Tom raised his hand and was quickly spotted by Justin. "Yes Tom."

"Are you saying that Squire is not his real name?" The other four were also slightly surprised at this new piece of information.

"No," Justin responded, and quickly went on. "Before anyone asks his real name - we don't know. This happened before any of us were part of the team and Kass refuses to tell us."

To stop any more discussion on the matter Justin continued, "I would like to invite all of you up to Kass' farmhouse in two evening's time," Justin continued. "I am delighted to say you have all passed tonight," he gave a special look and a wink to Elle sitting in front of him. "Come and meet with the whole team there and let us tell you about the Void."

There followed a time of celebration as the whole leadership team welcomed in the new recruits. There were handshakes and hugs being passed about. Daisy and Elle were in animated and excited conversation to one side, and shortly afterwards Justin and his daughter broke off from the others for a moment alone.

"I can't tell you how proud I was of you tonight," he said with honest admiration written all over him. "You deserve your place with the others, but it won't stop me worrying."

Elle was still exhausted but gave her dad a big hug. "Don't worry too much though," she said. "Look at these people I'm going to be with."

Justin looked at the bright new future around him and the life and energy within them was not lost on him.

Half an hour later the five tired and rather smelly new members headed home and Justin found himself on his own again.

He headed over to the other side of the Manor House to see George Brooker. He had some rather good news for him.

Paige had wandered off into the dark lane to cover the entrance to the barn and hide out in the undergrowth. The nights were getting lighter and the night was not yet totally dark. The evenings were also getting warmer and she reflected how much nicer it was being hidden in the summer months.

Kass was in the barn pointing out all the equipment he had been explaining to Bailey and talking non-stop about things which no one really needed to know.

Squire was already digging in his box and admiring the new weapons he found there. He pulled out a right handed holster and strapped it on, and then continued to fill his pockets with his normal travelling gear.

Once he was all done with loading up he headed over to the bench and picked up and scanned in a bracelet. It briefly flickered green and then the hidden voice in the room spoke up.

"Target one, green locked in."

Bailey looked around the room to see where the sound had come from, but soon gave up and started investigating the Fox Box as Squire had done a few minutes earlier.

"About fifteen minutes to a peak," Kass called to the other two. "Let's get saddled up." He too selected a bracelet from the wooden box on the bench and scanned it in.

"Target two, yellow locked in."

Looking over he saw that Bailey had put on two gun holsters and was tying the straps onto her legs. He couldn't help thinking the newcomer was putting the old hands to shame; in appearance at least.

Looking up she caught Squire's attention and asked, "You have only one gun. Do you always have just one?" The dream of last night was still fresh in her mind.

"Yes," he replied. "I don't think I can be lucky with two hands at once." He gave a smile and beckoned her over to the bench. When she was at his side he slipped a bracelet onto her wrist and then held it in front of the scanner. Bailey watched the crystals hidden in the metal flash a soft orange, and then disappeared again.

"Target three, orange locked in."

"Are you ready for this?" he asked looking closely at her eyes. She looked back just as hard.

"Totally."

One of the computer monitors on the bench gave a small beep and the display flashed up a new reading.

Magnetic field: Peak in 11.00 minutes

Kass had been filling his pockets with the contents of his bag on the bench but paused and turned to Bailey. "In about eleven minutes the Earth's magnetic field will be slightly stronger as it passes us."

She acknowledged him with a simple nod. Understanding how it worked was not important to her, only that it did.

He continued, "When that happens the systems here will send a very short, but very powerful pulse of magnetic charge which pauses the field as it passes. That should open the gateway for us."

The three of them headed to the floor in the middle of the barn and turned back to face the bench and Kass noted that once again Squire had forgotten his watch. He ignored the fact once again as he had his own and would do the timekeeping for all of them.

Squire had been watching the time carefully as it usually took him about ten minutes to slow his mind down enough for the transition. "We need to be ready," he said to her calmly, "It's time to be very still now and relax fully. Stare at the minute hand on the clock like we talked about yesterday and let your mind empty of everything else if you can."

Bailey did as she was instructed and faced the clock and focused. She had heard most of the procedures last night and the rest tonight, and she knew what to do.

"We should speak again on the other side," he continued. "If we don't meet out there we will see you back here. Stay safe and good luck."

Squire and Kass gave each other a quick glance and then faced the clock themselves. Time slowly drifted by and the three stood motionless.

After several minutes Bailey was surprised that she could see the minute hand moving just as Squire had told her it would. Butterflies bounced around in her stomach in anticipation as she prepared for the unknown. At the very edge of her vision she noticed the monitor change its display but couldn't read it with her eyes fixed firmly on the face of Doris.

Magnetic Field: Alternating

Initiating Grab

She knew the time was coming and clenched both her hands into tight fists.

The monitor ran its countdown and a low hum started to fill the room and got steadily louder by the second. Her mind was still but her heart hammered in her chest in a mixture of pure adrenaline and fear. The lights in the farmhouse flickered for a second although no one was there to see it.

She saw a sudden white flash - more in her mind than with her eyes. It only lasted a second and then everything disappeared and she was falling. The world around her had gone and had been replaced by a dark grey emptiness. She looked around her as her mind woke up again and saw nothing in every direction. She raced through the Void alone.

He became aware of them for the first time. He was always so busy with his work in his own fiery domain, but something had flashed into his mind like a fluttering candle in the dark but it was just long enough for him to see them. Three of them tumbling in the darkness, but something was not right. They shouldn't be here.

Very few things made him pause in his work, but now he did - his curiosity aroused. "Who are you, my little lost friends?" he murmured in a voice steeped with knowledge and age.

The first was a thinker. Oh yes, he was smart alright. He had found his way into this place and used it like a secret passageway whenever he wanted. Somehow he had a key to where he shouldn't be and he was learning fast. This was not good, but unimportant. He could wait.

The second, now that was different. He glowed with something that really wasn't good news; a *mal'āk* no less. He doubted that he knew it yet though, and good for him that he didn't. This one would have to be watched and taken care of at some time in the very near future. Despite his enormous power and knowledge, the Watcher experienced something he was not used to - fear.

He sensed the third, a girl, but she was cloaked in almost invisibility. He could read nothing at all about her at all which bothered him greatly. They had been marked. He would be watching and waiting for them.

The Watcher started to make his preparations. His manipulation of this domain was not going to be interfered with by outsiders.

Kass fell into darkness and gazed around him hoping the bracelets were going to do what Tinker had planned. For now, there was nothing to see so he relaxed and let some old memories of the Master run through his mind. He had only been a teenager when his tuition had started, and it hadn't taken long before he was in over his head.

"Could you tell me more about time please," Kass asked the old man.

Smoke drifted up from the old man's pipe making a thin stream of silver between the two of them. The Master looked up from the book he was studying and looked at Kass with wise eyes.

"All time has its boundaries," he started. "It is more than just the turning of a clock, or indeed, the time it takes our planet to make an orbit of the sun." Kass sat opposite and his eyes did not waver. He was an excellent student with a natural ability to absorb facts and figures.

The old man puffed his pipe once more before going on. "All things in time have a start and finish. The time of the universe seems to go on and on, but all actions within that time also have a finite time that they go on for."

He paused to give the young man a chance to take in his words. "So, for example, a car journey will take a certain amount of time, but our universal time started before it, and goes on after it. Therefore, all actions and activities within time also have their own measure of time."

Kass listened and accepted everything without any problem. "Can time be seen differently from different perspectives and places?"

The old man gave a small smile through worn, yellowed teeth. "Oh yes, indeed. I can give you an example; a very old one." The Masters eyes glinted at the prospect of the next lesson. "How old is the Earth do you think?"

Kass thought for a few seconds. "A few billion years I should think," he replied.

"Did science tell you that?"

"Yes."

"Do you believe science?" The Master watched Kass carefully, waiting for doubt to creep in.

"Most of the time I think I do."

"Ah good," the old man nodded. "But have you also heard that God created the Earth in six days, and rested on the seventh? How is this possible?"

The eyes of the young man glazed for a second and he looked down at the table. "I don't know," he replied. "One of them must be wrong."

Another long puff of the pipe greeted this. "Let me ask you this then young one. Do you think the creator of the whole universe and everything in it measures time by the turning of our Earth, or maybe something bigger?"

There was no reply from Kass.

The Master had set in motion a question that the young man would still be contemplating many years afterwards. "Perspective and places," the old man added.

As Squire floated through the Void he was aware that he could detect Bailey's mind really easily. He didn't know why but he concentrated on it and in moments he was speeding towards her. She saw him once he was close to her and offered a smile.

"I'm glad I didn't have to be alone too long," she called against the rush of the Void. "It's just like you said, there is nothing here."

Squire was now right next to her and grabbed her hand so they would stay together. "I don't think it's nothing really," he replied. "I think there is always a lot going on but we just can't see it."

It wasn't long before Kass came into view and was heading towards them. When the three were together Kass held his bracelet close to Bailey's. They pulled toward each other and clicked together. "Well knock me down with a feather," Kass said. "Tinker, you did it again."

They were all holding on to each other now and Kass was surprised that they were actually following procedure for a change. Another thought occurred to him and he called to his brother, "Try the gun."

Catching his meaning quickly Squire withdrew his Banisher and fired into the emptiness. The gun fired like a regular one, but the gel bullet shot out into the dark with a white burst of energy that eventually disappeared far in the distance. He turned again to his brother with a problem forming in his mind. "Those bullets contain the same energy as the Catching, but we can't send lost souls on by shooting them. That would just be wrong."

Kass had already given this some thought after Tinker had handed them over to him. "I don't think they will work like that anyway," he shrugged and raised an eyebrow. "We will use them for enemies only."

They would have to be content with that for now but were both impressed that the Banishers were clearly doing something special within the Void.

"What do we need to do now?" Bailey called.

Kass looked to his brother right alongside him. "Squire will pick something up I expect. He seems to be able to detect voices quicker than I do."

Squire was concentrating and listening to the sounds in his head. Almost straight away he found a clear voice. "I got one," he called. "Sounds like a boy." He looked at the other two. "Okay, let's go in."

Once again he focused on that one voice and closed all the other sounds away. The voice got clearer in his mind but then went again as the space around them began to change.

Colours and shapes now appeared and became more solid with each second. They found themselves standing on a grey platform of a train station. There were people all around them all wearing bright outfits but none of them moved. Squire went to have a look at one of them and confirmed his first thought, "They're plastic!"

Looking around at the station and the fields beyond it soon became clear they were standing in a toy train set and were small enough to walk around as if it was full size.

"This is amazing!" Bailey was looking at the toy luggage the plastic baggage handler was hauling on a little trolley. She went over to look down the empty tracks in both directions but there was no sign of any trains. Her smiles of wonder were cancelled though when she looked over at Kass and Squire. They were looking around and seemed troubled. "What is it?"

185

"Something's not right," Kass said and looked over at his brother.

It was a few more moments before both men realised what was out of place. "Bright colours," Squire said.

Bailey was confused. "What about them?"

"Things in the Void are normally drab and washed out," Kass explained. "This is not right. It's all a bit too real."

Squire was gazing at a smooth white sky from horizon to horizon and trying to work out why things were different. "It's like this isn't a nightmare, or even part of the Void," he said.

Kass nodded his agreement. "Lead on McDuff. Let's find your boy."

Squire climbed down from the platform and waited for the others to follow. He crossed over the tracks and onto the station platform the other side. "This way," he called over his shoulder.

They followed him inside the station house and found the one they were looking for. In front of them was a dark haired boy of about eight years old. He was lying on the floor playing with a train set. His eager face was so close to the station it was almost like he was a part of it. He moved figures around the platform talking to himself the whole time as he did. A steam train chugged though the station only inches from his eyes. He watched it in minute detail as it moved through and made whistle sounds as it left again.

Kass looked at this brother again, "This is not right."

Bailey's hands had come to rest on top of the guns hanging next to her hips. Hearing that things were not as they should be was making her edgy.

Squire squatted down next to the boy and tried to get his attention. "Hello there," he spoke in a cheery tone.

The boy looked up at him with vacant eyes. "Hello," he replied with a clear American accent, and turned straight back to his trains.

"This is a great train set," Squire went on. "I used to have one of these."

The boy looked back at him once again, and then cast his unseeing eyes at Kass and Bailey in turn. "It's alright I guess."

"My name's Squire Fox," he said. "Can I ask your name?"

Once again the empty gaze was turned his way. "Alex," he said, but this time he didn't look away. "You can play as well if you want."

His voice sounded strange; both sleepy and too deep for his size. Squire and Kass exchanged glances. Neither of them understood what was going on.

Squire tried again, "Are you lost Alex?"

The boy's expression never changed from the flat face and blank looks. "No," he said. "I'm just playing."

"I think he's dreaming," Bailey said. "The expression and the eyes. It's like someone sleepwalking."

"I don't think so," Kass gave her a look. "I don't think dreams bring you to the Void."

Squire and Bailey exchanged glances as they both knew differently. "Well, I don't know what to do so I'm just going to have to do it." Reaching into his coat Squire pulled out the Catching and looked around and caught Kass' eyes.

After a few moments thinking, and not having any better ideas he nodded back.

Holding the smooth chrome tube in front of himself Squire pressed the button. The device slid smoothly open revealing the glowing crystal inside. "I hope I'm doing the right thing Alex, I really do."

The boy did not respond or even look up from his playing. His attention was once again fully absorbed.

Squire spoke slowly and carefully

"For judgement's here and judgement's me,
Take you to where you ought to be."

There was no bright light and no sound from the Catching. The boy simply looked up at Squire and his eyes focused on him briefly. A second later he vanished and a few seconds after that everything around them faded away.

"What?" Squire exclaimed as he dropped once more into the Void.

The three of them drifted together as if they had all jumped off a high building at the same time.

As they were drawn towards each other again by the bracelets Kass called to his brother "What was that all about?"

Squire had put away the Catching and began explaining to Bailey why this run was different from the others they had done. Neither he nor Kass had any answers.

They were still no wiser when they landed on the barn floor with a bump fifteen minutes later. All of them were left sprawled on the floor and started sitting themselves up.

The slowing whistle of the magnets next them was accompanied by the loud ticking of the clock.

Squire was laughing. "Oh the joy of a glamorous landing," he smiled.

"It's better than coming in head first though," Kass added and was also smiling.

Bailey was brushing the dust from her now rather grubby white and grey leggings and also started to giggle. "I think I know why you two wear black."

Squire was still laughing but was looking over at the bench. Kass read his thoughts. "No," he said in a long, drawn out way.

"But we have to," Squire replied putting on his best pleading tone.

Kass knew he wanted to press the green button and inform everyone they were back safely. It had been quite some time since they had been able to send an all clear signal.

"As far as George is concerned you are laying in hospital with broken ribs. If you press that button things are going to turn ugly."

The point conceded Squire and the others removed their equipment and put everything away before heading to the barn door.

As they filed out and headed for the farmhouse Kass stuck two fingers in his mouth and gave a sharp whistle.

Down the lane they heard Paige running up to meet them. Once she was with them she looked at them carefully and was pleased to see everyone looked fine.

They wandered into the farmhouse and were joined straight away by Anna. The five of them settled down in the living room and went through what had happened on their run.

Anna seemed to be in high spirits. Everyone was back and there were no injuries for a change. Kass was also in a great mood. His concerns and doubts about taking an untested Bailey into the Void had been unjustified. If anything he had been very impressed with her.

Twenty minutes later the peace and high spirits were shattered when the phone started ringing. Squire was closest and answered the call with a cheerful "Hello."

"Squire?" It was George Brooker. "What are you doing there?" He sounded surprised, but at the same time he appeared uncharacteristically cheerful.

The sudden look of concern on Squire's face told everyone, except Bailey, who was on the other end. "I'm just sitting here with Kass and Anna chatting about things," he replied, trying to sound as matter of fact as he could.

George continued with the same happy tone, "Excellent. It's good to have you back so quickly."

"Thanks, it's good to be back." The sound of a good humoured George was unsettling Squire. It was unnatural and he preferred the grumpy version.

"How are you feeling? I expect you are still in a lot of pain." George's voice now took on something totally alien, compassion.

"No, no. I'm pretty good. I will be here for the meeting on Sunday."

"Good, I'm so pleased," George said. "I have some excellent news for everyone. See you there." The phone line went dead and Squire returned the phone to the coffee table in front of him.

"Interesting," Kass said. "Do I take it Mr Brooker is not his normal self tonight?"

"No," Squire responded, his forehead furrowed. "I've never heard him sounding so happy."

"I know why," Anna chirped up and all eyes turned to her. "We have five new members in the team after the testings today."

"Five!" Kass blurted. "How did that happen?"

Anna didn't want to spoil any surprises so simply added, "You'll have to wait until the meeting to find out as you chose not to be there tonight."

"I hate to put a downer on the evening," Paige interrupted, "Bailey hasn't been tested. We won't be able to bring her Sunday."

"She's right," Anna agreed. "Kass, can we run her through the testing tomorrow? No one will know and George doesn't take any notice of gunfire on the range anymore."

Kass was nodding to himself. "It's a plan," he said in his usual relaxed tone. "Fancy meeting us there at 8pm?" He glanced at Squire, then at Bailey.

Bailey was smiling, "Yes please. I want to do it."

It was agreed by everyone and plans were made. They would need to call in Ted and Justin as there had to be senior members of the team to oversee things. Ted was also the medical back-up in case of accidents so was doubly important.

Squire was looking at his phone in his hand, "I've just got a reply from Tinker. He'll be there to do the range."

When everything was in place, and the business for the day was done Squire took his group back home and left Kass to document the last run in peace.

Squire, Paige and Bailey found Daisy sitting in front of the television reading a book. The sound was on mute on the TV and the BBC News Channel calmly scrolled the latest stories at the bottom of the screen. As team researcher this was something Daisy always did just in case anything came up that affected the team. She looked up from her reading and was delighted to see everyone fit and well, and in good spirits.

Heading for the kitchen she told them all to sit down while she got drinks organised for them. Paige went to join her and returned moments later with a cold chicken leg from the fridge.

All the events from the testing were recounted by Daisy, who also informed Squire his total record had been equalled by Emily.

"About time," Squire exclaimed. "I can't believe no one has beaten it before." The reason his score had held for so long was the high average on every test. Kass had excelled on the mental agility part, but had lost all the good work he had done on the firing range. No one else had come close to Squire's averages even though individual people had done very well in certain sections.

"Looks like I will be doing the assault course sometime soon then," Paige had muttered. She tried to make out she was not really bothered her record had been broken but her eyes told a different story.

Daisy was laughing, "They all said you would but you are gonna have to go like the wind. Ted said Emily was like a whirlwind tonight."

They talked for an hour or so about the testing and Bailey was looking forward to her turn. "After that I will be a real member of the team," she smiled.

"You already are," Squire responded. "Maybe George would have a problem with it but you have already been into the Void, and he hasn't."

Everyone headed for bed soon afterwards. Daisy wanted to hear about the Void run but everyone was tired so they decided it could wait until morning. The lights were all turned out and Bailey settled down in her new bedroom for the first time.

X.

Bailey let out a whimpering cry and sat up in bed with a start. Her nightshirt was damp and her face was slick with sweat. She breathed hard and tried to convince herself she was safe.

The dream had been bad, even by her standards. Something terrible had been chasing her in the Void and even as she sat in bed she was trembling in fear.

She had never seen the dark stalker in her dream but she had felt its seething evil coming after her. The throbbing in her head was starting to slow as her heartbeat slowly returned to a more normal pattern.

She switched on the bedside light and gingerly slipped out of bed. Deciding a drink of milk would help her relax she crossed the room and opened the door. The Void waited outside where the landing should have been. As she looked out in horror two yellow eyes appeared and looked in at her. They stared right into her soul and she felt her heart stop and her body freeze. That stare contained pure hatred and evil and more power than she would have believed was possible.

She screamed then with a piercing sound that cut through the darkness and carried all her terror with it. She was still screaming when Squire finally shook her awake.

She laid there looking up at the concerned faces of Squire, Paige and Daisy. He sat on the bed with his hands still holding her shoulders. Tears ran from her eyes and into her hair.

"Easy now," he said. "You're safe. We're here."

Daisy turned to leave the room. "I'll get some water," she called behind her, and headed down the stairs.

"Holy crap," Paige said. "That scared the hell out of me."

Bailey was still in too much shock to speak. She looked back at the two of them looking down at her and just whimpered.

"Take your time Bailey," Squire said sitting up and letting the light from the lamp fall on her. "How often do you have dreams this bad?"

"Never as bad as that," Bailey replied in a quiet and wounded voice.

Daisy appeared with a glass of water and a wet flannel. Squire stood and she sat where he had been and wiped Bailey's face. The sudden cold water on her face seemed to bring her round and she lay still until all of her face felt cool and clean.

When Daisy had finished she sat up enough to take a drink from the glass of water she was offered. "Thank you," she said with the slightest hint of a smile.

"No worries," Daisy smiled back, "but I am so giving you some payback for giving me a heart attack just then."

This time Bailey's smile was broader and more like herself again.

"We can talk about it if you want to," Squire offered.

Bailey looked over and gave a small shake of her head. "In the morning," she said. "I've kept you up as it is."

"I'll stay with her," Paige said. "You two can go back to bed." The three exchanged looks and after checking she was alright Squire led Daisy out of the room.

Paige started pulling back the covers of the single bed. "It's going to be cosy," she said and added "move over fatty."

"What?" Bailey was smiling again at the term. She shuffled over to the edge of the bed and Paige climbed in beside her. "Now turn out the light and go to sleep."

Bailey flicked out the light and lay still for a moment. "Thanks Paige," she said quietly.

"No problem," came the soft reply. "Oh, by the way."

"Yes."

"You stink."

Bailey went to sleep with a smile on her face and slept peacefully until the morning.

Daylight streamed into Squire's room heralding a bright and sunny Saturday morning. As he slowly came around the sounds of

197

activity in the kitchen reached him. Daisy and Paige were speaking to each other in excited tones about the weekend and their plans. Turning to his side he reached for his phone to check the time and found he had a text message waiting to be opened.

Squire I wonder if you could pop over to the manor when you have some free time. Just let me know when you can make it. Thanks. George

"More trouble," he said to himself as he climbed out of bed and headed for the en suite.

Feeling more alive again he dressed quickly and headed for the landing and almost collided with Bailey. Her hair was still wet from her shower and she had that hot and fresh smell to her.

She shot a glance at Squire and offered a quick, "Sorry," before heading back to her room to dress.

She found the three of them downstairs in the living room with plates of toast and mugs of tea. They were all debating who should do which items of housework and their plans for the evening. Bailey went and poured herself some tea from the pot and went to join them.

She hadn't been sitting down very long when she exclaimed "Oh my God!" The talking stopped and all eyes turned to her, then followed the direction of her gaze and turned to the TV.

As usual it was silently scrolling the news channel. Paige picked up the remote and pressed the mute button. They had missed the scrolling item Bailey had seen, but the announcer then turned to that item for a report.

"A 19-year-old from Louisiana in the United States woke up yesterday from an 11-year coma. Alex Hullman has been in the Women's and Children's Hospital in Lafayette since a cycling accident left him with serious head injuries. Doctors there have expressed how pleased they are having all but given up on Alex ever making a recovery."

"Wowser," Squire said to himself in surprise.

Bailey addressed him, "You said something wasn't right when we were there, you commented that the colours were too bright."

"Yeah, he wasn't dead, only sleeping," Squire replied. He had his phone in his hand and was dialling Kass.

His brother answered on the second ring and was told straight away to put the news on. A minute or two later they were exchanging notes in excited tones.

"So that's why you couldn't send him," Kass said. "He wasn't dead."

"I just woke him up," Squire replied. "The Void isn't just for the dead Kass; the living can slip in there too."

He cast a long look at Bailey who was looking straight back at him. Unsaid words seemed to pass between them for several moments while Kass talked.

Squire continued, "Maybe people can dream into the Void Kass. There might be a whole lot more going on in there we don't understand."

"It's true," Kass was thinking hard at the farmhouse. The possibilities this opened up were huge. "If people in this realm can visit the Void in dreams then perhaps people there can come here in theirs."

"Good grief," Squire was rubbing his forehead. "How am I supposed to get my head around that?"

The two laughed gently although they both realised that they would have a lot more to do working things out. Kass announced that he would document everything as always but would be opening up a new section.

"See you later tonight at the Manor," he said.

"Sure will," then added, "George wants to see me."

Silence, then, "What is it this time?"

"Who knows, but I suspect I can fill you in later."

Hanging up the phone Squire spoke to Daisy, "Can you see what you can find out honey, but it can wait until after the weekend."

"Nah, I'll get on it today while it's fresh." Daisy's love of her research nearly always got the better of her and she relished putting some more pieces of the puzzle together.

"Okay," he added. "I have to go up to George's, he wants to see me."

"Can I come with you?" Bailey asked. She had heard about George and his grumpy ways but didn't want to be left on her own.

Getting up and heading for the kitchen with a pile of plates Squire called back, "Not this time. I think he wants me alone."

Paige followed him to the kitchen with the mugs. While they loaded the dishwasher she asked "Are you going to be okay?"

"Of course," he said, throwing her a quick smile. "You know me and George, right?"

"That's what worries me," she added. "I'm heading into town today. I'll take the others with me and meet you back here later on before we go to the testing."

Squire had done as requested and contacted George and arranged to be at the Manor House at 11am. He arrived a little late on purpose, rang the bell and waited at the imposing front door to the main building.

The door was answered by one of the staff in a stiff uniform and he was shown in to the drawing room. He was left there for a few moments feeling very out of place. It was such a grand room filled with paintings and sculptures and he ruined the look in his scruffy jeans and trainers.

George arrived shortly afterwards and was all smiles and welcomes. He asked if they could have tea outside and led Squire out through the French windows and onto a paved area surrounded by hanging plants.

They settled themselves into soft chairs at one of the heavy garden tables overlooking the lawns. Another member of staff brought out a tray of tea and left them sitting silently in the sunshine.

George looked over at Squire with a relaxed look on his face. "My friend, I have to take this opportunity to talk to you man to man. What I am going to say to you must stay strictly between us for now."

Squire sat forward and started to pour tea for them both. He said nothing though. This was unusual as George kept his distance from the team in general and only really got involved at meetings. On top of that his mild and pleasant manner was something to be careful of. He wondered what was coming and contented himself with making tea in antique china cups.

"I understand your distrust of me," George went on. "I have not made things easy for you these last few years." The gentle smile on his face was genuine and he seemed ten years younger than the last time he had met him. "You don't think I like you, do you?" His raised his eyebrows and waited for an answer.

Squire gave in. "Why would you think that George?" He tried his best to hide the sarcasm he was feeling and felt he was being baited into a trap.

"You have every reason," George nodded slowly to himself and sat back in his chair, and took in the warmth of the day. "I have made things anything but easy for you."

Squire offered him a cup of tea on a saucer and it was taken with a nod of thanks. "Sometimes things aren't easy though, are they George? I don't think I would have much patience dealing with me either."

There was a chuff sound from the old man now, the nearest Squire had ever heard to a laugh.

"I have to tell you some truths my friend," George went on. "Please, just hear me out because I need to clear the air."

Squire sipped his tea. It was vile. Some strange leaf brand that he couldn't abide. He put his tea cup back on the table and decided to give it a miss. He fumbled in his pockets for his cigarettes.

"The week before the Master was lost in the Void he had been acting very out of character." George's brow furrowed as he remembered. "He made me give my word that I would do everything in my power to protect you, and keep you as safe as our position would allow."

Now he had Squire's attention. If he could have popped up his ears further, then he would have. "You say out of character, how so?" Lighting a cigarette, he faced George with keen interest written all over him.

"He was distracted by something," the other went on. "I don't know what it was, but I could see it in him." He looked out over the lawn again and remembered. "He started to behave irrationally and you know the Master, he was not like that. It was almost like he had plans going on in his head that he couldn't speak to anyone about, not even me."

Squire listened and took it all in. "I can't say I noticed," he replied, "but we only really saw him when it was time for a Void run. He kept things to himself other than that."

"I wish I had tried harder to find out what was on his mind," George continued, "and I will not be making the same mistake again." As he finished he looked hard at his friend at his side. "Is there anything you want to talk about? He saw a shadow pass quickly in Squire's eyes and hurried on, "If you don't want to tell me that's fine, but please will you tell someone?"

Flicking the ash from his smoke Squire responded calmly, "When there is something to talk about I will." He wouldn't though. Kass had called him 'the sponge' many times for his ability to soak up other people's problems, and yet he was awful at sharing his own.

"Please do," George responded and offered a tired looking smile of resignation. "Now," he changed the subject in a more upbeat tone, "that was not why I asked you here today." He shuffled his large frame in his chair almost as if he was starting the meeting afresh.

"In the past years you have done a great many things that have put you in great danger. I understand this is just the way you are but it has been hard for me to watch. I gave my word after all."

Squire was looking around for somewhere to put out his cigarette but didn't want to just flick it into the immaculately kept garden. He resorted to balancing it on the tea tray instead.

"Finally the time is coming for me to give this all up," George waved his hand in the air like a conductor. "I am seventy-two now and I can't keep doing this forever. The time has come to follow the Master's last wishes and place you in charge of the Void Team." His eyes met with Squire's and locked there. "You will make a great leader, I know it."

"You want me to lead?" Squire asked flabbergasted. "I have trouble looking after myself let alone the rest of the team." He started to look uncomfortable. "Surely Justin or Ted would make better leaders than me?"

"That, my friend, is not what the Master wanted." George rang a small hand bell on the table and put it back down. "His instructions were clear."

"So you want me to take over the team. What about you?" Squire was totally taken aback by the meeting. He had expected another severe ticking off but was instead being offered the top job.

A maid had arrived at the table following the summons. She waited until George addressed her, "Would you bring Mr Fox some different tea please, in a mug and I suspect he would prefer something that comes from a tea bag." The maid immediately turned and headed back into the house.

"I will retire, of course." George smiled. "I will stay in touch with everyone naturally, and where possible I will attend meetings." He paused to make sure he had everything covered. "Oh, and I will still control the finances and keep everything paid for until you get used to it and feel ready to take over."

"Will we still be able to use the Manor for testings?" Squire asked.

George looked back and the smile on his face spread. "You decide that Mr Fox. It will be yours to do with as you wish."

The maid arrived with a mug of tea on a silver tray and laid it on the table in front of Squire. His face was a picture of surprise at the time and he didn't say anything. After the maid had left them he looked straight at George. "Are you saying I am to have the Manor?"

"It is not mine to give," George reassured. "It was the Master's, and his wishes were clear." Squire was testing his tea and seemed to approve. "Let me spell it out for you in all its glory."

George produced a pack of cigars from his jacket and offered one to Squire and took another himself. The younger man lit them both and they blew pungent Cuban smoke into the air.

"We have some new members," George began. "For one month you will train them and teach them as much as you can about the Void and its ways. After that you will retire from doing any runs yourself and instead will lead the team."

Squire's eyes had begun to shift around as he thought it all through. "No more Void runs?"

206

"Definitely no more Void runs." George was firm. "Kass will lead the teams entering the Void and you will lead the whole operation from the outside. In return you will have the Manor House and a starter payment of five million to keep things going."

There was a loud cough from Squire who had to sit forward suddenly to clear his throat.

"If you will permit," George added, "I would request one wing of the Manor and live there. I will not get in the way, and will do what I can to help with the running of the place."

It was all too much to take in. Squire puffed on his cigar and considered what it might be like to be a millionaire and owner of Shillyford Manor. He had sudden visions of a Ferrari and a private helicopter sitting out the front.

"I know this is sudden," George said, "but may I ask what are you thinking?"

Squire was lost in thought for some time and even his tea and cigar were not helping. "If I'm really honest I don't want it." He pressed on before George could interrupt, "Money, power, leadership; I'm none of those things. I'm just a scruffy guy that likes an easy life. Kass would make a better candidate. He's clever and thinks hard about things and would be good for the team."

George had expected the response but was ready. "How about if I added that the scruffy guy is also funny, likeable, trustworthy and honourable. The team would follow you to the gates of Hell itself and back and your new team will do the same."

Squire had his head down and his cigar clamped in his teeth. "You're not going to change your mind, are you?"

George leant his elbow on the arm of the chair and tipped himself forward, "No Mr Fox, I am not. I believe in you and so do your team." He allowed himself to relax back into his chair. "It is a shame that you do not."

There was silence for a few minutes as both men thought quietly and watched the clouds drifting across the garden. Finally, Squire spoke up again. "Very well. I want to meet the new people as soon as possible. Once I have I can decide if they are strong enough to run the Void, and who will be leaders in time. If I have to retire from Void runs I want Kass to do the same quite soon. He can help organise as he's brilliant at that kind of thing.

"You will have plenty of time I assure you, and I think you are going to like the new team. Justin was very impressed with them." His tone then changed to a more formal but friendly one. "He also told me about what has been happening to you. A miracle cure at the hospital is something I would have liked to have known about." He kept his eyes on Squire. "I understand why you would want to keep it from me, and you must also know that Justin is very worried about you. He slipped up while telling me about the new member testings and ended up telling me what happened." George shifted again in his chair. "He would never have betrayed you. The team are loyal to you more than you would believe, and that is why your position as leader is so important."

Squire switched the subject now. George had opened up to him and now it was his turn to do the same. "Did you see the news this morning?"

George had crossed his legs and was slumped back in his chair as if he had already retired and given up on being formal. "Yes, I did see the news yes, but which bit?"

"The coma boy in the U.S."

"Ah yes, I did see that. Amazing. I wonder how his family are reacting to it. I imagine a lot has changed in the world since the boy last saw it."

"It was me George. I found him in the Void last night." Squire looked over and received a concerned look back.

"You went in last night? I did wonder and suspect as much when both Kass and yourself were missing from the testing evening, and your loyal bodyguard of course." Even though he was slightly annoyed he didn't show it and finally allowed himself a smile. "I take it then you had a green run?"

Now Squire also allowed himself a smile, "Of course, as if we have anything but green runs." The atmosphere was light and happy and Squire considered how the future relationship with George was going to change. He wasn't the ogre he suspected after all but more like a worried parent.

"Someone in the Void that was alive in this world. How is that possible?" George's question had been keeping Squire busy since he discovered Bailey had met him while dreaming about the Void.

"The body isn't in two places I don't think," Squire ran a hand over his chin and realised he needed a shave. "When we jump to the Void from the barn we take our bodies, but I don't think that is the only way in. I think it's possible to enter in mind only and then you 'live the dream' as it were."

Even as he talked more pieces of the puzzle were falling into place. "If Bailey can dream herself into the Void then she can't be killed there, but when we go there for real we can." His mind was racing now, "the boy Alex was safe as only his mind was in there."

"Who is Bailey?" George was looking straight at Squire now and could see he was deep in thought.

"Oh, you will meet her tomorrow," he replied without looking up from where he was staring at nothing in particular.

George laid the remainder of his cigar on the metal table, "I will look forward to it." In one morning he had understood more about his companion than in all the previous years of his involvement with the project. Now he looked at a thoughtful and troubled man beside him.

"If it's okay George, could I be excused? I need to see if I can find someone."

George pushed himself up to his feet and beckoned Squire to do the same. "I have taken enough of your time," he said. "Of course you can go but please remember; the door here is always open."

They walked together through the garden and eventually came to the front drive. They shook hands and then Squire drove away. It dawned on him it was the first time he had ever considered George as a friend.

Half an hour later Squire sat on the park bench and watched the passers by, letting his mind wander. She wouldn't come of course; he already knew that. He didn't make the rules of their meetings. She would appear when it was right for her and nothing he could do was about to change that. He gave up after an hour or so and started to walk home with his head full of clouds. They understood so much more than the people he saw walking past him, yet they knew almost nothing. Were they any nearer to proving the existence of Heaven? No. They had discovered the Void and found it to be just as full of questions.

He spent the afternoon making notes. He had never had to be a leader of anything before as he always did everything on impulse and he now found planning things a lot harder than he expected.

He had been joined by the three girls later in the day. They were full of smiles having had a great time at the cinema and were looking forward to the evening.

Paige asked what the meeting had been about with George, and Squire had dismissed it as just another debate about all the things he needed to do better. The subject was soon dropped and they got down to planning food and the evening's entertainment.

They arrived slightly early for the testing at the Manor House and found Tinker already there setting up. By 7.45pm everyone who was needed had arrived and Squire thanked everyone for giving up their Saturday evening.

"It's very nice to meet you Bailey," Ted had said with his white smile glowing. The introductions had been short and on a need to know basis. At this stage it was being treated as purely an extra testing session for someone who was unable to make it last night because of other commitments; like being in the Void.

The day had been warm and sunny but clouds had come rolling in from the west in the early evening and the air was now close and humid.

"She's going to be messed up in this heat," Ted laughed. "As if this thing isn't hard enough already."

"Don't stress yourself," Paige commented. "She's going to be fine." There was a look in the ex-record holder's eyes that said she expected her assault course time to take another battering tonight.

Bailey had gone off to get changed and reappeared in grey workout shorts and vest. If nothing else at least she had inside information and came dressed for the occasion.

Ted prepared himself and checked his stopwatch. "I will give you your first instruction and start the time," he said. "Are you ready?"

Bailey nodded and moments later was pulling herself up the frame with just her arms. She made easy work of it and was soon trotting over the balance beam. It was clear she was not only strong but agile and quick.

The snake also caused no problem although she was now sweating freely. She didn't slow throughout the whole course until she came to the cement bag. Using every bit of her upper body strength she hauled the bag onto her shoulder and jogged down the course.

Ted looked at the time and threw a glance at Paige. She knew from that glance how quick Bailey was going and had to admit that agility was just as important as strength. Emily had beaten her time with sheer speed and flexibility but Bailey was going to beat it on just style alone.

When the final whistle went there was applause from those watching and they went to congratulate their friend who had slid to the floor exhausted.

Paige offered her a bottle of water and it was taken with a hand that shook with fatigue. "Did I do okay?" she asked while taking a long gulp from the bottle. Sweat ran down her face like a boxer after a fight and there was no doubt that she was in excellent shape.

"You did fine," Ted said, "but before you get too comfortable you need to get yourself in to see Daisy for the next part."

The mental agility session didn't seem to give her any concerns either. They knew she was clever, and she was soon recovering from the assault course and going well with the mental questions.

Her breathing was back to a normal rhythm by the time she stood in front of Tinker at the firing range and she was pleased to be outside where it was less stuffy and there was the slightest hint of a breeze.

Paul McCoy explained how the course worked, and gave her the choice of one gun or two as he had the previous evening. Bailey took two straight away and before she had any further instructions had ejected the clips and was counting the bullets.

Tinker could see she was no stranger to guns and gave Squire a look of approval. She was soon standing at the start and the test began.

The first target popped up 30 metres away and Bailey was off like a cat. Halfway there she fired with her left gun at full run and saw the small black hole appear in the white target. At the same time the second target popped up to her right and she fired at that with her right hand gun.

Nobody ever hit the third and fourth targets because they were still trying to manage the first two but Bailey pitched into a sideways roll and fired twice in quick succession.

"Holy rubber goods Batman," Squire said out loud, "that's incredible!"

"Advantage of two guns," Paul added. "She has great skill with both."

Bailey didn't even get halfway around the course when both guns jammed open showing her she was out of ammo. She had run and rolled around the course faster than anyone they had seen before and didn't even look puffed out. She walked back to Paul and laid the guns on the table next to him.

"That was loads of fun," she said smiling brightly. "Wish I had more ammo to keep going."

Tinker picked up his clipboard and started to head out to check the targets. "Maybe another time we will run it with extra clips and you can go head to head with Mr Lucky over there." He threw a glance and a smile at Squire who had the all time range record that he had set with his single gun. Right now he didn't look like he fancied the challenge.

Anna ran the morality test and that turned out to be the toughest part for Bailey. All the others had their church upbringing behind them which had taught them a great deal about the rights and wrongs in life. Having not had that Bailey found some of the choices the questions offered quite difficult and was glad when it was over.

When she was finished everyone had gathered outside and were sitting on the grass chatting. She went to join them and was rewarded with another bottle of water.

Justin gathered all the results together and added those from Anna last. He made notes and sat checking things for a time while

215

everyone else waited. It was almost dark on the lawn when he finally came forward and gave them the news.

"Okay Bailey," he started. "I suppose I should start with the important part first. You have passed in all the sections." There were murmurs of approval from everyone sitting around her. She was wearing a huge smile and was delighted.

"In other news," Justin continued, "we will need to work on that morality score in the future as that section was a little touch and go." He gave Squire a wink and moved on. "Your time on the assault course was very fast indeed. In fact, it was the second fastest we have ever had."

Paige scowled at Bailey and then started laughing. "Well done fatty," she called with a big smile on her face.

"Mental agility," Justin went on, "was also very good, so well done on that. Not as good though as the firing range. Squire, I'm sorry my friend," he said looking up, "your record has finally been beaten. 100% targets hit."

There was celebration from everyone as Bailey became a legitimate member of the Void Runners. They all offered their congratulations and Squire's smile was bigger than anyone's. "I knew it," he said to her with smiling eyes. "Totally deserved, and well done."

Bailey was overjoyed. "I'm so glad I didn't let you down," she said earnestly.

Squire rubbed his chin and turned serious. "Well actually, there was one thing." A slight look of concern appeared on her face. "I have actually seen you looking better."

She suddenly realised he was joking and looked down at herself. Her shorts and vest were damp and grass stained where she had thrown herself around the firing range. The cement dust only added to the look. They both started laughing.

"One last thing," Justin had to call to make himself heard above the noise. "Squire, you have another naming to do I'm afraid. Your all time record has been broken."

Now the atmosphere picked up another notch and there were pats on the back all round for the new champion of the testing. They were all in high spirits but eventually people started to head home after a very successful evening.

The Foxes walked back to their car at a gentle ambling pace. "I've never seen anything like that at the firing range," Squire said, "that was unbelievable."

"I thought the assault course was great too," Daisy added knowing it was going to annoy her sister.

"Oh," Bailey said turning to Paige, "I'm sorry about beating your score."

"That's fine," she replied, "oh, by the way,"

"Yes?"

"You stink."

XI.

Sunday morning rolled in overcast and grey but was still warm and pleasant. Justin led the morning service at the Shillyford New Hope Church like he always did, bursting with energy and passion. His belief was contagious to those that attended each week and they would leave on a high note full of positive thoughts to start the next week.

Bailey was attending her first service and had surprised herself. "I thought it was going to be really dull and formal," she said to Paige next to her.

"Nah," Paige responded. "You're thinking of Bells and Smells. Sit, kneel, stand and all that. We tend to rock out a lot more here."

Sarah Naylor then sang Oceans in her clear and pure voice and Bailey had her first hint of a power she didn't understand. Peace washed over her and the negatives in her life seemed to pale. To her it was like a drug and she sucked it in.

After the service everyone gathered for teas and coffees and Bailey stood chatting to Justin. He was delighted she had come along and introduced her to Tom, who was full of smiles as always and still had a handshake as hard as his faith. Neither of them knew that the other was part of Justin's new team, and would have to wait until later to discover that.

Squire stood against the back wall of the hall with his cup of tea in his hand. He watched the comings and goings around the room, and played a game with himself trying to work out who the new recruits were. He suspected Tom straight away, strong and thoughtful and already a good leader. Ashley too seemed to radiate peace and confidence, and had more interest in the worries of others than her own.

He caught sight of Paige over the other side of the hall giving Emily a piggy back around the church. Emily, he thought. There was another who would be interesting, peaceful, kind and considerate.

He was knocked out of his thinking when Ryan came over for a chat. "Hello Mr Cool," Squire greeted him.

Ryan did his half smile back and they shook hands as always. He had been playing bass guitar in the band and was always so composed and in control. "How was the sound today?" he asked. He was always concerned with the band sounding as good as possible, and loud too.

"Epic as always," Squire replied. "I could feel that bass in my stomach."

Ryan was pleased. "That's great. So have you been up to much this week?"

Squire almost wished he could talk about his week when people asked. He resorted to his normal reply, "Nah, work and not a lot else really."

Slowly conversations came to an end and people drifted away to get on with their Sunday lunches. Squire collected the girls and they headed to a pub for their dinner and as the sun had managed to come out they would spend the afternoon in the beer garden chatting and mixing with the locals.

"See if you can manage not to be late tonight," George had called after them on the way out of the church.

Daisy had smiled back in her typical angelic style. "You know he will be George, he always is."

Naturally he was late. Kass and Anna were staring at the empty living room of the farmhouse but it wasn't helping as there was not going to be enough room.

"It doesn't matter," Anna said cheerfully. "We can all squeeze in somehow."

It would certainly be a bit cosy that evening as there were more people than chairs. Kass had half a mind to light the fire, but put the idea off as people could end up sitting in front of it. "Whatever happens," he noted, "the existing members will have to get their usual chairs or there will be a bun fight."

Justin had arrived first with Elle. He was clutching a folder of paperwork and looking excited, whereas his daughter was not saying a lot and looked apprehensive. Anna headed to the kitchen with Elle trailing behind her and they put the kettle on and got cups out ready for the start of a major tea making session. Ted and Tinker followed shortly afterwards and joined Justin, who was standing in the middle of the living room, and began talking pleasantries.

Soon afterwards the girls arrived. Ashley had picked up Emily on the way and they entered both looking slightly sheepish and nervous about what was coming. They had walked into a strange house which was filling up with people, some they knew well and some not so well.

"Don't get comfortable there," Kass had said to them after they sat down. They looked up at him now even more on edge. "All the chairs have owners here," he said light-heartedly. "We will sort out the seating arrangements as everyone arrives.

Having overheard the conversation Tinker took his chair by the entrance to the living room and Justin sat in his on the other side of the door. "Elle can have the arm of my chair," he volunteered.

Ryan and Tom were next and joined the huddle for a few minutes before heading off through the archway to the dining room and fetching a couple of chairs from there. They set them down in front of the arch but left enough room for people to go in and out. Ashley saw it happen and wondered why she hadn't thought of that.

She stood with Emily and the two of them talked quietly and waited for everyone else to arrive.

Anna and Elle started to circulate with drinks and the various coffee tables started to fill up and the general noise of background talking steadily grew louder.

George was there shortly afterwards and things got under way. He asked if everyone could sit down somewhere so they could see who was there and who they were waiting for.

All around him the team started to get settled and George scanned the room. He was smiling broadly at the sight of so much energy around him and the youthful faces that had finally started to balance out the old timers.

Ten minutes later the meeting should have begun. Ted had arrived after attending an emergency up at the hospital and had to shift Ashley out of his chair. She went and sat on the arm of Emily's chair and felt more nervous and unsettled still.

George looked at Kass and then at his watch and then at Justin. People were still talking quietly in the room and the waiting went on, but soon enough another car arrived outside and the noise level would soon be raised some more.

Paige and Daisy both entered first with Bailey close behind. Paige took Daisy's chair and sat on one edge so Daisy could squeeze in next to her. Bailey looked around the room and saw nowhere to sit. There was a moment of awkwardness as she was clearly on full display as the only one standing.

Justin called over from the other side of the room, "Girls, I'm sorry you are going to have to move again."

Ashley and Emily got up once again and went to join Bailey in the middle of the room and their sense of not belonging deepened further.

When Squire finally came into the room there were calls of greeting and smiles from all over the place. He went to the existing crew that he knew and exchanged quick handshakes and a hug for Anna before heading over to his chair and sitting down.

Bailey didn't hesitate and moved past the other two and sat down on the arm of his chair and felt the feeling of clammy embarrassment start to subside. Emily and Ashley then sat on the floor in front of the fire between Squire's chair and Ted's.

Justin opened the meeting officially and began by thanking everyone for coming and welcomed all the new members to the team. He then said that he would introduce everyone on the Void Runner team and would then announce the new members to everybody.

"You already know who I am," he began, "so we will miss me out. For any that don't know George," he pointed his arm to his right, "he is our Chairman and looks after the financial side of things. Next to George are Paige and Daisy Fox." Both girls looked up and around the room. "These two provide a great service to the team and operate on the support side. Paige is head of security and Daisy is in charge of research. I expect most of you recognise them from church."

Looking opposite him now Justin continued, "Opposite me is Paul McCoy that I expect you all know. In the team he is better known as Tinker, and his job is to create equipment for us and is responsible for all things technical."

"Next to him on the arm of the chair is Anna, and in the chair is Kass. They look after headquarters here and on top of that Kass is also a principal team member and the brains of the outfit. If Kass asks you do to something you need to be listening and acting. We are not overly strict here, but we will take a very dim view if anyone is not taking instruction from the leaders of the team."

Now Justin turned to the far side of the room. "The smiling gentleman in the corner is Ted Dawes. He is head of all things medical and is the Director of Mendip Hospital. If you get injured you will see him, but additionally he can now be your doctor for anything else if you wish. Your health and welfare is of great concern to us so please use the people around you." Ted flashed his white teeth and nodded to each of the newcomers.

Now Justin turned to the other corner of the room. "Last, but not least I am sure you all know Squire Fox." There were general nods in his direction. All the new members knew him from their time at church. "More than anything else you must appreciate," Justin went on, "that Squire is the most senior member of our operations team and his requests must be followed without fail. Your safety falls to him as you will be finding out very soon." Justin eyed the new team members one at a time and saw from their faces they were all taking everything in. "I will now hand over to our chairman to continue."

George then spoke up for the first time. "Thank you Justin and may I welcome each and every one of you to the Void Runners and I hope we are all going to enjoy working together. Justin has selected you all for a very special purpose, which we will explain in more detail shortly." His eyes took in the new team as he spoke to each of them. "You may consider this now as your occupation should you wish to, although you are free to continue with schools, college and jobs. There are a couple of things I need you to understand.

Firstly, you will be working for us from now on. For want of a better way of saying it, Mr Fox senior over there is your boss. He doesn't act like one most of the time," he cast Squire a friendly smile, "but please do not doubt for a moment that he is. There will be no paperwork so please don't wait for a job description or a contract. This is a secret organisation and must stay that way. Finally," he made eye contact with the six new Void Runners, "what you do in this team can be extremely dangerous. A very substantial salary will be paid directly into your banks and will reflect the job you do. Please do not rush out and spend it all though as this will also arouse suspicion from friends and family."

There were smiles and excited looks from the new members now. No one had mentioned anything about pay and this was a real surprise for them.

"I have one last announcement to make," George went on, "but before I do perhaps you could introduce yourselves so we can start to get to know you." His eyes seemed to rest on Tom as he finished speaking so they started there.

"Um," he began, "I'm Tom Stonley and I'm 21. I come from the village and I work in electronics with my dad. As I think you all know I'm also the youth group leader at church." Having said all he thought was important he turned to his left and waited for the chain to continue.

Next to him was Ryan who was well known for being quite quiet and thoughtful. He began in his normal, unassuming style, "I'm Ryan Grey and I'm 22. I'm a carpenter and live in Highgate." Glad to have got his piece over he also turned to his left.

Sitting on the floor in front of the fire were the two girls, and they went next. "I think I know everyone here. I'm Ashley Lord and I'm 19. I am on a university break and doing religious studies and I'm doing charity work at the moment." Her earlier nerves were starting to evaporate having found everyone to be so friendly. Like the others before her she now looked to her left.

"I'm Emily Watts. I'm 18 and studying full time still. I didn't know what I wanted to do with my life really so I'm really excited to be part of this team." Her bubbly spirit and joy was apparent immediately and she gave a little smile as she finished speaking.

Moving left once again all eyes fell on the one most didn't know. "Hello, I'm Bailey Moreton," she started nervously. "I'm 24 and I passed the testing last night." She didn't know how much she should say, but went ahead anyway. "I only met Squire and the girls a couple of days ago in the village." Happy she had said enough she fell silent.

Finally, all eyes went to the other side of the room and the last of the new recruits. "I'm Elle Naylor, Justin's daughter as I'm sure you all know. I'm 15 so still at school and hating it." There were some smiles around the room at this. "I know what the team does so I have a head start and I can't wait to be a part of it."

Justin had been watching from his chair and now addressed the room. "Thank you everyone." He opened his folder and shuffled some papers. "Now, let me explain what it is that we do so secretly up here."

Justin spoke for nearly an hour about their discovery of the Void and the hope that there was a way to find a way to find Heaven. He also explained the dangers involved and the cost in lives their search had suffered and the procedures they had put in place to keep everyone as safe as possible.

Having covered everything, he addressed the newcomers again. "If any of you want to drop out then now is the time to do it." He looked at each in turn but saw only determination and enthusiasm in all of them. "We look after each other here," he went on, "so please stay close. We need to build trust and strong bonds between us as much of what we do cannot be discussed anywhere else."

He explained the need for total secrecy once again, even from family and friends. If word got out to the general public the lives of the Void team would suddenly get more difficult. Once he had covered everything he could think of he handed over to George once again.

"Thank you Justin," George started. "As you know I am Chairman of this team and have been since the Master formed it so many years ago. It falls to me to organise your instruction and training and everything from there on." His eyes scanned the room and he spoke slowly and with his usual authority. "However," he said, "I am retiring from the team having been a part of it for the last thirty years."

Around the room now there were looks of surprise and shock from those that he had worked with for so long. "This new team," he went on, "is young and exciting, and I am neither of those things." He smiled softly before going on. "Finding a new Chairman is no easy task with so many talented people amongst us, so the choice of my replacement is the one the Master chose many years ago." All eyes were fixed on George now as this was major news for the existing members. "For the rest of this meeting and for all meetings after this I will now hand over to your new Chairman and Captain: Squire Fox."

There were some gasps in the room, not least from Daisy and Paige. Bailey sitting on the arm of his chair looked down at him and beamed. After a few moments Justin broke ranks and was the first to his feet. He headed over to Squire and shook his hand and offered his heartfelt congratulations. He was followed by everyone else in the room. Paige and Daisy both gave him a great big hug and were smiling broadly; their example was then followed by Bailey who seemed equally as thrilled.

When the hush had died down, and Kass had mumbled loudly "We're all dead," they awaited the new Chairman.

Squire composed himself and tried to organise his thinking. He had not expected to be dropped in it so suddenly and had to hand it to George for giving him such a build up. As always, he did the next bit on impulse.

"Well, thanks everyone, and thank you George," he nodded at the old man. "All of you guys that have been here for a while know what you do and you do it well. There will be no changes that I can see so please just keep doing those things and making life for us Void Runners that much easier."

Now he looked at the new recruits. "As for our new team; I need to get to know and understand you a lot better so I will try and arrange a meeting with each of you in the coming week. We can organise dates and times on your way out so please make sure you come and see me. Every evening that you are not busy and are not meeting with me will be spent here with Kass learning the basics and anything else he feels the need to teach you."

Turning now to Paige to include her Squire issued the next request. "This Saturday may be the first day everyone here is available. Could I ask all our new members to meet up with Paige and Bailey for some essential retail therapy as it appears we have a design guru sitting with us." There were general nods from everyone. "You will all be kitted out with new clothes for this project, so have a think about how you want to look and we will see to it that you get it."

Paige was looking carefully at each of the new people she would be taking shopping and imagining how she could transform them like she had done to Bailey. She already knew how they dressed most of the time and looked forward to the challenge of making them look and feel amazing.

Squire continued, "By next Sunday I hope to have two teams set up based on your individual skills and abilities. One team will be headed up by Kass, and I will take the other." He looked around the room. "Meetings and training this week and as soon as we are all set we will make our first visit to the Void together as a new team." There were excited smiles now from everyone. For a change the whole operation was going forward with purpose and direction.

Kass was then asked to run through the last run the team had made. It was normal practice for full details of the week's activities to be announced at the Sunday evening meetings so that everyone had the same news and information.

The new members listened in amazement as Kass recalled finding Alex with his train set. The small boy with the grown up voice was returned to the world and also made headline news at the same time. "This was a first for us," Kass explained. "Never before have we found a presence in the Void that was actually alive. We come across many things on our travels but they have always fallen into the same groups: the dead, and the dreams and the nightmares they have around them." Kass looked over at his brother. "There are also lost souls that are alive. The Void is not only a place of death."

"Perhaps," Justin added from the corner of the room, "it has nothing to do with death at all. That may be all we have found so far, but what we find are the souls of people. Maybe it is possible for our souls to leave our bodies and enter the Void."

It was as though every one of the existing members had the same thought at once, but it was Ted that said it aloud. "Sasha."

The atmosphere in the room changed at once. George Brooker looked like he had been physically hurt and the Foxes cast their eyes down suddenly.

"What is it?" Bailey asked. It was obvious to all the new members that something had happened: something none of them understood.

"Move on please," Kass said quietly without looking up from his knees.

Ted was still considering the possibilities this new information may have for the team. "I'm just thinking perhaps we should explore this further," he said to the room in general.

"I said move on," Kass repeated firmly. He looked over at Ted and then took in the others in the room and noticed how many still had their heads down. "This is too painful for too many of us and we will not discuss it further."

Justin heard the warning in Kass' tone but ventured further. "I understand fully how we feel about this, but I wonder if we owe it to the new members of the team. They are part of this team now and they should be given an explanation."

The room fell quiet and the tension in the room mounted. Most realised Justin was correct. The six newest members sat within the same room, but none of them had any idea what was going on.

"Then you will explain to them Justin," Squire said finally raising his head and looking over at his friend, "but not here, and not now." The look in his eyes left no one in any doubt that the subject was closed. He looked at the confused faces of the new members. "I am sorry," he began. "There are some things that are hard to talk about, but you will be told in due course. For now, we have had a busy evening and I think we have a lot to look forward to. Unless there is anything else I am closing the meeting there." He glanced at everyone quickly before getting to his feet as a signal that it was time to go. As soon as others started to do the same he sat straight back down again.

With the meeting over a queue formed at Squire to sort out dates for the meetings with the new members. Bailey was sitting right next to him and informed him they could have a meeting anytime.

"We will catch up later," he informed her, "but I have a task to complete before we depart. From this point on your name within the Void Runners is Dreamer. You do not have to use it if you don't want to."

Bailey was delighted even if she didn't understand it. "Dreamer Moreton," she whispered to herself and tried to decide if she liked it.

Emily was right by Squire's feet so she went next. "I'm free most evenings so I don't mind, and you have to name me as well." Her shy smile was mixed with excitement.

"I cannot name you until I know you," Squire said, "but don't worry, I won't forget to name the assault course record holder."

Ashley was added to the diary for Monday evening, with Ryan and Tom on Tuesday. Elle would be straight after school on Monday so would be the first in line.

Meeting places were arranged as none of them could be at their homes. The secrecy of the project had to be protected so neutral ground was selected and agreed on.

George also caught Squire before he left and complimented him on his plan of action at such short notice.

"I'm no good at planning George," he replied. "It's better when stuff just happens."

When everyone else had left Squire sat and chatted with Kass and they compared diaries for the week. It was going to be a bit full on but they were both looking forward to it.

Kass was quietly amused with the speed things were happening. "So if strange old ladies and everything else wasn't enough we now have a new Chairman." His tone was soft and kind and he seemed genuinely rather pleased with things.

"I don't want to be Chairman," his brother replied. "I certainly didn't know it was going to happen this quickly."

Kass nodded to himself. "You will be fine, and if nothing else it will be quietly chaotic for a while."

When they were all done Squire collected Paige, Daisy and Bailey from the clutches of Anna in the kitchen and escorted them out.

The short trip back in the car was full of loud talking and laughing.

"So much for another ticking off," Paige said laughing. "Why didn't you tell us George was handing it over to you?"

"Yeah," Daisy piped up from the back seat. "I thought we were friends and all that."

Squire was laughing along too. "I was told I couldn't say anything. I didn't know it was all going to kick off that quickly."

"Blimey," Paige went on. "What a change from the deadly meeting last week to this one. I seriously thought George was all set to kick you out of the team."

It was barely a five-minute drive home but in that time Bailey hadn't said a word.

When they were all back in the house Paige and Daisy headed off to bed and Squire headed to the kitchen for a smoke and more tea. He was joined a few minutes later by a thoughtful Bailey who pulled out a chair and sat down at the kitchen table.

He watched her closely for a few seconds and saw the worry in her eyes. "What's up?" he asked in a soft tone and pulled up a chair opposite her.

She looked up briefly and met his eyes. "It's nothing important," she replied, but the lie was clear.

"I am in charge now, and that makes me responsible for a change," he went on. "If something is up I need to know about it. I can't help if I don't know."

She rubbed her hands together and looked like she was going to stay silent, but then changed her mind. "What if I'm not on your team?"

Squire looked back slightly surprised. "Is that what's worrying you? I'm sure you will be fine whichever team you are in.

The way you handled yourself on the testing makes you the least of my worries."

"Of course I'm worrying," she replied and Squire saw that she was totally serious. "It does matter though," she finished.

He hadn't even thought that far yet but he reacted on instinct. He reached across the table and laid his hand on hers and gave it a squeeze. "Could you maybe worry about something else," he said quietly, "because you won't need to worry about that."

She looked up and gave him a crushed smile. She couldn't tell him about the dream in case he thought she was mad, but it had felt a little too real to her and she had also seen Kass there before she even knew who he was. Her dreams were becoming more real since meeting Squire Fox in them; something neither of them had an answer to.

Squire let go of her hand and gave it a quick pat before getting back to his feet. "Right," he said while scanning the kitchen. "Forget the tea, I should be celebrating. Would you care for some wine?"

She nodded and smiled quickly. "That sounds like a great idea."

They headed for the living room where Squire put on some Muse for them to listen to and served a mature strong red for the two of them.

"We didn't organise when my meeting was going to be," she said, feeling the need to be more positive.

Sitting in his favourite chair Squire raised an eyebrow. "I doubt we need to have a meeting, but if you think we need to, why don't you tell me all about you."

So she talked. She told him of her family let downs and how she had battled endlessly to do well both at home and at school. Her evenings were an awful memory full of loneliness and sadness. She had tried to be popular at school but she was not liked there either. Being clever and hardworking did not go hand in hand with having friends.

By the time she had started work she was in the athletics club and also a member of a local gun club. She didn't like the macho theme going on there but it helped to get her frustrations out of her system. She imagined the targets she blew holes in were her dad and she almost wished he was there for real so she could show him how his failure as a parent had made her feel.

The red wine softened her up and loosened her tongue. For the next hour she sipped her wine and her pain and hatred came flowing out.

Tears fell at times when she talked about her greatest let downs; her mother and father and all the nights she had sat alone upstairs sobbing herself to sleep. There were the happy moments too though; her graduation and her job at the museum.

"I have no happy people moments," she said. "I've done some great things but I always had to celebrate them by myself. I didn't have people around me I could share those happy times with."

237

She looked up at Squire who was patiently listening in the chair opposite her. "Until now," she added.

It was early morning by the time she had shared her pain and she was feeling better. "I've never told anyone this stuff before," she said.

"Why not?"

"Because I didn't trust anyone enough," she replied and finished off her wine. "I've trusted people in the past but they just used it to beat me with. I'm more careful now."

When she had no more to say they headed to their rooms and the house was quiet again. Bailey slept soundly all night. She had poured out her demons and they had fled from her in the night leaving her in peace.

The following day had started late for Squire and he found the house empty when he got up. He spent the day planning ideas for the team and its training and spent an hour on the phone to Kass making sure they both knew what they were doing.

Later that afternoon he sat on a swing in the park gently rocking it backward and forwards. It was a good place to think and unwind and he needed both. He was still troubled by the old lady and her words that bounced around inside his head that he had no answers to. Feelings of anxiety were starting to grip him and he tried to push them away by focusing on things he had some control over.

The weather had changed and the day had been a lot cooler and a gentle breeze blew off the duck pond and filled the air with freshness and hinted of rain.

Looking up he saw Elle bowling towards him in her school uniform and her bag slung over her shoulder. She dumped her bag and sat on the swing next to him and smiled. "Did I keep you waiting long?" she said.

"No, just got here," he replied. It wasn't strictly true but he had been waiting for someone else initially.

"Oh good, I'm glad," her bubbly personality came shining through. "I thought the stupid bus was going to make me late."

Squire asked her to talk about herself and at first it was a little slow going. She gave basic facts about the subjects she did and didn't like and then talked about her hobbies. All of this he listened to and absorbed and slowly she started to relax. Within half an hour he had dug in deep enough to start to hear what actually made her tick.

"It's so crap sometimes," she said.

"What is?"

"Being the Pastor's daughter," she responded. "No one ever tells me their secrets or anything because I may disapprove." She had started now and was getting up some steam. "I have to try so hard not to do things wrong all the time in case it reflects badly on my family. All my friends can watch bad stuff on TV, gossip, swear and I have to be little Miss Nice."

Squire detected the deep set frustration lurking inside her and suspected that in fact most teenagers were full of the same sorts of feelings. "Look what your frustrations have given you though," he said. "You are a credit to your family which surely can't be a bad thing."

"I know," she responded, her voice still holding a bitter tone, "but it's still not fair."

"Well," he offered, "I am not your parent, but I am your friend. You cannot drag your frustrations around in the Void. You need to be you and you need to be at peace with yourself."

"Do I have to be good all the time?" Her question seemed strange to him, but as he hadn't lived her life it was hard to judge how much it was eating into her.

"Just be you, that's all I ask." He rummaged in his jacket for his cigarettes and having found them he set one to work. "You may be fifteen Elle but you put yourself forward for a task that is for adults." He blew smoke into the air and felt his head clearing. "No one asked you to apply," he said watching her closely. "You chose this path and now you have to stick by your choice."

Elle calmly rocked her swing with her arms hugged around her. "So I need to act like an adult," she asked back.

"No." his reply brought her chin up to look at him. "So many people have this wrong. Being an adult doesn't mean you have to be serious all the time. Carry that young part of yourself with you always and enjoy fun and games and the odd bit of mischief. The adult part you have to adopt is to accept not everything is fair in this world, but to do the best with what you have and not find excuses when things go wrong."

Elle considered the words and would still be thinking about them as she lay in her bed that night. "So be young and have fun but think about my actions and reactions?"

Squire nodded slowly from his gently swaying perch. "Nicely put, but also consider Elle; the world may be a better place without bad TV, gossip and swearing, so don't blame your father's position. Be thankful for it."

"I guess so," she replied quietly. "I think the frustration is that I don't quite fit in with my friends because I'm different."

They both swung silently on their swings for a minute before Squire spoke again. "Perhaps being different is what makes you special?" His question brought a smile to her face. "Consider how you must look in their eyes, not just your own."

Elle felt some of the invisible chains that had been holding her back falling away. She felt somehow renewed and her spirit was lighter. When she saw her father walking towards them she said, "I'm really happy to be in your team."

Justin asked how everything had gone and got a big smile from his daughter and thumbs up from Squire. They both left him alone on the swings shortly afterwards with Elle calling back cheerfully, "Thanks for the meeting boss."

Even though her age and life experience was lower than he would have liked Squire was pleased Elle was on the team. What role she would play, or how she would fit in he did not know but her cheerful good spirits would be good to have around.

The next meeting was with Emily, and Squire was sitting outside the chip shop five minutes early. When she had arrived he had brought them both fish and chips and they had found a spot sitting on a low wall outside the Town Hall.

She was much easier to talk to and seemed to be quietly full of peace. Her home life was excellent and her school work was average although she didn't really enjoy it. She had given up gymnastics a year before when it was getting too obvious everyone else in the club was so much younger than her and she seemed like a giant in size to them.

Her complexion was very pale but clear and her blue eyes appeared to have a sleepy look to them. At barely 5' tall she was compact and slim but full of power. Squire had read the notes on her assault course run and was totally impressed. Having someone that flexible and agile may be very useful to the team and he also picked up on her caring instinct.

"I want you to meet up with Ted," he said and scrolled though his phone to give her the number. "I need a really good first aider in the team and with your caring abilities I think that will suit you."

Emily had slender eyebrows and they now bunched up on her forehead. "I don't really like that kind of thing, but okay." She finished with the smallest of smiles and Squire knew she didn't feel confident about her role.

"You care about people don't you?" he asked as he rolled his chip paper into a ball.

Emily was still only halfway through hers. "Yes, well, the people I like."

Aiming at the rubbish bin ten feet away Squire lobbed his paper ball and felt the joy as it bounced off the edge and fell in. "People you like and care about may get hurt where we go. Imagine what a bonus it will be if you can do something about that."

Beside him Emily continued nibbling at her chips. "Yeah, I know. I guess that would be a good thing, as long as I don't faint in the process."

They both laughed and Emily was pleased with her meeting. She didn't really want to be a first aider, but she did want more than anything to be in the team.

"Do you know enough about me to give me my new name yet?" she asked with a tone of hopefulness.

He smiled to himself. "No, but I am getting there."

The meeting came to a close on a light note and she promised she would call Ted and arrange it tomorrow and thanked Squire for dinner. She wandered off home still eating chips and left him sat on the wall making some notes before he too headed off for the last meeting of the evening.

Ashley was sitting in the bar of The Swan Pub even though Squire arrived early. She looked pleased not to be on her own too long and enquired how his day had gone. She was easy to talk to and was kind and genuine. Her concern for the others was also clear and before long Squire has also asked her to meet up with Ted and learn first aid.

She seemed pleased straight away, "Oh yes, I can do that."

"Are you squeamish?" he asked.

"No, not too bad I don't think," she said and her smile was relaxed.

"Are you afraid of anything else?" Something in her eyes had given it away. He was slightly concerned he could see too much of himself hiding in the look she had given him.

Ashley pondered the answer for a moment. "Well, yes, lots of things." Her eyes shone and she shrugged her shoulders. "You will have to help me with those." Her smile was soft and sincere but Squire still felt something going on deeper.

"I feel fear Ashley," he said calmly. Her expression changed briefly before once again she regained herself and tried not to feel disappointed. "Even now you are pushing yourself beyond your comfort zone."

"I know, but I don't want to let you down," she replied in her bravest voice.

Squire could see her passion and determination but went on. "You will only be letting me down if you don't ask for help when you need it. Please don't wait for me to ask if you are okay. I need to know when you're not."

"I will," she replied. "I promise."

Giving her a half smile he continued, "I expect you will break that promise. Fear is not weakness Ashley. Don't be ashamed of it."

Once the meeting was over Squire drove her home and then headed off to see Kass at the farmhouse. He was already forming some ideas in his head and needed his brother as a sounding board.

When he arrived at the barn Tom and Ryan were still there with Kass and looking amazed at the equipment. They had run through the basics and seemed eager to get on with it for real. To save time later Squire asked Tom to join him outside so they could have their quick meeting and right from the start it was clear there was a future team leader in the making.

"What worries you the most?" Squire asked once they had got the initial pleasantries out of the way.

Tom seemed to almost radiate his energy and enthusiasm in his words and in his gestures and actions. "Just letting people down I suppose," he said after giving the question some thought. When

Squire did not speak again Tom continued, "I have a bit of an idea what to expect now, but from what Kass was saying there is no way of knowing what we are getting ourselves into beforehand." Lit up only by the single lamp outside the barn, it was clear to see the passion in Tom's expression. "It just makes me a bit nervous."

Squire knew the feeling well. "I have run the Void a thousand times Tom and I am still nervous. If it is any help for now, do not worry how you will react to things. Kass and I will guide you and train you until you are as good as we are or better."

When they were finished Tom swapped over with Ryan and the last of the meetings got under way. Ryan was the quietest and humblest of all the new team. He answered all the questions he was asked, but every time his replies hinted at something unspoken.

"Ryan," Squire said as he began to close the meeting. "Why do I get the feeling you do not feel worthy to be in the team?"

The other cast his eyes down for a moment as he tried to put the right words together. "I suppose everyone else is bringing something more special than me to the party."

Squire watched him carefully; all the time weighing his words and body language. "I don't see that. Can you explain?"

Once again Ryan looked down before continuing. "Tom is really courageous and strong and encourages those around him while Emily, well she has the likable factor and she's funny and caring. Elle is really talented for one so young and you can tell there is more going on in her head than she reveals. Ashley has a heart as big as her body and is spilling it wherever she goes. As for Bailey; I don't even know where to begin with that one." When he finished he looked up and hoped Squire wouldn't agree that he was the weakest link.

He didn't. Instead he calmly lit a cigarette and considered everything Ryan had said. At last he gave his verdict. "I wonder what kind of a person can spot all of those things in others and yet not see the gifts they carry themselves." Ryan looked quietly surprised. "You see; it takes a special kind of person to unravel people as quickly as you have done; just the kind of person I need in the team as it happens. The Void affects people in different ways and having someone there who can spot things and react to them is really important. Do not doubt yourself Ryan. Your skills are just as important as any of the others and I will have need of them."

When they headed back into the barn a few minutes later Squire was convinced he had an excellent team of people and looked forward to working with them and setting them on their way.

The boys left very late, seeming to have almost endless questions about the procedures and previous Void stories. When they finally headed home Squire sat and chatted with Kass and filled him in on his ideas going forward. Two teams, two leaders. There would be one medic in each team as well as someone handy with a gun in case things turned bad.

Kass liked the plan but raised a major issue that was worrying him. "We only have one Catching," he said. "If we can't free lost souls with one team what's the point of going?"

Squire just smiled. "I have a theory on that my friend, but we will have to wait and see if I'm right on that one."

Bailey ran across the rocky ground at the speed of a jaguar. Her feet found safe places to land with each step but the sound of pursuit was loud in her ears. She turned and saw them; hundreds of them by the look of it. They came down the ravine like angry thunder calling for her blood.

"They knew we were coming?" she asked herself aloud before running on.

On her heels came the dead in their masses. Their carnal rage was obvious and she knew why. The backpack she carried was what they wanted and they knew its purpose.

She pulled out one of her guns and twisted to fire behind her, but at the same moment she missed her footing on the rocks and was sent sprawling to the ground. She tried to break her fall on the rough surface, but the gun in one hand and the backpack in the other made it impossible. She hit the ground hard going down chest first and banged her chin on the rocks.

Her vision went hazy as she tried not to pass out. "Please God, not now," she cried. Her body refused to move but a pair of black boots stopped in front of her eyes. She wanted to look up but she was fading and they were coming. Everything went black.

She jolted awake with a start. Wide, staring eyes took in the room and her surroundings. She was in bed and her heart was thumping out a decent rock track amid her ragged breathing.

She switched on the bedside light and lay back looking at the ceiling and waited for her breathing to return to normal again. She recounted the dream again in her head while it was fresh and made sure she didn't fall asleep again until she had it firmly fixed in her memory.

The details she didn't understand, but Void dreams were becoming more common, although they didn't seem to happen to the rest of the team. Now she had another to add to her collection and she made sure she remembered as much detail as she could before finally dropping off again.

All the new members received a text message on Tuesday morning asking them to report to the Manor House at 8.00am Wednesday. Any members either at school or working were to call in sick. They were all to bring spare clothes.

In an uncanny twist Wednesday would have more sick involved than many of them wanted.

Kass had sent the global text after considering the problem of how to get a feel for how people would react to their first Void experience. Confident he had just the solution he prepared transport and made various phone calls to make sure the day would be useful.

Tuesday morning was a busy one following the news that George Brooker had purchased another house in the village for the new female members of the team. The four-bedroom townhouse in Orchard Close was in need of some work, but was vacant so anyone who needed somewhere to stay had a base.

Kass was on site by 10.00am and met Paige and Bailey there. They went around the house working out what was needed and started work on a very long shopping list.

Bailey had first choice of bedroom and had selected a south facing one to catch the sun in the morning and was busy planning her room.

After lunch they were joined by Ashley and Emily who also started chipping in with essential items for the shopping list and not long afterwards they were all heading to Highgate to shop for beds and furniture as well as the kitchen items. It would take a few days before anyone could actually move in but for the ladies it was an exciting adventure.

They sat on the floor of the living room that evening with an Indian take-away and talked about how they would arrange the house and couldn't wait for the furniture to start arriving.

As they were finishing off the food they had their first visitor. Squire Fox was shown around the house by three highly excited ladies who explained what the curtains would be like and where everything was going to go. He tried to look interested but could not keep up with their enthusiasm. He smiled at how happy they all were and thought they would work well together.

"We brought you a new mug," Emily piped up, "For when you come and visit." The beaming smile on her face was evidence enough that she was clearly delighted with the idea.

With that he was escorted back down the stairs and to the kitchen by the three new home builders. Rummaging through one of the many boxes on the kitchen counter Emily produced a mug with a look of delight and offered it up for inspection.

"World's greatest boss," Squire read aloud and looked back at the beaming faces in front of him. "Very good," he offered back with a hint of a laugh. "I will try not to let my mug down."

There was no milk to actually make tea so everyone decided it was time to head to their respective homes for the night. As they got their things together to leave Squire turned to Emily, "I have your name for you."

Looking back with her eyes bright Emily waited with anticipation. Ashley and Bailey also stopped what they were doing and waited.

"From this day forward," he announced, "your Void Runner name will be Shine." This was greeted with silence while everyone

251

tried to figure out if this was a good name or not, so he added "because you do."

XII.

Wednesday morning dawned bright and fresh and various cars waited outside the Manor House for Kass to arrive. Everyone had got out of their cars and were milling around talking to each other and wondering what they were going to be doing for the day.

Just before 8.00am a coach pulled into the driveway and headed towards the house which caused even more discussion. Shortly afterwards Kass rolled up in his BMW having collected Squire and Bailey on the way.

Once out of the car Kass gathered everyone towards the waiting coach and ushered them all in once he had made sure everyone was there. Having barely decided who was sitting where and got themselves sat down the coach was pulling away with Kass standing up at the front with the driver.

They were soon heading out of Shillyford and on route to the motorway. Kass had moved forward between the front two rows and was asking for some hush.

"I'm sure you are all wondering where we are going today," he called in a raised voice. There were nods and murmurs of agreement to this. "Well it's very simple really. We are going to Alton Towers where you will be going for a ride or two."

Now there were excited faces looking back at him and most were smiling. A few, which he noted, were not smiling and had slightly wary eyes.

The coach journey to Staffordshire was uneventful and gave everyone a chance to get to know each other and bond. Kass had also booked food for the coach trip and there was plenty for people to pick at as the journey rolled on. By the time they had arrived and got into the theme park the day had turned grey and heavy clouds threatened.

"This is good news," Kass turned to Squire beside him. "I knew the forecast was going to be like this."

Squire also gazed heavenward and could feel the odd drop of rain falling. "This is good news because?"

"Wait and see," Kass said with a glint of something in his eye that could well have been mean.

The day got steadily darker as the group headed for the Oblivion ride. Kass had planned well; the schools were still running and the gloomy day had kept people away. They would not have to fight any crowds today.

As their first ride came into sight Tom dropped back to speak to Kass. "The guys are asking if we can send some people back to the coach to get our coats?"

Kass stopped and called everyone to gather round. When he had the group around him he asked, "Who wants to go back and get coats?" Hands were raised by everyone except Squire, who was wearing his.

Looking at the group of faces again Kass went on, "This is an important lesson for you." Everyone watched him. "Do you think where we are going you can head back to collect something you forgot?" Faces that had been bright and cheerful started to look a little warier. "Do you think where we are going the sun will be out all the time and we will be warm?" By now the message was sinking in and there were some resigned faces gazing back. "You will continue as you are because you need to remember this lesson."

As the group turned and headed off again Squire muttered, "Brilliant Kass, great lesson, you mean git."

The queue for Oblivion was almost non-existent as it was still relatively early in the day. Ashley looked more nervous than anyone else, but took her place knowing backing out was the end of her journey with the team. As they sat waiting for the ride to start the heavens opened and the rain came pouring down. Kass removed his collapsible umbrella from inside his coat and he and Squire watched from the start of the ride and smiled to themselves when the screaming started.

After three runs on The Oblivion, Kass led them all to The Air ride. He was watching them all carefully for signs of stress but so far they only looked soaked. Ashley was not walking properly and seemed to be suffering. Her wet hair stuck to her very pale face and she didn't seem to have the energy to move it. Ryan too was looking a bit sick but was still cheering and encouraging the others on.

They only ran The Air ride twice, but that was enough to add Elle and Bailey to the ones looking a bit worse for wear. By now they were all soaked through and the cold was also adding to their troubles.

After the first run on The Smiler, Ashley asked if she could get off. The front of her T Shirt and her lap were now decorated with sick and her eyes were rolling. Squire and Kass helped her off and sent the others around again. They led her on wayward legs to a bench and let her sit down and start to recover.

"Do you think I could borrow a coat please?" Ashley asked. Her face was very pale and her lips shivered. "I'm freezing." Her bare arms bore witness to the statement as an array of goose bumps battled the cold rain.

Kass knelt down in front of her; his long hair dripping wet. "If I give you my coat I will also be freezing. This is not my lesson to learn Ashley, so you will sit there shivering until we finish. This is not me being mean. This lesson may save your life in the future."

Ashley looked back at him knowing he was right, but already sure she had learned the lesson. She wondered if the others were feeling as cold and fed up as she did.

After the third run on the Smiler the whole group were allowed to get off. Only Tom and Shine looked like they could keep going, but they were shivering and clearly cold and tired. Bailey and Ryan had also been sick and Elle had turned nearly grey in her efforts to keep everything in her stomach.

Now they were all asked to head back to the coach and everyone was happy to be getting out of there. The rain still came teaming down and the group of soaking wet recruits walked stiffly back. There was no talking now; they were all too cold and miserable and only wanted to be warm again.

Once they had all been checked on board the journey back to Shillyford got under way. They all took turns heading to the back of the coach to change into their spare clothes in the toilet. It was harder than getting dry and dressed in a swimming pool cubicle and they emerged looking rather twisted. Kass and Squire got stuck in to the food but they were the only ones. It seemed the others had no appetite left.

There was very little talking on the return journey and a few had fallen asleep to escape the sickness they were still feeling. When they finally arrived back at the Manor House everyone collected their wet things and got off the coach tired and looked slightly fed up. For most it was their first experience of trying to get on with things while soaking and cold and was not one they wanted to repeat too soon.

For the last time that day Kass gathered them around him. "You have done well today. You have survived and learnt some useful lessons." He looked at each of the team in turn and saw that they had grown stronger as a team during the course of the day. "The

Void is tiring and dangerous and this has been a good exercise for you to see it is not all sunshine and flowers. Tomorrow I need you all to report to the Army base at Hendon at 10.00am, where you will have some more excitement under the watchful eye of Paige." Nervous glances went around the team. "If any of you need directions let me know. Other than that enjoy the rest of day and don't forget to keep practicing slowing your minds down and watching your clocks."

Kass and Squire sat in his kitchen at the table drinking tea that afternoon, and the atmosphere had turned more and more subdued as the time went on.

"Kass," Squire looked into his brother's dispassionate face, "I think I'm starting to lose it." He fiddled with his empty cup for a while before leaving it alone and reached for his cigarettes.

Kass was also thinking about things deeply. "Why do you say that?" he asked in his normal calm, measured tone. He didn't need to ask really; he had never seen his brother struggling so much.

Squire fired up the smoke and blew a trail of grey cloud up to the kitchen ceiling. "The old woman, the healing and Bailey knowing what she said." He shook his head. "There is so much I just don't understand and I think it's going to get much worse before things sort themselves out."

Looking into his brother's worried face Kass could almost feel the questions bouncing around inside that normally peaceful head. "Do you want to run through the things the old woman said?"

Looking up once more Squire considered the question before putting his cigarette out in the ashtray and responding, "No, it's giving me a headache. I need to go for a walk and clear the cobwebs away."

Kass left shortly afterwards; his older brother was solemn and silent by the time he did. Before heading home, he dropped into both Ted and Justin and passed on his concerns.

"He's so distracted at the moment I actually wonder if he's safe going into the Void," he told Justin.

Justin too had noticed the difference in his friend. "I'm not so sure George picked such a good time to drop the Chairman bomb on him." He pushed his glasses back up his nose and blinked quickly a few times. "You are right though, he is distracted."

They all agreed to keep as close an eye on him as they could manage. The pressure of a new team, a change in leadership and the old lady were taking a toll.

The rain earlier in the day had made the park smell lush and fresh. It was also empty save for the ducks on the pond. They had now fallen silent as the evening deepened. Squire sat on the bench

259

taking in the peace of the place as the last light began fading from the sky and looked down at his trembling hands.

Black wings of doubt and fear beat in his head as he went over and over problems he could not answer. When he was working with the team or busy planning he was alright, but these quiet times were killing him and he could feel his emotions beginning to get on top of him. More than anything he needed the old woman to come along and give him some guidance; he was now desperate for it.

He reached into his right pocket for the pack of cigarettes he knew were there. He was depending on them more and more these days but he didn't have the willpower or the strength to try and cut them back.

"Don't worry so Mister." The voice was soft and quiet next to him on the now almost dark bench.

Squire had to hold himself steady as a sudden rush of emotion washed through him. He felt tears rising but forced himself under control to confront the old lady once more.

"Am I going to die?" he said softly facing the dark figure next to him.

The old lady breathed in gently. "That was the only thing that was guaranteed from the time you were born."

He couldn't see her in the gloom sitting next to him on the bench, but if he could have, he would have seen the kindness in her eyes and the care in her face.

"You know what I mean," he went on. "I mean soon."

Again there was a pause and the fresh smell of the grass and trees around him seemed to sink into his soul a little. "If you knew the answer to that," she replied, "would it change what you are going to do?"

Squire once again started to feel for his pocket and the cigarettes hiding there. "Do I have a choice in this?" He pulled out the packet and the lighter next to it.

The old lady smiled briefly in the shadows, "Oh yes, you've always had a choice in everything Mister." Squire withdrew a cigarette and replaced the packet. "Every event is unfolding as it was destined to be and putting into place future events that are also destined to be."

"Why are you here then?" he fired back quickly. "If everything is destined to be then why are you here steering things?"

"Very good Mister. Very good." The old lady was genuinely pleased with the response and nodded to herself. Perhaps he was not such a fool after all. "There are complications."

Squire lit the cigarette and his eyes flicked up toward her. For a split second as the lighter flint sparked he saw not an old lady next to him: the face was much younger and white, but as soon as the flame of the lighter caught, the old lady was there looking back at him just as he remembered her.

"Complications?" He took a deep pull on the cigarette and tried to replay in his mind what his eyes had registered for the briefest of flashes. A trick of the light?

The shadow next to him replied calmly once more. "They are not yours to worry about, but you play a part in two worlds and that takes a little steering as you call it."

Squire sat back and considered while puffing away on the cigarette in his hand. "I don't know what I am supposed to do." He looked out at the dark park around him. "If you want to steer me so much why don't we start with some answers?"

"I already told you, you know all the answers Mister." The voice next to him was as calm as ever and seemed totally at peace with everything.

Squire felt the first touch of annoyance but knew he would get nothing from her. He had to find the answers for himself. "The bit I don't understand," he went on, "is how I remember all the things you say, yet I can't remember ordinary things from day to day."

Her reply was as soft and measured as always. "Oh yes, memory can be a powerful thing." When she spoke again her tone had changed and implied she was coming to the point of her visit to him. "The time is getting close. You must find the Dreamer."

"The Dreamer," he responded from the dark bench. "Bailey. She is the Dreamer; she's always having deep dreams." He looked towards her next to him but could barely see anything now. His spirits started to rise at the prospect of unravelling part of the mystery.

"Then find her." The old lady's reply was so soft he hardly heard it.

Squire knew she was part of this from the moment she announced those dreadful words to him. "I already have though. She's at my house right now."

"No." The statement was flat. "She found you. Now you have to find her."

Squire sat puzzled once more and was unable to answer. He smoked as he thought about this new riddle. His earlier feeling of triumph had fallen flat once again.

"Know this also," she went on smoothly. "The path you must take is going to mean you will need outside help. When that time comes you will have it." He could tell she was facing him and watching but he didn't turn to look. He listened and pondered. "Do not doubt it Mister," she added. "Doors will be opened for you."

He tried to respond but his head was suddenly filled with something as leaden and solid as anaesthetic. The world was going dark and he was falling. His eyes closed as his body started to slump but he forced one last thought out. "Will I see you again?" Sleep took him then. His arms flopped down and the still burning cigarette dropped from his fingers into the grass.

"You never did Mister."

There was silence then. In the distance cars went past in the town and the ducks tucked their heads down for the night.

Billy Flitton found him there two hours later. His shifty eyes took in the scene quickly. All day he slept so that he could prowl all night and he was adept at his task. Burglary, robbery and muggings; they were his profession and he had become rather good at all of them.

Taking a shortcut through the park to see if there were any drunkards coming from the pubs that needed relieving of their valuables he had stumbled quite by chance on a sleeper.

He approached slowly knowing there was someone there on the bench but not sure how conscious they might be. Once he was close he flicked on a small pen torch he kept for his night time excursions. The guy on the bench was out for the count; looked almost dead. He took in the clothes and all his skills told him what he needed to know.

"Nice new clothes." His whisper was deep and husky. "That spells wallet." He moved closer and started reaching towards the jacket of the sleeper in front of him.

"No." The soft voice came from the trees behind the bench. It was a woman's voice.

Billy Flitton jumped and dropped his pen torch. He looked into the darkness suddenly alert and surprised all at once.

"You don't want to do that." The voice from the trees was flat and calm and seemed to have no fear of him at all.

Billy stood up tall and growled, "What are you going to do about it?"

The air around him suddenly started to crackle with energy like electricity. His surprise was then replaced by fear when the light came. It flew at him from the trees in a burst of force that made him stagger blindly backwards. In the light was a figure, and the figure was the light.

Billy Flitton turned and ran.

Bailey slept fitfully. Twitching in the dark of her room she heard voices and saw images that came and went in blurry, surreal flashes. She wriggled and writhed as she tried to awake from the dark dream she found herself trapped in.

There was a woman there. She didn't know who she was but sensed something like déjà vu about her. The Watcher had summoned her and she had come at his bidding. She smiled in eager anticipation of the task she had been selected for.

The Watcher was there but there was no one to see. Bailey could sense his menace and evil all around as he passed on his thoughts to the woman.

"We have a problem," the voice said from everywhere. "There is a *mal'āk* coming to us. That should not be possible. He must be taken care of."

The woman smiled some more and her eyes yearned to be the one to take care of the problem. "What is your bidding Lord," she purred in return.

Bailey fought again in her sleep and her eyes were closed tight and her body tense.

"We will bait him," the voice rumbled again. "You will be the bait my young assassin."

"Yes," the word was held long by the woman. "How will this be done most wise one? If he is truly a *mal'āk* he will know me for who I am."

"He does not know it yet and he will only seek to rescue you." The all knowing voice had planned, and planned well.

The woman laughed in wicked joy. "Rescue me?"

"Yes," the voice returned in quiet satisfaction. "You will be the bait and he will seek to free you. When he does you will kill him." There was a pause while she laughed again. "You must not fail in this task."

The woman once again smiled her crazed smile and looked forward to her task. "How will we lay this trap my Lord? What must I do?"

The presence around her shifted slightly but the dark menace only increased. "It has all been taken care of."

The voice withdrew but the Watcher looked on to savour the next part of his plan. The woman was aware then of others around her. Men came slowly towards her with their faces bent on their purpose.

Bailey flinched sensing the dark thoughts pouring over her. She wanted to escape but she was held transfixed on the scene; just like the Watcher.

"I will not need helpers," the woman looked around her and laughed.

The men came on but they had not come to help. The first to arrive at her side went to strike her but she was too quick and chopped him down with a quick flick of her arm. The defence would not help. Even as she did so she was hit from behind and then again from in front.

She went down under a flurry of blows and understood her purpose and stopped trying to defend herself. Yes, she would indeed make convincing bait.

The men surrounding her continued to rain down blows on her and she took them all while trying to smile. Pain roared through her as punch after punch landed on her body. She was soon only semi-conscious and the beating slowed. She was thrown to her back and hands pinned her down and she was raped again and again.

The Watcher looked on and enjoyed every moment while Bailey was staggered by the brutality of the scene and wanted to flee.

Still they attacked her and the whole time they went on beating her she bent her whole spirit on the task in front of her. She lay there bleeding while fists jolted her head from side to side and still she smiled.

Bailey finally struggled away from the images that hurt her very soul and floated away into the darkness. Her twitching body relaxed and finally peaceful sleep came to her. By the time she would awake the dream would be gone and only a vague, dream-like memory existed.

The Police picked up Billy half an hour later wandering in the town centre after numerous reports were received of a screaming man in the street.

When they arrived they expected a drunk or a partygoer; the normal paperwork and a night in the cells to sober up. What they found would stay with them for many years.

A regular visitor to the station, Billy Flitton was well known to the Shillyford Police and many other towns around too. The Billy they found that night was different; his eyes were wild and his face was contorted in madness. His hands clenched and unclenched and he was clearly terrified of everything.

An ambulance was called and took him away but he would find no help with the medical staff at Highgate Hospital. He would spend the remainder of his days in a cell with soft walls and an endless supply of medication to keep him sedated.

A damp and stiff Squire Fox woke up as the first rays of the morning sun lit the sky. He had spent the night laying on the bench in the park and now his body complained about the stiffness of his bed.

He rolled off the bench and slowly struggled to his feet feeling rather confused and groggy. A pen torch lay at his feet that he couldn't remember being there the night before. He gave a shrug and wandered off in the direction of home, determined that a warm shower and a cup of tea was high on the list of things to do. When he opened his front door twenty minutes later he was greeted by a concerned household.

"Where have you been?" Paige called coming over to look at her rather dishevelled father.

He brushed the question aside and made for the kitchen and was followed by Bailey and Daisy. Concern was carved on their faces as they waited for answers. His behaviour was getting steadily stranger as the days went on.

Flicking on the kettle he turned to face his worried audience. "I fell asleep in the park. It's no big deal really."

"No big deal," Daisy exclaimed. "People who have a house and a bed do not normally fall asleep in the park, and spend the night there." Her views were agreed with by the others.

"She was there again," Paige asked. "Wasn't she?"

Squire was loading a cup with a tea bag but paused. He remembered again the meeting and the things she told him. She had said the time was getting close; his time. He still had no idea how any of it made sense and tried to push it from his mind to focus on his plans for the day.

When he turned around with his tea there were three faces looking back at him. He realised he hadn't answered the question and they were waiting. "I was just tired," he said looking at them. "I must have nodded off."

He left the kitchen and knew none of them had been convinced by his response. He sat and watched the news for the next fifteen minutes drinking his tea and then headed for the bathroom.

Paige, Daisy and Bailey were busy getting ready for their morning appointment at the Army base.

"What is going on with him?" Daisy asked the others. "He knows he can trust us." Paige agreed but knew there was more going on than any of them knew.

"He does trust us," Bailey replied. "I wonder if he might be trying to protect us." The dream of him battling overwhelming odds was still fresh in her mind. Had she dreamed a premonition and did he know what was coming?

Hendon Army Camp was not the prettiest place for a morning out but it had its uses. Paige was in her army uniform and had waited for each of the team's cars as they arrived at the security gate. She gave directions where to park their cars and each time gave a signal to the security office and the barrier was raised to allow them through.

When they were all together Paige escorted the six newest members of the team to one of the barracks and found them all army combats and boots to wear.

"None of you are to discuss what we do in any way while you are here," Paige told them as they tried on different boots. "We are here as guests on a team building exercise so do not stray from that idea please."

None of their clothes fitted too well and with their heavy boots they all looked and felt like the worst army unit yet. Paige led them away into the woods nearby where they were met by Kass, who had Squire and Daisy as observers.

"Good morning everyone," Kass greeted them while trying to keep a straight face. They each greeted him back although they felt ridiculous. "Today you will run the army assault training course and we will watch and time your efforts."

Behind him there was a large log wall but beyond that they could see nothing. "Please be aware that as a team you will be going into many physical situations and we need you to survive them. We don't train you like this just for the fun of it so do your best and we will see how you come out. Are there any questions?"

No one spoke up so Kass took them all to the start. "In a moment I will blow this whistle and you may begin." He held his clipboard in front of him and gave his whistle a sharp blow. The Void Runners were away.

The log wall posed few troubles as it was relatively easy to climb, but even after the first few seconds it was clear who the front runners were. Tom landed on the other side just seconds ahead of Bailey and they both ran for the next obstacle.

By the time they had reached the tunnel crawl under the wires everyone else had cleared the wall and the spectators walked along the side watching carefully. At the rope swing over the water it was still Tom and Bailey out in front but a second race was on between Ryan and Shine. Where he had strength, she had agility and they were level pegging most of the way.

The course took a nasty twist up ahead with a deep and wide trench filled with wet mud. Tom launched into it but came to a halt as he sank to his knees in the mud and fell forward. Bailey used a different tactic and waded with long strides and fought against the resistance. Only halfway over the trench the pair of them were crawling on all fours and dragging themselves forward. They were both still trying to haul themselves out the other side when Ryan and Shine also reached the trench and waded in.

Ryan followed the style of those in front and adopted the crawling tactic and used his strength to drag himself through the trench. At his side he saw Shine overtake him. She used her forearms and shins to support her weight and almost appeared to skate over the mud.

On the far side of the trench was a twenty-foot-high rope netting wall that was made even harder being wet and muddy. By now Bailey had surged ahead with her higher fitness levels and was climbing the ropes quickly.

Just reaching the bog trench behind them were Ashley and Elle. They were both almost worn out and struggling to keep pace with the ones ahead. Ryan too was fighting to keep up with Shine but was determined and struggled on.

Kass, Squire, Paige and Daisy walked along the course in comfort and were highly entertained watching the struggles unfolding.

"Bailey is going to finish first," Paige said to the others. "Tom is stronger but will run out of puff." Her lead at the front was growing as she jumped into the water splash and climbed into the concrete tube tunnel the other side. Tom was labouring but kept going and was being rapidly caught by Shine. Her combats were too big for her but she charged on regardless.

Way at the back now Ashley and Elle still crawled and dragged their way through the mud trench. Neither had the energy or strength to wade through so they slithered over slowly on their fronts. Ashley knew the race was up and turned to Elle when she reached the far side. Instead of heading up the rope netting wall she offered her outstretched hand to Elle. Together they made it out of the bog and encouraged each other slowly up the net. Kass and Squire gave each other a look and moved on.

At the end of the course Bailey began the very last set of obstacles and jumped up to the monkey bars which would take her thirty feet over the top of an algae filled pool below. Tom had finished the abseil slide and was plodding heavily after her. Right behind him was Shine.

Less than halfway over Bailey finally hit bad luck when her oversized combat trousers started slipping from her waist. She considered letting go and taking her chances with the pond, but in the end she chose to keep going and hope for the best.

Tom reached the monkey bars and his far superior body strength soon had him closing on Bailey ahead. Shine too was closing fast and her lightness and speed made the task easy for her.

Ryan knew he would be fourth and decided to try and finish in good shape rather than chase the others. Way behind him Ashley and Elle worked together to complete the course and used the easiest routes possible. Neither of them attempted the monkey bars opting for wading through the pond. It proved much slower but they were barely at a walking pace by the time they got that far.

Bailey dropped off the monkey bars and only had the short dash up the hill to the finish, but as her feet hit the ground her wet and muddy trousers dropped to her knees. She reached down and tried to haul them up and run at the same time but only succeeded in falling over. Tom didn't hesitate and used all his remaining energy to run up the hill. Bailey would finish second with one hand holding her trousers up.

Further back Shine finished the bars but was exhausted. Her energy levels bottomed out and her legs failed almost completely. She resorted to a heavy legged jog to the finish and was followed closely by Ryan who still looked still fairly fresh.

The four of them sat panting on the ground at the finish line and looked back down the course for the last two. It would be a long wait.

When Ashley and Elle finally walked over the finish line and collapsed on the ground Kass stopped his watch and added another note to his clipboard.

As the team sat or lay sprawled on the ground the group of Kass, Squire, Paige and Daisy walked up the slope to meet them with serious looking faces. "Remember," Kass said to his brother at his side, "your very best acting please."

"Oh no," Shine said quietly to the others. "I think we may be in trouble." The others watched the leaders approaching with serious faces and waited for the verdict. All too soon they arrived at the top and Paige stood with her arms crossed and looked very unimpressed as she looked at the group in front of her.

Squire came forward; his face stern. "What the bloody hell was that?" he blasted. He looked one by one at each of his team with

275

his eyes hard and his brows forward. Six suddenly very worried faces looked back. They were all totally exhausted and had not expected the angry reception they were now getting. Squire looked like he was going to blow up and it was the first time any of them had seen him annoyed. "That was a total bloody disgrace," he went on and let his fury carry through them. They looked back; their faces cast down and devastation in their eyes.

"Two of you," Squire blasted again and paced backwards and forwards. "Just bloody two of you I am satisfied with." He paused for his words to sink in and took the opportunity to light a cigarette. In front of him his team waited in shock for the torrent to continue as they sat feeling miserable in wet and smelly clothes.

Squire went on still at full force. "Paige told you this was team building." He took another puff on his smoke and glared at them. "Kass said 'as a team' and asked if there were any questions." In front of him the message was getting through. "Most of you buggered off and left your team struggling behind!"

Now the lesson sunk in and heads and eyes started to drop. "Ashley and Elle are the only two that worked together to complete the course," Squire went on. The anger was fading now from his voice. "When you are in the Void you had damn well do a lot better than that or people are going to end up being left behind." With that he turned on his heel and walked away in the direction of the barracks. Behind him was stunned silence.

When Squire was out of earshot Kass calmly turned to the team and said quietly, "Lesson learnt?" His eyebrows were raised making his eyes bigger than normal. Six very dejected heads nodded with sullen eyes.

"I do hope so," Kass went on. "You will pay a price for your failure here today. Two of you should be exempt so you can choose to take your punishment individually without Elle and Ashley, or as a team and they join you?"

The group at his feet looked at one another and they all knew which option they were supposed to choose.

Elle quickly spoke to the others, "It's okay, we will all stick together from now on," and she cast a look to Ashley for approval. When she got a nod in return she called to Kass, "As a team please."

"Very well," he replied. "I think you have already suffered but I expect you to learn and remember these lessons." He looked at the mud covered and wet group in front of him. Ashley and Elle were covered from head to toe. "The showers are closed to you so you can get changed in to your normal clothes and go home as you are."

The group looked at one another but accepted it could have been a whole lot worse than going home damp and a bit smelly. Their clothes would get covered in mud and be filthy but they could live with that.

"Right, go and get changed then." Kass watched as they got themselves up and left for the barracks without speaking.

Daisy was first to crack and her face creased up. "You said best acting and he went for the Oscar." A smile broke her face and both Kass and Paige tried to contain themselves.

Paige added, "I've never seen dad that angry before. Even though he was acting it was pretty scary."

"The lesson was important though," Kass replied as he led them back down the slope. "Sometimes as a leader you have to be tough."

Squire Fox kept walking. When he reached the barracks he was halted by a thin call behind him, "Squire."

When he stopped and turned he found the sorrowful face of Shine looking up at him. "I'm so sorry," she managed before her face crumpled and she broke into tears. The leader of the Void Runners suddenly felt horrible.

Behind her now came the other five and they all gathered around him and offered their apologies. The boys looked annoyed with themselves but the girls were devastated.

Slowly he raised his hands and spoke very gently and softly to them. "Stop now and let me speak to you." He looked at the faces around him. "Do you realise how important you all are? Both Kass and I are desperate to keep you all safe and alive and for you to learn and think." He paused to finish his cigarette. "We dropped you plenty of clues today but you did your own thing. If you do that in the Void someone is going to end up dead, and that is a thought I cannot even think about."

Those around him started to brighten slowly and would remember the day and the lessons it brought. "In other news," Squire went on. "Bailey that was a great effort today and if not for the wardrobe failure you would have come first." The smallest of smiles appeared on her face along with bright blushes.

"Tom, Ryan," Squire looked between the two. "You both went very well and gave it your all. "Shine, look at you," he gave her a smile. "You are tiny compared to these guys but you stayed with them the whole way." He now looked and found Ashley and Elle. "You two did your best, but you did it right. You helped each other." They both looked slightly relieved. "Imagine how much better you would have done if you had all looked out for each other." He could see that they all understood. "I trust as a team you will improve your time next time we are here. Now, go and get changed and enjoy your afternoon."

As he turned to leave Ashley called out, "Kass said we are not allowed showers."

Squire paused and gave them all a quick look and a smile. "Then you got lucky today. He was going to make you all swim the algae pond first." With that he left them and headed for the car park.

They turned and walked off to go and get changed and the mood had lifted. They talked quietly and were recovering themselves

279

when Paige came trotting up. "Hey Bailey, wait up." The other stopped and waited for her friend.

"I guess we really blew it today," she replied.

"Not only that," Paige said with a smile, "You stink."

The beds arrived in the afternoon along with a lorry load of other furniture. Ted and Kass had come along to help the girls unpack and start putting things together and spirits were high in the new house.

Ashley was upstairs with her face buried in the instructions for constructing her bed while Ted laughed and told her instructions were for girls. Half an hour later he was looking for some himself to find out what had gone wrong with the drawers he had been making.

Shine had left Kass putting her bed together and was busy downstairs unpacking the flat screen television and was eager to have it up and running quickly so they could have some music while they worked.

By lunchtime Justin, Sarah and Elle had arrived to help out and the place started to take shape pretty quickly.

"Where is Squire today?" Justin asked no one in particular.

Paige put a shiny new toaster on the kitchen counter and then changed her mind and moved it to the other side next to the tea making things. "We're not really sure," she answered. "He spent the night in the park but was with us for this morning's assault course."

Kass had stopped by the kitchen on his way outside with more empty packaging and heard the news. "Was there an old West Indian lady involved last night at all?" He had his eyebrows raised at full salute for the question and was disappointed there was not a better answer.

"We don't know," Daisy put in from behind him. "He was being a bit evasive about things."

Kass cast a look back at Justin and the two of them passed mental thoughts to each other. They both intended to have a little chat with Mr Fox and see if they could find out something more. The old lady appeared to be at the bottom of a lot of the confusion going on.

XIII.

Squire was the only one to walk to the barn that night. His habit of unwinding on the way was something he wanted to hang on to. Bailey had driven there with Paige and had passed him on the way.

He wandered past the Anchor Pub and ignored the lads stood outside having a smoke and talking a little too loudly. He wondered why they tried so hard to convince each other they were laid back and easy. He could see with a glance the masks they wore to hide their real selves but he left them to their banter.

As he turned into the lane and began the last part of the walk to the barn Paige whispered loudly from the undergrowth. "Hurry up, you're late."

"What's new," he responded quietly and continued on his way. Once inside he found everyone else was already there and Kass was organising kitting the team out. All the first timers were wearing jeans and trainers and sweat shirts. Shine had a light jacket but the others seemed to have forgotten their lesson about being prepared. The day had been pleasantly warm and deceived them into thinking the Void would be the same.

Bailey was wearing the same as before and stood out from the others with her bright colours and style. She looked up and saw Squire enter and went over to meet him. "Are you ok? You look troubled."

He let his face relax and pushed the worries clouding his mind away for now. "Yeah I'm fine, I was just thinking," he replied and moved over to meet with everyone. He greeted them one by one and checked in with Kass.

"They have all scanned in and armed up," his brother said and passed Squire a bracelet for himself.

Putting it on Squire scanned it in. "Well done Kass, have you briefed them?"

"Target blue: Locked in"

"Nope," Kass replied while calmly sitting on the bench adjusting his watch. "That would be your job I think." He finished with a small smile before picking up his bag of travelling gear and dropping the various items into his coat pockets.

Squire turned to face the others and found them all looking at him and waiting. It was time to find out how well they had been trained. He started to walk towards the Fox Box to fetch his own things but on the way he called to them all. "Magazine check please."

Immediately they all drew their guns and ejected the magazines and checked they were full before snapping them back into place.

Strapping on this own gun now Squire called again, "Notes." Now Tom and Elle both produced small note books and pens and held them up for inspection. It was their job to document anything and everything that might be important.

"Good," Squire smiled. He loaded up his things and went to face the Void Runners. They stood in a semi-circle in front of the bench and waited for his instructions.

"Please don't forget," he went on, "There are no electronics in the Void. If you have phones or watches that have batteries, please remove them and leave them here." There was no movement from anyone so he suspected they had all remembered.

"What we do is dangerous guys," he looked at each of them one by one. Kass watched on from beside him and noticed how solemn and quiet everyone was.

"Very soon Kass will let us know when we aim to head in." Squire turned to look at his brother. "How long are we in for?"

Kass took in everyone with a quick glance, "Thirty minutes."

"When we drop out," Squire went on, "take a few moments to see what's happening around you and then we try and locate each other. If things don't work out you may be in for half an hour of falling alone, but after that you will return here."

There was silence from everyone. There was genuine fear flowing through the group as for most, this was a new experience. Bailey looked quietly confident to one side.

Squire went on now but emphasised each word to make sure everyone understood. "You may well hear voices and other stuff in your head. Do not, I repeat do not try and listen or focus in on them until we are all together. If you focus on something you will be drawn to it alone. That may turn out alright, but is more likely to go really badly so please don't do it."

Everyone acknowledged him with a nod so he went to take his place with them. "Good luck everyone, and please try and relax."

Kass was looking at the monitors and looking for a fluctuation. "Ok, I got one," he called without looking around. "We have thirteen minutes to wait and watch." He also now went to take his place with the others and together they all faced Doris. "You know what to do everyone," Kass said. "Good luck everyone. See you again on the other side."

There was no sound now except the ticking of the clock. The eight Void Runners stood facing it and stared intently at the minute hand. Each had their worries, some more than others. The new members tried to slow their hammering hearts and all the training and breathing exercises now took effect.

Slowly the minutes ticked by and the silent group around the clock remained motionless. Another noise soon started to fill the barn as the electro-magnets charged up ready for a burst. Tom could hear his heart pounding in his ears as could some of the others but they all remained still. He wanted so badly to see what was on the other side of this and forced his breathing to remain steady as he watched the minute hand gently moving.

Magnetic Field: Alternating

Initiating Grab

There was a sudden white flash.

Ashley tried to remain calm as the clock continued to turn in front of her, but her heart started hammering in her chest when the two electro magnets started charging up. Her mind started to wander but she battled to keep it under control knowing within a few seconds her life would change forever.

There was a sudden flash of white light and then she was falling. Endless swirling grey surrounded her as her clothes and hair were caught up in a freefall rush towards nothing at all.

She tried to look around but the speed of the wind made her eyes stream and her long blonde hair whipped her face in a frenzy. She knew all too soon that she was alone and there was no one else in sight.

Her stomach had not recovered from the falling sensation and now her pulse joined it. Everything around her seemed to close in and press on her already suffering body as panic started to take over. Her lungs didn't feel like they were absorbing enough air even though she breathed quickly. It was like trying to breath through a wad of cotton wool and to compensate she tried even harder which sent her head into oxygen overload.

The adrenaline rush altered time and the two minutes she had spent in the Void felt like ages. Still she was alone and there was no one in sight.

Terror closed in on her mind as she fought with too many sensations at once. She clenched her teeth and closed her eyes and an involuntary pained noise escaped her as her mind started to go dark and close down. She was aware then of a strong hand grabbing her wrist. "Gotcha." Ashley opened her still streaming eyes and looked to her side and into the face of Squire Fox.

"Relax," he called over the wind. "You're safe."

Feeling anything but safe she called back, "I don't feel well." Shock and fear were etched on her face and startled eyes stared out at him.

Squire understood all too well. "Breath slow and easy and ignore what is going on around you. Your mind is in overload and causing anxiety and panic."

"But I'm falling," she yelled back. Her face was still contorted in a mixture of fear and relief that she was no longer alone.

His face didn't change and he looked back calmly with his coat flapping behind him. "Are you?"

Ashley looked down at her flapping shirt and her wild hair all around her. It was like standing against the strongest wind she had ever encountered and she called back with a hint of sarcasm, "Well obviously!"

"Perhaps," he called again, "you are still standing stationary in the barn and the Void is the bit that is moving past you."

She thought on that for a second and almost immediately the wings of terror that were beating in her mind started to quieten. Almost at the same time she saw more of the team floating towards her surfing on the wind of time. Kass was there with Bailey. Elle and Tom were with them and looked pale but there was no sign of Shine or Ryan.

"Are we really stationary?" Her question was loaded with hope.

Squire shrugged beside her. "Who knows," he called. "I find it helps to think that way though and try and overcome what my eyes and mind are telling me."

"I don't know how you can be so calm in here," she called once again sounding much more like her normal self. "You must be so brave."

Squire smiled slightly and he also watched the approach of the others. "I am not calm," he stated flatly, "and far from brave." He looked into her face and saw so much of himself hiding there. "I am just like you."

As the sound of the electro magnets slowed Shine gulped hard and fearfully looked around her. She had braced herself for a turbulent ride through the Void, but was instead still standing in the barn alongside Ryan.

"What went wrong?" Her voice was small and thin and she felt immediately like she had let everyone down.

Ryan too looked disappointed and dejected. "I suppose we are not ready," he said trying to work out if he had done anything wrong. "Could you see the minute hand moving?"

"No," she said straight away. "I could do it in the week but tonight I was just staring and nothing happened."

Ryan was taking off his gun holster and was heading over to the box to put it away. "It didn't move for me either," he called back to her. "I was too nervous I think."

She went over to join him and also started un-strapping her holsters. "I'm so gutted," she said at his side. "Are we going to be in trouble?"

Laying his gun back in the box Ryan too was thinking the same thing. "I hope not," he replied. "We can't do anything now except wait for them to get back."

They took off their bracelets and left them on the bench as they didn't know if they were supposed to scan them back in or not. After that they found a patch of straw covered floor to sit on and wait the half hour for the others to get back.

Six Void Runners fell through the emptiness together. They had all linked hands and were facing each other in a ring.

"Ryan, Shine?" Squire called over to his brother.

All eyes then turned to Kass. "I suspect they didn't make the jump," he called back. "First time is never easy."

"Okay then, here's what we do," Squire looked around the ring. "In a moment I want you all to be quiet and listen to things in your heads. You will hear fragments of things going on and it's not easy to pin them down. If any of you manage to pin down one clearly and can get a steady flow of speech let us know."

They all went quiet then but it was only a matter of seconds before Tom spoke up. "I can hear a woman," he called to the group.

Kass and Squire exchanged a glance. They were both thinking how quick that was. Everybody else had given up trying and had stopped to hear what the next step was.

"Great," Squire called. "What were you hearing?"

"It was a bid muddled, but sobbing I think and sounded like a call for help." Tom was not really sure how well he was supposed to hear things, but to him that one noise was clearer than the rest of the background sounds.

"Everyone hold on to whoever is next to you," Squire addressed them all. "Tom, focus on that voice as much as you can and make it as clear as you can in your mind. It should take us to it." He took in the team with his eyes as he spoke. "When you feel the speed of the wind slowing down it means we are going to appear somewhere. Try to make sure you are falling feet down into the wind or you may end up landing badly."

The team were all linked and once more nerves started to break out. Elle had hardly spoken a word and was doing all she could to remain calm.

"If this goes to plan we will arrive somewhere in range of the voice." Squire went on. "No one is to do anything unexpected please until we work out where we are and what is going on." He looked around the group and made sure he had everyone's attention. "Finally," he added before giving Tom a nod to proceed, "No one is to shoot anything or anyone unless they are definitely an enemy."

Kass was smiling to himself throughout. It seemed funny to him that the one giving the instructions was so terrible at following them himself.

Tom closed his eyes when Squire had finished and the top of his nose pinched in his efforts to concentrate. Everyone else kept their eyes open and looked around waiting for something to happen.

Within a minute the Void wind had slowed to nothing and the grey around them was slowly replaced by dark trees and woodland. They had arrived in a gloomy and wet forest. The ground was wet and bog like, although it was covered in dull green ferns and moss. The trees were dark and foreboding and seemed to be leaning in on them in the half light of late evening. Even the air felt wet although it was pleasantly warm.

The Runners now stood with their feet gently settling in the sodden ground and looked all around them.

Kass held up his hand gesturing for quiet. They all listened, but the only sounds were of those of dripping water from the trees and the rustle of the wood around them.

"Please," a quiet sob broke the silence. "Please, someone."

Everyone turned in the direction of the sound and Squire immediately headed off slowly towards it. The others quietly formed up behind him and Kass and pushed through the undergrowth.

They hadn't gone very far when they came to a small clearing surrounded by trees and bushes. Squire slowed down to gently creep forward. As he entered the clearing he found the source of the quiet sob.

A woman in her twenties lay in the dirt in the centre. Both her wrists were held with metal manacles and these were then chained to a stake that had been driven deep into the ground.

Coming into the clearing Bailey was getting the most intense feeling of déjà vu but couldn't place where or why. The hairs on her arms and neck bristled as she looked at the woman on the ground. Instinctively she became more alert and wary.

The woman's long dark hair was soaked with wet mud as were what was left of her clothes. She had been beaten severely and seemed to be barely alive. Her whole body was covered in a mixture of wet mud and blood.

Squire now moved to her side and knelt beside her and was followed immediately by Kass. The others moved forward but hung back almost to avoid confronting something they didn't want to see.

"Hello," Squire spoke softly in front of her face. "Can you hear me?" There was no response from the woman. Her swollen eyes remained closed and her breathing shallow.

"Tom," Squire asked. "Notes. Ashley, here."

Kass stood and moved aside to allow Ashley to move into his place in front of the woman. Tom had his notebook out and was writing everything down feverously.

Kneeling in the wet earth beside the woman Ashley looked at Squire and awaited the instructions she knew would be coming.

"Can you do anything for her?" His question was soft and imploring knowing she had barely begun her medical training.

Ashley slipped off her backpack and opened it up and removed an extensive first aid box. "I'll try," she replied with nervous eyes.

Opening the kit, she looked for anything that might be useful although the woman looked to have been beaten senseless. Most of the injuries were likely to be internal but she pulled out sterile swabs and begun the process of cleaning up the woman's face.

The silence from the others was then broken by movement in the woods all around them. Something, or many somethings were heading towards them.

Kass took the lead and ushered everyone to attention. Bailey was at full alert and was scanning the trees all around them. There were shadows in the trees coming straight for them from all directions and the Runners fanned out to protect the woman and Ashley in the centre of the clearing.

The first figure came into view. A heavy set man in farmer's clothes came forward slowly. He carried an old fashioned pitch fork with three long prongs and he walked into the clearing with his eyes fixed on Tom, who was the nearest.

"Back away," Kass said gently to Tom as he himself edged forward. He watched the approach of the man and tried to gauge the danger to the group but the oncoming threat gave no sign of either good or bad.

Suddenly the man lunged and the pitch fork came up. Tom tried to spin away but the strike caught him badly in the side with a sickening stab sound. He went down into the mud with his shirt ripped open and blood flowing from three small puncture wounds.

"Enemy?" Bailey called out quickly to Squire. Other figures had arrived in the clearing and looked equally as threatening as the first.

"Very enemy," Squire called and drew his Banisher. "Take them out!"

Bailey's guns were already out and she fired at the first man before he could lunge again. A shot rang out along with a white burst of light. The man was hit in the chest and immediately his whole body turned to glowing orange ash that held the shape of the man for a second and then slowly drifted apart.

Shots now rang out all around as the group fired at the humans that entered the clearing. Squire stayed in the centre and protected Ashley and the woman, but fired at anything he saw move in the trees.

All around the group within the edge of the clearing were bursts of orange flame as the approaching humans were banished, but still they came.

Kass was, as always, unarmed and went straight to Tom. Almost laying next to him he grabbed him and called urgently, "Hang on for a bit. You're going to be fine."

Tom didn't look fine though. He had gone deathly pale and his breathing was uneven. From behind him, and now covered by Squire came Ashley. She did a commando crawl to his side and immediately started trying to stem the bleeding.

Bailey now stood over the woman lying in the mud and was a living hell to any enemies that came within the clearing. She had her arms out on each side and slowly rotated while looking from side to side. Anything that moved in the shadows was fired at. The other Runners had dropped back into the middle and aimed into the gloom. Every time one came in to view Bailey would dispatch it with barely a glance.

The attack lasted only a few minutes. Twenty-two enemies had been destroyed in short order by the weapons Tinker had supplied. Most of the kills belonged to Bailey who stood like a statue in the middle even after the last of the humans were gone. She was also the only one of the group that was not soaked and covered in dirt.

"Hang on Tom," Kass called now in the sudden quiet and gripped his hand. "We're here."

Ashley pushed her wet, muddy hair out of her way and continued to try and stop the bleeding but was having no luck. Every time she wiped at a wound to try and cover it with a gauze pad fresh blood would poor out. She was looking more and more flustered.

All the others now came to his side to assist their fallen team mate.

"I don't think you need that," Elle's voice was quiet and calm.

Ashley didn't take any notice and continued to work as fast as she was able. Nothing was working and Tom was bleeding too badly. She was starting to get emotional with the frustration of not being able to help, and once again mild panic started to appear.

Squire reached out and grabbed her blood covered hand and held it still against Tom's side. He slowly looked over to Elle who was at their side motionless. He saw that her eyes were unfocused and she looked miles away in some kind of trance. Ashley fought against his hand stopping her working but he held it firmly but gently.

"Elle?" Squire asked. "What is it?"

Now everyone in the group turned to Elle and noticed the fixed vacant stare. She said only one word. "Pray."

There was no reaction at first. It wasn't what anyone had expected to hear. Looks were cast around the group quickly and slowly the idea sunk in.

Kass spoke first. "All of us?" This was a first for the experienced Void Runner. Potentially they were a lot closer to Heaven where they were but it had never occurred to him praying could help.

Again looks were cast around which ended at Elle kneeling beside them. She continued to stare at nothing.

"No," Squire said quietly and looked to his side at Ashley. "It's you. You are the healer." He carefully let go of her hand and moved away slightly to give her some room.

Ashley looked back confused but ready to try anything. She laid both her hands on Tom in front of her and closed her eyes. At the same time Elle reached out her hand and laid it on Ashley's shoulder.

The others sat silent and still and waited. After a few moments and with her eyes still closed Ashley's face relaxed. Her previous distress was replaced by an almost sleep-like peace and tears and mud were mixed on her cheeks.

Almost at once the bleeding from Tom's side slowed and stopped. The others watched with growing amazement and as the minutes passed the wounds also closed to leave barely a mark where the pitch fork had stabbed him.

Elle took her hand away from Ashley and her eyes suddenly focused. Ashley also opened her eyes and saw for herself what had happened although she had already seen it in her mind.

There were tears of joy and smiles from everyone as the badly injured Tom slept peacefully in front of them.

"Elle," Kass asked looking at her.

"Yes," she responded quickly.

He asked the question everyone was thinking. "What did you just do?"

Elle looked back at Kass and then looked at everyone else. They were all looking at her and she didn't know why. "What do you mean? How did Tom get better?" The look on her face of confusion told everyone that she had no idea what had just happened but the questions would have to wait for another time.

Squire had turned his attention to the unknown chained woman and was moving back to her. The others soon joined him leaving Tom sleeping behind them.

Squire turned to find Ashley. "Do you know what happened?"

She looked a mess but her smile was bright and her eyes sparkled. "No, but it felt amazing whatever it was." Looking down at the barely breathing woman she added, "Do you want me to try again?"

Squire knelt down once more and put his face close to the woman's on the ground. "Can you hear me?"

Her cracked and swollen lips started to move then. "Please, help me?" The voice was weak and it was clearly causing her great pain to speak.

"No, don't," Bailey called quickly and suddenly. The rest of the team all turned to her in surprise.

"Why not?" Squire spoke calmly but with urgency.

Bailey looked troubled as something deep in her mind refused to come out. "I don't know," she replied. Her eyes had the look of pleading in them. "Something's not right."

"These animals did this to her," Kass responded. "We have to help her Bailey."

The woman on the ground groaned some more for effect and observed though a partially open eye. She felt the pressure of the stiletto blade on the inside of her left sleeve and prepared for her strike. When they released her the one called Squire would get it first. She would bury the blade in his heart before the other fools could react. After that, if she had time the bitch with the guns would get hers. She would open her throat wide and feel the spray of her life blood on her face before she was finally gunned down. She tried hard not to smile in anticipation.

"Bailey?" Squire called again. "I need more to go on than just a hunch. This woman deserves a chance surely?"

All eyes were firmly fixed on Bailey. "No," she said slowly. "Don't do it." She looked pleadingly between Kass and Squire. "I know it doesn't make sense but I really mean this."

"I believe her," Elle spoke up quietly from the back of the group. "It doesn't make sense but I do."

The prisoner felt her annoyance growing. If her idiot friends had stuck to the plan and entered the clearing after she was freed instead of getting themselves killed things would have been fine. She could have then taken every one of these impostors out one at a time.

She wanted so desperately to slice them all open and watch the life flow from them. The forest clearing would run red and they could watch each other slowly die. As it was she was trying to think of other ideas as the bitch one seemed to be getting her way.

Squire took two steps towards Bailey and stood right in front of her. "Don't move," he said quietly. She did as she was told and remained stationary and waited for him to continue. Instead of saying anything he just stared straight into her eyes. She felt suddenly exposed without knowing why. The impulse to look away grew quickly in her as she battled with that gaze. Within moments it was over.

"She stays chained," he said turning back to the woman. Bailey's shoulders relaxed at once and she felt a great weight lift from her.

"I don't understand," Ashley asked confused. She looked at the others for help. "Surely we have to help her if we can?"

"No," Squire said calmly back to her. "Bailey is right. Something is wrong here."

The woman on the ground snorted gently but never opened her eyes. "Fool. You shouldn't be here. You should be dead."

Squire looked up at his brother on the other side of her. "I don't like the sound of this."

Kass was also concerned. "We don't have time for this anyway." He looked at his watch and saw that they were down to the last few minutes. "Whatever we do we need to send her before its too late."

"No!" the woman called out loudly. He swollen lips split open from the effort. "Leave me here. Just go and let me be."

Kass gave Bailey a hard look and raised one eyebrow. He had no idea how, or what she knew, but she appeared to be right. "Send her now," he called to his brother.

Nodding his understanding Squire ushered everyone back. He walked a little way from the woman and felt sadness at her suffering. She now fought against her chains with a sudden energy trying to break free.

With the others spread out to the sides of him he reached into his coat pocket and pulled out the Catching. He held it out at arms length and pressed the button to release it. The four sides slowly opened and as soon as they were flat white light flickered up in the gemstone in the middle. In a second a bright beam of light had shot out and enveloped the woman on the ground. She immediately turned to flames that held her shape for a few seconds and then slowly faded until there was nothing left except the manacles chained to the post.

"No way," Squire said in almost disbelief.

The others looked just as surprised but they didn't have long to think about it. The forest was fading quickly around them.

"Quick," Kass called. "Link up and someone grab Tom."

There was a flurry of movement as they all raced to join up before they were dropped back into the Void.

Shine and Ryan were getting on well and had got to know each other much better while they waited for the others to return. They had shared stories and found they had quite a bit in common when it came to music.

The talking stopped when the sound of the magnet plates began their charging cycle. They both jumped to their feet and looked at the monitor which was busily scrolling.

Target green: Acquired

Target yellow: Acquired

Target blue: Acquired

Target black: Acquired

Target red: Acquired

Target orange: Acquired

Withdrawing Targets

The charging was now at full power and there was a brief "popping" sound as the other six members of the team landed back in the barn.

Ryan didn't know which way to look when the team arrived back. Everything went suddenly surreal. Tom was being lowered to the ground by Kass and looked asleep. His waist area was covered in blood and his shirt was ripped. The rest looked like they had crawled through a swamp with the exception of Bailey. She stood with a dangerous look in her eyes and her hands close to her guns.

"Bailey," Kass called over. She looked up immediately. "Amber please."

She walked over to the bench and pressed the amber button without delay. Elsewhere in Shillyford the message was transmitted and Justin and Ted would be called to the barn by it.

Shine was rushing over to Kass to help him and Ashley with Tom and she nearly collided with Bailey on her way across the barn.

Seeing that everyone was alright Squire gave quick instructions. "Everyone relax and be calm. We are safe again. Could someone give Paige a quick whistle."

Bailey was already at the door, but only managed to open it for the oncoming security officer who also had the amber message. "Is everyone okay?" she asked quickly as she rushed into the barn.

Bailey closed the door again and turned to follow Paige. "Yeah, we're fine."

Kass was stood at his brother's side and they were both watching Ashley tending to Tom. "What happened in there?" he spoke softly to his brother alone.

"I dunno," the other responded, "but look at her."

It was obvious why. The previously nervous and fearful one they had taken with them that evening had returned different. Her tear and mud stained face was a vision of serenity itself and she looked almost glowing.

Shine was at her side and was also wondering what had changed in her friend. "Are you okay Ashley?"

The response from her friend was just a smile that lit her eyes in deep sparkles that tried to tell a story her mind had not yet understood.

The barn door then opened again and Anna bustled in carrying two large flasks of tea and coffee. She took in everything quickly with her eyes before going to the bench and setting down the flasks. Paige was retrieving cardboard cups, sugar and milk from the storage cupboard in the cellar and would soon be helping Anna to serve everyone.

"I'm really sorry." Ryan had arrived to stand in front of Squire and looked like he had just missed something important.

Squire looked back with a quickly relaxing expression. "Neither of you have anything to be sorry for." He looked at Shine down on the floor and got a gentle smile back. "We will not speak about the trip until the others arrive," he added as Paige offered him a steaming cup of tea.

"I was wrong," Kass again spoke softly to Squire and received a questioning eyebrow in reply. "About Bailey. She was incredible."

Squire looked up and found her un-strapping her guns over by the Fox Box in a simple matter of fact way. She didn't look flustered at all.

"Yes she was," he replied. "She will lead the team when I am gone."

Kass turned his head quickly back to his brother. "Gone?"

Squire stopped just short of taking a sip of tea. "I mean retired," he corrected.

Kass watched his brothers' eyes closely and saw some sort of discomfort pass behind them. He would be laying awake thinking about that look for many hours later that night. There was something more there than just a slip of the tongue.

Fifteen minutes later the Runners were sitting on the floor, most in damp and muddy clothes for the second time that day. Their numbers now included Justin who had arrived quicker than normal in his rush to make sure Elle was safe. Ted was also pacing around and had collected Daisy on the way. She was now ferrying drinks around from the freshly refilled flasks.

305

Tom had woken up and was confused but was otherwise fine. He asked lots of questions to Ashley but was told to wait for the official meeting to start.

With everyone settled Squire called to everyone for attention. All heads turned to him straight away. He puffed on a cigarette as he perched on the edge of the bench with the clock ticking away behind him.

"This is an Amber debrief meeting," he announced to them all. "We have these to quickly confirm facts between ourselves and make sure we share the information with Justin and Ted."

Squire continued to smoke and talk as the others looked on and Daisy had settled down with her notebook. Ted was also ready to make notes and waited eagerly. He knew there had been some action from the mess everyone was in and the various team members who looked bloody.

"This is not a question and answer session," Squire went on. "I will state the facts as I saw them happen and will at times ask for your individual input to clarify things. I expect some of what I am going to say may come as a surprise to some of you that were actually there."

Anna still passed around the group with drinks and had found blankets for any that wanted them. Elle was still wet through but was now wrapped up warmly next to her father.

Squire began the debrief in a matter of fact tone and as he spoke he looked around the group. "We jumped in just after 8pm this evening. We lost Ryan and Shine immediately. I suspect nerves interrupted their preparations for the transition." He looked from one to the other and they both nodded in turn. "Once in the Void Tom picked up on a moaning woman and we followed his lead." Ted and Daisy made notes while he spoke, and Paige and Anna listened intently to all the things they were hearing about for the first time.

"We arrived in a dark and wet wooded area and soon found a clearing. There we found a woman in her twenties badly beaten and chained to a stake in the ground." Daisy waited in anticipation for a name or anything else she could go and research later, but that bit never came.

Squire continued. "Ashley tried to administer first aid to the woman but we were then aware of others approaching from all sides. We stood guard and waited. The first of the human men to enter the clearing had a long hay stacking type pitch fork and used it to stab Tom in the side." All eyes had turned to him now sitting on the floor taking it all in. Those that had not gone into the Void now understood the blood stained and ripped open sweat shirt.

"Tom was seriously wounded in the attack," Squire went on. This was big news. Ted looked up and could only see someone with no injury at all.

"The intruder was then shot with a Banisher and he turned into burning ash that drifted apart and vanished." This news would be fed back to Tinker and was a massive step forward for the team.

"We were then attacked by maybe a couple of dozen other humans who were also armed with general farm-like weapons." Squire paused as he relived the moment back in his mind. "That's when Bailey happened."

Before he could continue Kass began to gently clap his hands from where he stood at the side of the barn. Within seconds the other Void Runners had joined in and were looking at Bailey sat on the Fox Box. She in turn tried her best to look humble but was bursting with pride inside. She looked at the others and then to Squire at the bench who had also joined the applause. Finally, her smile broke though and she beamed.

After a minute everyone settled down to continue and Squire went on. "We took out all the enemies, with a little help from Bailey." There was gentle laughing in the barn. "We then turned our attention to our injured team mate. Ashley tried her best to stem the bleeding, which was by now pretty serious." Ted again looked up and was amazed how good a job she had done. He looked totally fine.

"Elle then went into a trance like state and told Ashley to pray." Justin looked at his daughter beside him, but she looked totally bewildered by the statement. "Do you remember any of that Elle?"

She looked around at the others and then back to Squire. "No," she said in a quiet voice. "I don't remember that at all."

Squire went on again. "Ashley closed her eyes and Elle put her hand on her shoulder. I'm not sure what happened then, but the effect was hard to believe." He was looking at Ashley now. "Can you tell us what happened?"

The still tranquil Ashley smiled back. "Not really. I know I prayed and then when Elle touched me I was suddenly filled with so much peace." She tried to remember back to that moment. "It was like any doubt was taken away and I knew that whatever I prayed for was going to be answered and that through me Tom would be healed." She stopped then as she really couldn't describe it any better than that.

Justin put his head down and closed his eyes in relief and thanks. Once more this team had showed him that his faith was real and that this evening a miracle had been performed.

"Tom," Squire called. "Could you show us your injury please, for those that were not with us." Tom stood and lifted his shirt and turned around so that everyone could see the three small red bruise marks in his side.

Squire waited for the still amazed looking Tom to sit back down before going on. "Having little time left it was decided to send the woman on after a discussion regarding setting her free or not." He then looked troubled as he sat on the bench and stopped talking for a while to think. "I used the Catching, but," he paused and his eyes were far away with his memory back in the Void. "She burned."

There was real surprise now from those that had not been there. This was a first. Justin couldn't hold back his question. "If she was a captive and had been beaten by these people," he paused. "Then why was she sent to what we think of as Hell?"

Before anyone could answer Kass cut in. "There's something else." He looked over at his brother who was turning slowly to look at him. "You didn't say the words."

"What?"

"The words," Kass went on. "The Catching just lit up before you said anything."

"I must have," Squire returned and looked over to Bailey to confirm it.

Bailey looked back now also realising that Kass was right. "He's right. You didn't say anything."

All eyes turned back to Squire who was busy lighting a cigarette. "Okay," he started again. "We will have lots to discuss at the Sunday evening meeting. What happened to Elle? What happened to Ashley? The Catching." He paused and looked at the faces looking back at him. "Why would someone that was evil be chained down, and why were we attacked by those that did it?"

He slid off the bench and shrugged. "We will think more on this but for now that is the end of the evening." People started to fidget and get ready to move. "Tomorrow I want all of you Void Runners to go with Paige on a shopping trip and get yourselves kitted out with any clothes and gear you need or want. In the evening we will make another jump and see if these mysteries deepen or sort themselves out."

As people started to get to their feet Squire added one more statement. "Remember please that tonight we saw some incredible things. Dreamer," he looked over at her. "You now have the position of Guardian and Ashley; you are the Healer. Thank you everyone and see you tomorrow back here at 7.30 with your new clobber on."

They calmly got their things together and departed after making arrangements with Paige for the morning. The wet and muddy team shambled out and headed off to get washed and changed and finally only Kass and Squire were left behind.

"That was some evening," Kass began. He was at the bench and was carefully replacing all the bracelets into their box one by one.

Squire sat on a hay bale at the side of the barn and had been thinking. "You know what's even crazier?" He looked up and found Kass calmly looking back. "If we hadn't had Ashley, Tom would be dead." He lit up another cigarette before going on. "If we hadn't had Elle, Ashley couldn't have done it, and if we hadn't had Bailey I think we all might be dead."

Kass was thinking and nodding to himself. "Let's hope for an easy run tomorrow." He started to check the barn was all shut down and that everything was in order before getting ready to leave.

Squire also got up and started heading for the door. "The meeting on Sunday is going to be a long one."

Kass walked his older brother to the door and laid his hand on his shoulder. "I can give you a lift home if you want?"

"No, it's fine," he replied. "The walk will help me think."

311

They left the barn and Kass latched the door. Squire continued to walk and started heading down the lane.

"Don't think too much," his brother called behind him. "I think it might be bad for you."

The walk home was quiet and uneventful and by the time Squire reached his front door he had decided he didn't have all the answers.

Bailey had gone to bed already but not before setting the washing machine going with her Void gear inside. She was the cleanest of the lot for sure.

Paige and Daisy were in the kitchen talking about the shopping trip and some plans for colours and styles but looked up when their father walked in.

"Hey Paps!" Daisy called with a smile. "Want some tea?" She got to her feet and gave her dad a hug before going to the kettle.

"Yeah, tea for the win," he smiled back and sat himself down opposite Paige.

The kettle popped and burbled into life and Daisy grabbed a cup and started putting things together.

"Sounds like you had a wild time tonight," Paige offered. "Nice way to introduce the new ones to the Void." She did her best to smile and Squire realised how badly his daughter wanted to be going in too.

"It was pretty crazy for sure," he replied. "The main thing is we all came back safe, even though we had a close call."

After half an hour of talking they all headed to bed as another busy day was coming.

XIV.

Saturday morning was bright and glorious and would turn out to be the warmest day of the year. Bailey had been up first and was busy arranging transporting all her things to the new house. They now had beds and furniture and had planned a big food shop for the afternoon with Ashley and Shine. She didn't need anything from the shopping trip today but was thinking spare clothes would be a good idea if they were going to need to be washed so often.

By nine o'clock Paige and Daisy were also up and nearly ready to head off to meet the others.

"We should call you the Gunslinger or something like that," Daisy joked with Bailey, who simply smiled in reply as she laced up her boots.

Looking back up to Daisy she said, "It wasn't just me shooting you know. The others were doing fine as well."

Having seen Bailey at the firing range Paige wasn't so sure the others would have had too much to shoot at. "Come on you pair of losers, we need to get a move on."

"Almost done," Daisy said from the hallway mirror as she dragged a brush through her long blonde hair.

Paige headed for the front door and waited for the other two to join her. "You can drive this time fatty," she smiled and offered Bailey the car keys.

The door closed behind them and soon they had driven away to meet up with all the others for another retail therapy session sponsored by George Brooker.

Squire sat on the edge of the bed lost in thought. Fresh warm air came flowing through the open window and everything pointed to today being a warm one.

He could hear birds outside and they brightened his already subdued mood somewhat. Too many questions banged around in his mind from yesterday and he had struggled to sleep with so many things to think about. He took some comfort knowing Kass would also have found dream time elusive.

In his hand he held the small and limp hand of Sasha. Turning back to look at her he wondered what she was busy dreaming about. She looked so peaceful as her eyes roamed around fixing on nothing. Squire envied her tranquillity.

"I don't know what to do," he told her. "So much is going on and none of it makes any sense."

Laying her hand back at her side he got up and started to walk around the room with his head hung low. "The old woman can't be real," he went on. "But somehow I also know that she is." He continued to pace about with his mind filling with thoughts he needed to talk about. "She cannot be from here if she is real; she knows far too much about things, but she could still be in my imagination. If I shut my mind off to her and refuse to believe in her I think things will be easier for me." He stopped in front of the window and lifted his chin. Below him Highgate Park spread out under a bright new day. "What do you think Sasha," he went on. "Should I follow her?"

"Yes."

The small voice from the bed snapped him out of his mind wandering like a shot and he spun around so quickly his neck cracked loudly. "Sasha!"

Rushing to her bedside he sat down and picked up her hand again. He looked into her face closely to see if there was any change. "Sasha," he called quietly.

Laying on the bed her eyes looked out without seeing and there was no response at all. He lifted her hand in his and held it against his chest and pleaded with her. "Sasha." Still there was nothing and no sign that any part of her was conscious, but he was certain that the small voice had come from her.

Reaching over to the wall he pressed the call button and then rubbed Sasha's shoulder gently. "Come on kid," he whispered. "Please Sash."

The door to room 220 opened and a nurse came in looking flustered and ready for anything. Seeing Squire sat on the edge of the

316

bed she went over to him. "Is everything alright Mr Fox?" Even as she asked the question she was looking at Sasha and finding everything looked to be fine.

"She spoke," he said looking at the nurse. She was in her forties but the years of care and devotion had taken their toll on her.

"Are you sure," she said looking surprised, and again looking intently at the vacant eyes of the girl on the bed.

Squire nodded and followed the nurse's gaze. "Yes, I'm sure."

The nurse started to back away and said she would return in a few minutes. Squire could do nothing but wait and keep trying to get a response.

A few minutes later the nurse returned with one of the doctors and was explaining to him that Sasha had spoken. Seeing him come in Squire had stood and moved out of the way.

The doctor moved in close and carried out some quick checks before turning back to Squire Fox. "You say you heard her speak?"

"Yes, I did," he responded. The doctor tried to look passive but his face was full of doubt.

The doctor stood and made eye contact with the nurse before looking back at the visitor. "Did you see her speak?"

Not for the first time in the last week or so Squire had that horrible feeling he was the only one who believed in himself. "No, I didn't, but I know I heard her."

The doctor relaxed his shoulders in resignation. "I'm sorry Mr?"

"Fox," the nurse added for him.

"I'm sorry Mr Fox, but that is not possible." The doctor turned to leave and the nurse gave Squire an apologetic smile before she also turned and left the room. He had been dismissed as if he was no more than a school child. The thought occurred to him that if he had imagined Sasha speak so clearly the same could also be said of an old lady that was keeping him from sleep at night. He was already highly over-tired and this new twist was hurting him badly for so many reasons.

"Sasha, I heard you," Squire said to the empty room and looked back at the girl on the bed with his emotions on edge. She hadn't moved and gazed at the ceiling giving the odd twitch every now and then. He walked to the bedside and gently patted her hand. "I'll come and see you again soon little one." Without looking back, he turned and left the room. He paced down the corridor and tried not to dwell on yet another moment he couldn't explain. It didn't feel fair and all he wanted was to understand, or for someone to help him.

Leaving the hospital in a bit of a daze he found his Mercedes in the car park and headed off to see if he could find his brother.

George Brooker's account was being dipped into once again in the name of fashion and kitting out the team.

Paige was having a great time picking out things to wear for the others but was getting a little carried away. The sad part was that she was also having fun with the team as well, as they were slowly finding out.

Tom and Ryan had both been sent off with Daisy and Bailey with strict instructions not to come back empty handed. They had gone away laughing and looking happy and Tom showed no signs of any injury from the evening before.

Ashley came out of the dressing room with pink cheeks. She stopped in front of Paige who stood with her hand rubbing her chin. "Paige," Ashley spoke quietly so as not to attract any attention. "I know you are the clothes expert but do you think this is such a good idea for the Void?" The shoulder-less slinky white silk dress she stood in would be impractical at anything except dinner.

"No, not at all," Paige replied with a cheeky laugh. "I just wanted to see what you looked like in it." She gave Ashley her best wink. "Go back in and put the next thing on instead."

The relief on Ashley's face was obvious and she turned and headed back to the changing room.

"Oh, Ash," Paige called after her as she reached the curtain. "It does look good on you by the way." Ashley smiled quietly to herself and pulled the curtain closed to part with a dress she could never afford.

The next curtain along slid open and Shine jumped out with a flourish. "Tada," she called and beamed a huge smile. Her tight, light blue trousers and T shirt went well with her eyes, but that was all.

"No," Paige said immediately. "Next."

Shine gave a quiet shrug and the smile vanished as she turned and headed back behind the curtain.

Elle too was getting the same treatment and didn't like anything she had been given. While the others were trying on their things she had done some of her own picking and smuggled the stuff into her changing room.

Ashley emerged once again and straight away Paige raised an eyebrow. "Hold the phone," she said as she admired her choices. "I think you need to do a twirl now or something."

Ashley rotated a full turn and seemed quietly pleased with her next outfit. White and black pinstriped trousers and pale blue crop top. "I'm going to get a bit cold in this top," Ashley said but Paige simply waved her away.

"Bag it up Ash," Paige responded. "We need to get an extra set of those but you are done in here."

After many more choices Shine finally emerged in something that suited her style down to the ground. A pair of rainbow three quarter leggings and a white work out top. Now both Ashley and Paige agreed they were excellent and Shine's smile was bright and cheerful.

Only Elle remained and having decided she didn't want anything she had been given she emerged from the curtain in the things she had chosen. A tight black woollen dress that was very short, and a pair of black tights. She held her arms out so that she could be inspected by the others and gave a quick twirl.

The other two were silent and studied the plain style that suited her perfectly. Elle faced them and her eyebrows asked the question.

"Well," Paige began carefully. "It is the best thing we have seen so far to be fair." She looked at Ashley next to her then back to Elle. "There is a problem with skirts and dresses in the Void though. Not all that practical."

Elle was not ready to be beaten yet. "It's a stretchy dress so it will let me move easily and apart from that it's what I want."

After another few moments thought Paige had to concede. "Let's bag it and tag it girls. For now, we are done."

The boys had no problems further up the shopping centre and were doing what they were told. In quick order they were kitted out in chinos and polo shirts. Daisy was happy she had got the boys to sort it out as they were so much easier than girls.

They had wasted time in a joke shop trying to find something to test on Squire and Kass and had then moved on to the jewellers.

They had left there some time later both sporting very expensive fully manual watches that were now something of a rarity. They had chosen stylishly modern looks with the practical auto-winding function knowing they would never remember to do it themselves after years of allowing batteries to do it.

Next came their shoes and Tom soon found some brown dusters that went with his burgundy chinos and Ryan had gone for casual looking trainers. The girls had marched in as they were finishing, so the boys hung around and helped them pick.

Ashley ended up with black ankle boots but the other two both went for trainers. For Shine it was the obvious choice as she was the sporty type and it went well with everything else. For Elle the white trainers she picked looked odd at first, but they did suit her casual 'don't care if they don't match' attitude.

Last but not least came the coats and Paige made tracks to where her dad always got his. Ashley picked out a huge flared long black coat and the others were busy trying things on. Tom's dark red American sports jacket gave him the educated and rugged look and Ryan went for a similar style in deep green. Shine and Elle both went for waist length black bomber jackets and at last they were all done. With their arms loaded with bags and boxes they made their way back to the cars and then headed off to find a pub for some lunch.

Kass sat in the garden of the farmhouse and watched his brother carefully. The mature garden had been carefully tended by Anna for years and was a blaze of colour. Bumble bees bounced heavily from flower to flower as the heat of the day increased and pungent smells wafted on the light breeze.

The garden table and chairs nestled under an apple tree and the shade was a welcome for the two men sitting there. Anna had brought out a tray of tea and a plate of biscuits and had left them to their talking. She knew when to stay and when to leave and this was definitely not a day to hang around and be polite.

Squire had sat for a good deal of time staring at nothing special and smoking. His forehead was deeply grooved and his eyebrows pushed right forward in an attempt to shield his blue eyes from the glare of the sun.

Next to him Kass waited. He knew the drill with his brother. In his own good time he would figure out the thoughts in his head and they would come spilling out.

"Hey guys," a loud voice came from the patio doors. They both looked around and saw the beaming being that was Ted coming over to them. His smile and casual off duty stroll marked him as a man enjoying his weekend. His jeans and T shirt were another sign that this was the relaxed Ted everyone enjoyed so much.

He reached the table and pulled a chair out for himself. "I didn't know whether to go for shorts today," he said with his normal cheery tone.

"Thank you for sparing us that," Kass gave him the smallest of smiles back.

Ted laughed. "You guys," he sniggered. "How 'bout you Squire my man. How is our Chairman today?" He had turned to his friend next to him and reached out a hand and gave his shoulder a friendly squeeze.

Squire looked up but the troubled look never left his eyes. He figured Anna had called in Ted on his day off to come and see what was going on. He reached for the table and the pack of cigarettes laying there. "Sasha spoke."

Ted's bright wide eyes shot open and he learned forward at once; the mirth and joy gone for a change. "You serious?" He could never be sure when these guys were taking him for a ride, but the expression on Squire's face did not look like it was in wind up mode. "I don't get it. How is that even possible?"

Kass watched from the other side of the table and tried to assist in getting the medical officer up to speed. "Squire was there earlier today. Says Sasha spoke while he was busy rambling to himself." Ted listened closely. "Doctor came and checked; basically blanked it and said it couldn't have happened."

The thoughtful look did not leave Ted's face and he turned once again to Squire. His tone was careful and slow. "And you're sure you heard Sasha speak?" There was no accusation in the question; he genuinely just wanted clarification.

Squire's squinting eyes turned to the big Jamaican next to him. "I know it was her Ted. I know how dumb it sounds, but I know."

Kass looked at both men one at a time and saw the trust there.

Anna had arrived with coffee for Ted and he briefly acknowledged her with a nod of thanks. He looked back to the man by his side and leant forward and placed his forearms on his knees.

"Let me tell you something my friend," he began, his tone still soft and warm. I heard from a good friend that he saw an old lady that no one could see." Squire looked up from his blank stare and turned his focus on Ted. "I would have struggled to believe it if it hadn't been for the fact that my friend was miraculously healed of broken bones and other injuries."

Ted looked around while he searched for more words and his eye caught a group of butterflies fluttering around the lavender bush. "Listen my friend," he started again. "I've seen you do things I didn't believe were possible and the tales you two have come back with from the Void with are incredible. If I were you, I would be wondering if I was going mad." He nodded to himself and gave Kass a quick glance next to him. "You are not going mad my friend. If you say you heard Sasha speak, then I say she spoke and Amen to that."

He saw the pain of doubt draining from the face of his friend; saw the wall come tumbling down as Ted's words and compassion broke through.

Ted reached forward and patted Squire's knee. "I believe you my friend," he said softly. "Do not doubt it."

"Do not doubt it Mister"

The transition in Squire continued. The anguish was gone from him and his eyes were filling up. He retained control though; just. "Thank you Ted," he said quietly but could say no more for the moment. Anything else was going to open the floodgates.

"We saw a miracle happen in front of our eyes last night," Kass changed the direction of the conversation to give Squire a chance to recover his composure. "Things are also happening in the Void which to others are just as unbelievable, and yet we saw it - all of us."

"The pace of things is gaining," Squire said to them both. "The new team are going to be amazing and I don't worry about them at all." He looked to his brother at his side. "I think there are things I have to do and no matter how much I try I'm still not sure I have much choice."

"You've always had a choice in everything."

Squire had relaxed and looked more like his old self again. Ted's words had cut through the fog of doubt that was making things so difficult for him to see.

"Whatever happens," Ted included both men now, "We will all be here for you guys in any way that we can."

Anna appeared at the patio doors and called across the lawn. "I've made some experimental cakes. Do you guys wanna try them?"

"Do we have a choice in this?" Kass whispered to the two men with him.

"Nope," Ted whispered back looking from one brother to the other. "Maybe we will be okay if we wash it down quick with more coffee."

"I feel better knowing we have a doctor with us," Squire added and saw that Anna was now heading towards them carrying a tray. When she got to the table she laid it down in the middle.

"There you go boys," she said with a smile.

Kass lowered his eyebrows to look and saw three blobs that must have been the cakes his wife had mentioned. "Wow, looks good," he uttered in his best, most positive tone. "Do I get an Amen boys?" The other two agreed at once.

"I hope you like them," Anna added before stepping back to leave again.

"Ah," Ted said looking up, "Would we be able to have some more coffee here as well please." He finished with a big smile and tried to look pleased with the whole situation. Anna continued back to the house with a bounce in her step.

The three men all leant forward now to inspect what had come out of the oven. "Experiments," Kass observed.

"Yep and by the looks of it these are right up there with Frankenstein," Squire agreed.

Ted was looking around and came up with an idea. "How about the yard behind the barn?"

The others turned to look and agreed the plan was worth the risk. They all reached forward, grabbed a cake and then stood to fire. Kass was fastest and his cake was soon soaring through the sky and over the fence. It landed in the yard behind it with a sound like a snowball hitting a wall. The shock of the impact made Ted laugh as he launched his cake, but it failed to make the distance and crashed into the fence with a loud bang. Squire's cake may have been more experimental than the others and simply came apart on the launch pad. His brother was in the flight-path and got showered along with thirty metres of garden behind them. They sat down quickly and tried not to laugh too loudly.

When Anna returned with three mugs she found the men having a bit of a giggle about something. Squire's shoulders were bouncing up and down in his effort to keep the laughing in and Ted's eyes were watering.

"Hey, messy eater," she scolded Kass. "You've got cake all down you."

Kass was unable to speak. He had his lips tightly sealed together which made everything even funnier to the other two. He simply looked down at himself and brushed chunks of cake out of the creases in his black T shirt.

"Did I miss a joke?" Anna chirped back.

"Not one we could repeat in front of you," Squire replied and tried not to make eye contact with the others.

It was still funny an hour later when Ted and Squire got up to leave. They helped Kass clear the table and took everything back indoors and would all reflect on their painful ribs from excessive laughing.

They discussed briefly the oncoming jump later that day although there was little they could do to prepare. Kass had put a call in to Tinker earlier and requested more bullets for the Banishers, but other than that they would have to wait and see what was going to come.

"I hope it goes fine for you boys tonight," Ted said as they reached their cars on the driveway. "You stay safe yeah."

"Of course we will," Kass added watching from in front of the house. "Don't you be late," he added looking straight at Squire as he got into the Mercedes.

Closing the door and calling back through the open window Squire called back, "Of course I will. It's me."

The girls finally moved into their new home in the afternoon and immediately put their new clothes away. Paige had insisted they have at least two of everything as things would need washing and would also get damaged. She had also added some items for those days when people just wanted something a little different.

Ashley was in her room and had a special drawer assigned for her Void gear. She had laid everything out carefully and removed all the price tags and labels and couldn't wait to try it all out. Her two long black coats hung in the wardrobe which would be packed with her existing things very soon.

Paige wandered into her room and inspected her handiwork. Ashley looked up from her sorting and smiled but also noticed the brown designer bag being offered to her.

"What's this?" she asked with a little excitement in her voice. She must have forgotten a bag somewhere she thought. Looking in the bag she saw the white dress she had tried on earlier. She looked up in shock at Paige. "Why?"

"I have a feeling about it," the other replied casually, "and you did look good in it."

Ashley had taken the dress out of the bag and held it up to the window to look at it again. It was beautiful. "I don't know what to say," she replied. "Thank you."

Paige just nodded with a smile and headed out of the room to help drag more things up the stairs from the cars.

Shine was busy all over the house but seemed to have adopted the kitchen as her favourite. She moved things around and cleaned anything that didn't already look sparkling. She had packed her clothes away quickly with Elle helping her. Her bed was made with all new bedding and the net curtains were up.

"I think we should make up the last bedroom and it can be yours," she suggested to Elle. "Not for all the time maybe, but after

Void runs you can come home here with us rather than having to get a lift home."

It was a great idea and Elle was excited about it straight away. "Would I be able to do that? That would be so amazing." She rushed off to look at her new bedroom to be. It was the smallest and a bit gloomy but she loved it at once. She couldn't wait to get started on it and spend more time with the older girls. She felt at home with them and had liked them from the start.

When Squire walked into his kitchen later that afternoon he surprised Bailey who was almost ready to leave with her things. Her last job was to recover her clothes from the washer-dryer to add to the rest of her things back at the new house.

She was slightly startled when he had walked in behind her but recovered quickly. Stepping away from the table she revealed the box she had been carefully planting there. The small black gift was complete with its own red bow on the top.

"Hey Dreamer," Squire smiled. "I didn't expect you would be here. What's this?" He was looking at the box in the centre of the table and then turned back at her.

She was looking sheepish and started to skirt around him to head for the door. "I just wanted to leave you something," she faltered, "to say thank you for having me and taking care of me." She continued to back towards the door with her eyes sparkling, "and so many other things that I can't put into words." She then turned to go.

"Bailey," he called gently to her. She stopped and turned again while still backing away.

"What did you do to me?" Bailey asked. "I mean, back in the Void, when you looked in my eyes."

Squire remembered, but had given it no thought at the time. "It's a gift," he replied. "Sometimes I can see the truth of things when I do that. Don't ask me to explain any better than that though because I can't."

"Well I felt it," she said quietly, "like I had walked naked into a crowded room. I don't think I could have hidden the truth if I had tried." She edged back another step. "My gift back isn't quite as amazing, but I hope you like it all the same."

Squire returned his gaze back to the black box on the kitchen table.

"Don't say anything please," she called back. "This can be a no words present." She turned again and didn't slow down until the front door was closed behind her.

Squire went to the side and picked up the kettle and gave it a quick shake. It felt heavy enough so he put it back down and switched it on. He then pulled out a chair and sat down and picked up the hand sized box.

Removing the bow, he opened the box to reveal another harder box inside. He tipped it out and saw the logo Rado and knew what lay inside. Flipping the cover up he saw the black and titanium watch held within on its ceramic black strap. He was no expert but knew these things cost thousands. He also suspected that this had come from Bailey alone, and not from the bank of George Brooker.

Squire thought it was just as well this was a no words present. He really had no idea what he could have said anyway.

XV.

The team started to arrive at the barn not long after 7.00pm. No one wanted to be last and they all needed time for preparation, and to get their minds focused.

Tom and Ryan arrived first in their new clothes and once again Kass was left feeling rather outdated. They were followed in dribs and drabs by the others. Everyone was excited and their nerves seemed no less than the previous night.

The girls looked amazing in their bright colours and when Squire finally arrived, last, they all stood to attention like it was some kind of fashion show. Kass realised they were waiting for his approval and smiled to himself.

Squire had a good look at all of them in turn and gave each of them a smile and a short nod. "You all look amazing," he said and went to the Fox Box to get his things.

Bailey was already there loading her gun magazines with new bullets and as he came closer she saw the glint of titanium under the coat sleeve on his left wrist. After the briefest of smiles to herself she looked and caught his eye and mouthed to him silently "no words." She went back to her guns then and tried to take no notice as Squire joined her.

He collected his things one at a time and filled his pockets as always and then strapped on his gun and belt. "It's amazing," he said to the open box and then turned and moved away. For Bailey those were all the words she needed and she smiled quietly to herself.

On his way to the bench he stopped in front of Elle. She looked up at him looking back down at her. "Are you sure about this?" He asked quietly enough that no one else noticed or paid any attention. "The dress I mean, in the Void."

Standing there in her stretchy black dress and trainers and gun belt she looked quite the picture. She considered carefully what she wanted to say. "You said you wanted me to be just me in there," she smiled. "This is how me looks here, so this is how I want to look there."

It was an excellent answer and Squire respected her even more. Amazing on the assault course, miracle in the Void and now she was going to follow her heart no matter what other people might think. "Bravo Elle," he said sincerely. "I am privileged to have you in the team."

Elle's smile was reward enough and she turned to find Shine. The bond between them was growing strong very quickly.

At the bench he found his brother as usual watching the monitors. He looked up and offered Squire a bracelet. "Are you all good?"

"Yes, I am indeed," the reply was bright and much more like his old self. "This is a fabulous team Kass," he added. "I can't believe how much I care about them already."

Scanning in his bracelet Squire turned to face everyone as he had the night before. "Okay everyone," he called.

The talking stopped straight away and everyone turned to face the bench. Squire went on then with the briefing for the evening with Kass stood at his side. "Most of you know what to expect this time so I hope some of the nerves will be more settled." He threw a quick look at Ashley and then continued. "Shine and Ryan, please don't stress about not making the jump like last time. Just relax and I am sure you will be joining us tonight."

"Fifteen minutes," Kass said from beside him without taking his face from the monitors.

Squire noticed that most of the team had parted with their coats and put them to one side. "It may be cold where we end up people," he called. "Don't be fooled just because it's so hot in here."

The team in front of him cast looks at each other but seemed happy to take the chance. It was really hot in the barn this evening and trying to relax when you were overheating was no fun.

Shine had her first aid pack on, as did Ashley, but she had opted to keep her long black coat on. Tom and Ryan had removed theirs and were happy to take the chance they could be cold or wet for an hour or so.

"I think they feel the heat more than us old folk," he said to Kass beside him.

His brother nodded in agreement. "I don't think they would feel the cold as badly either. Let them take the chance though. They won't die from cold in an hour."

"Okay," Squire said heading over to join them. "Positions and ready everyone." As he walked to find a place for himself he gave Ryan a friendly pat on the shoulder for encouragement. He then went to take his place next to Shine and gave her a wink when she looked at him. "It will be okay," he said quietly to her.

She gave him the smallest of smiles back. She was pleased he had taken the effort to come and speak to her knowing she would be worrying when he didn't have to. Relaxing a little more she stared at the clock with deeper resolve.

Kass had also taken his place at the end of the line and looked at everyone in turn to make sure there were no last minute issues. As his eyes scanned past Shine and then Squire he noticed the glint of something shiny under his brother's coat. He raised an eyebrow at that revelation. His brother hadn't remembered his watch for years.

As the magnets gave their giant pulse there was a brief white flash and then Shine fell. Her initial delight at making it into the Void this time was replaced in a matter of seconds in a rush of feelings and emotions. She had known what to expect but it was one thing hearing about it and quite another to be thrown headlong into it.

Luckily for her within a minute Elle came floating into view and the two were drawn together. "Shine!" she called excitedly as they approached each other. Her smile was huge and when they latched on to each she shouted, "I'm so glad you're here."

Shine wanted to call back but it felt like the wind of the Void would rip her words away from her. She gave Elle a hopeful grin back and tried to give the impression she was fine.

Elle was busy rethinking her choice of the woollen black dress that was refusing to behave itself in the wind of the Void and decided that falling feet first was not going to go well.

In the next few minutes the whole team were moving together and everyone called out to one another. Ryan remained quiet and calm on the outside and didn't show either his relief that he had made it or how sick he was feeling.

Tom was looking out and checking for everyone when he caught sight of Ashley in the distance. Her blonde hair steamed out behind her along with her billowing black coat. He had the feeling it was like watching a superhero in flight and wondered if that was why Kass and Squire also had cape-like coats.

Once they had all linked up in a ring Shine and Ryan got a chance to look around them at the swirling grey emptiness. They soon got used to the feeling of falling at high speed and suspected free fall parachuting would feel something like it.

"Like before," Squire shouted out to them. "Listen to things in your heads now. This time, if you get something just take us there and don't worry about breaking the chain to tell us about it."

They each closed their eyes now and focused as hard as they could on the jumble of meaningless clips of voices they heard. Once again it was Tom who was quickest. He tuned into voices that were clearly German. He knew a little of the language and he decided he wanted to hear what they were saying. As soon as he made that connection the whole team were pulled in that direction.

The wind slowed to a stop and the grey of the Void was replaced by a bleak sky from horizon to horizon. The ground materialised under them, sandy soil covered with rough patches of washed out grass.

The team looked around waiting for everything to take shape but before it did the smell found them. As one they reacted to the sickness in the air and tried to cover their faces with their sleeves or their hands.

They stood in a field that was covered in dead bodies; thousands of them. As they looked around in shock it was soon clear all these people had died of massive malnutrition or worse. Skeletal bodies lay piled up. Some had scraps of clothes while others lay naked. Flies hummed in the air and the scene was pitiful.

Kass scanned further around and soon picked out the barbed wire fences and the lookout towers further away and knew where they were. A hundred metres or so behind him lay a cluster of industrial looking buildings as well as huts and tents. He saw the tall chimney in the middle of it all and knew that was where the gas chamber would be.

The stench of death clung to his throat and nose but he forced himself to endure it. "Concentration camp," he said to the others who all looked equally appalled.

They had been there less than a minute and yet all they wanted was to be gone. Tom was horrified that he was responsible for bringing them all to this place. He lifted his shirt up and covered his nose and mouth in an attempt to stop the smell but it didn't help much. Everywhere he looked waxen death glared back at him.

Squire looked at the group quickly. His first responsibility was for the safety of the team and this was going to be stretched to breaking point very quickly.

Shine dropped slowly to one knee and pitched forward as the contents of her stomach poured out onto the ground in front of her. Even as the others saw it and tried to respond Elle collapsed in a heap in the dirt. She was as white as a sheet and the sights and smells had proven too much for her. Ashley was first to move and went to her even though she could feel her own stomach reaching and convulsing in revulsion at everything around her.

A loud snarl broke through the chaos as a guard dog leapt silently over a pile of bodies straight at Bailey's back. She had no chance to evade it. The German Shepherd's powerful strike pitched her forward as the jaws closed in on her neck.

Everyone froze with the suddenness of the attack; except one. Squire Fox drew his Banisher and fired in one smooth motion. There was no time to think and no time to aim. Instinct alone moved his right hand before any of the others even had time to move. Even as Bailey hit the ground the body of the dog on her back turned to burning ash which then poured over her in a wave before slowly disappearing.

The second dog leapt unseen by everyone and caught Squire's right arm in its jaws and yanked him off his feet. He was hauled to the ground and the maddened dog twisted and jumped, but didn't release its grip on the arm of the team's leader. His gun fell uselessly from his fingers.

Bailey looked up and saw it happen in surreal slow motion. She was flat on her front with ash flowing out around her and her arms pinned under her body. She saw Ryan and Tom draw their guns and aim. They couldn't fire though; it was too easy to hit Squire. She reached out and went for her gun with her right hand but even as she did there was a white flash and the dog turned to burning ash.

Kass was knelt at Ashley's side and in his hand was the Banisher he had pulled from her holster just seconds before.

The sounds of barking in the distance grabbed everyone back to reality again. Coming from the building area raced another six crazed German Shepherds. Kass squatted in a position to try and cover Ashley and Elle. Squire tried to pick up his Banisher with fingers that didn't seem to be working properly. His arm was bleeding badly and blood ran from his sleeve and down his hand. Finally, he managed to get a grip of the handle and pick it up but had no idea if he was going to be able to pull the trigger. His fingers were numb and pain throbbed up his arm.

Bailey was up and had her guns drawn, as did Ryan. They both went to the front of the attack path and were determined to be the front line. Tom also moved off with them with his Banisher in his right hand.

The dogs came on fast dodging in and out of piles of the dead. Bailey aimed but couldn't get a shot. "Wait till they're close," she called. She braced herself with both guns aimed forward. Ryan did the same, his heart beating fast and strong.

Kass called over to his brother, "Give your gun to Ashley," but only received a shake of Squire's head in return. Torn between covering the girls on the ground or his stricken brother he ended up staying motionless. Everything had happened too quickly.

Shots rang out now from the front as Ryan and Bailey both opened fire. They shot rapidly and white bolts of energy streamed out at the dogs but most missed. They came on in a rush of black and brown thunder. Tom took the first one out and then Ryan got another but the others didn't slow down.

They were right on them now and the first of the dogs leapt up towards Bailey. She fired as she threw herself backwards and was covered in another wave of ash a second later. She landed heavily on her back and the air was blown from her lungs in a jolt. Ryan took down the next but was quickly running out of ammo.

One dog jumped over Bailey on the ground and landed among the group and straight into the sights of Squire. He tried to pull the trigger but nothing happened; his useless finger didn't have the strength to move it. His heart lurched for a split second as he realised the danger but then Shine pitched over the top of him and rolled forward and fired. The dog burned up instantly.

Ashley was right next to it but couldn't see what was happening. Elle had opened her eyes and was looking dreamy and confused. It was as much as Ashley could do to stop her getting up and moving.

With only one dog left the team huddled backwards into a group and it was only a matter of time before they dispatched it. After the final shot rang from Ryan's Banisher the group were once again plunged into silence.

Squire lowered his pain riddled arm and rested his gun on the ground with a wince. "Shine," he said through the pain. "Thanks."

She walked back to him wiping sick from her chin with her arm. "Anytime," she said with a smile. "Are you okay?"

"Holy Moses guys," Tom said with disgust. "I'm sorry for bringing us here."

Ashley was helping the pale faced Elle to sit up. "You need to stay still until your head clears," she said to the sleepy looking face of her friend. "Tom, can you sit with her? Squire's hurt."

Tom moved forward along with Ryan and they propped up the swaying figure of Elle.

"We need to get your coat off," Kass said to his brother. Blood was dripping from his fingers at an alarming rate and he was going to need some attention quickly. Squire shook his left arm free first and then allowed his brother to carefully remove the right. Shine was removing her back-pack and the medical kit from inside. "You're going to be okay," she said while trying not to be sick again. Her stomach was queasy and the smell was not helping.

Ashley too had arrived and together they looked at the injury on Squire's forearm. The dog's teeth had ripped a gory line of holes that looked deep and bled freely.

Bailey understood at once why Squire had been unable to use his gun. The damage was serious on both sides of his arm and there was probably nerve or tendon damage.

"You finally hit something," Squire said looking up at his brother. "About bloody time."

"Don't mock," Kass replied dryly, "I was aiming for you."

"We need Elle," Ashley said but already knew she was in no state to do anything for now. Instead she started ripping open cleaning swab packets so they could make a start cleaning up.

"Bailey," Kass called out looking around for her. "Go round all the guns and empty them to make sure you and Ryan have full clips."

"Do you think we will be needing them again?" she called as she went into action. She hoped the answer was no. Another attack like that one and they really would be out of bullets. On top of that Elle was out of it, Shine was sick and Squire was injured.

Kass considered for a moment. "I don't hear a fat lady singing and we are still here. To me that means this is not over."

She and Ryan went to work straight away and started emptying clips from all the guns that were being passed to them by Tom. Squire's magazine only had one bullet missing and this was transferred to Bailey's first gun. The two worked carefully to make sure they had most of the ammo but that the other guns would have some too, just in case.

Squire sat on the ground trying to avoid looking at his arm. He was okay with injuries as long as they were not his own. Now he felt light headed and queasy and wanted to lie down and be better again. Shine noticed how pale he had gone and dumped herself down right in front of him. "Here," she said to him while pointing at the end of her nose. She looked right back into his eyes and anytime they started to wander she would repeat the process.

"Here," she called again sharply. Squire noticed this time her fingers were running red and his head swam even faster than before.

The wounds on both sides of his arm were still bleeding freely and Ashley had begun to bandage them up as quickly as she could. There were thick pads underneath the wrappings but they were going red very quickly.

"We've got trouble," Tom called back to the others. He was looking over to the buildings and watching a movement now coming from them. Kass, Ryan and Bailey joined him straight away and followed his gaze.

German soldiers were appearing from the buildings and gathering together. There appeared to be over forty of them slowly moving together, some in SS uniforms.

"What are they waiting for?" Ryan had drawn his guns once again but was standing firm.

"Us I think," Kass responded. He looked behind him to see how his brother was doing. He was pale and washed out but was in no immediate danger. Elle had some colour back in her face but was on her knees holding her stomach and retching. Ashley had finished with her bandaging and looked like she was trying to make a sling.

"I think we need you with us," he spoke down to her. Laying her sling to one side she got to her feet and looked at the small army of German soldiers ahead of them.

"Shine," Kass called and she looked around at him. He handed her one of the guns that still had nearly a full magazine. "Stay here with Elle and Squire." She took the gun and laid it on the ground where it would be easy to reach.

"Here," she demanded at Squire again and put her finger on the end of her nose. While he looked back a little dazed she took a

346

quick look at Elle and saw she was still okay and seemed to be improving.

"If anything happens to us," Kass said to Shine, "Try and hold them off for long enough for the time to run out." With that he started walking towards the buildings and the group of soldiers watching them from afar. The rest of the team went with him with their hands close to their holsters.

As they walked it was almost impossible not to look at the death all around them. Dead eyes watched their progress from sunken sockets and all of the group were affected by the sights they had to see.

Onwards they went, sometimes stepping over bodies and still the soldiers just watched them. From their distance Kass couldn't see any weapons and was rather glad of it.

"If you see or hear another dog we form up into a tight knot so that we can fire without hitting each other," he called back to the others. They were all braced and fully alert for just that possibility.

Kass stopped the team twenty metres from the group of Germans. As he looked at them he noticed the officers' once crisp, black uniforms were now covered in dust and falling to pieces. The other soldiers seemed to be doing no better and none appeared to have a weapon between them.

"English?" one of the officers called out. His black SS peak cap was battered and worn.

Bailey's hands rested on her guns. They were all in a group and would be easy to hit even if she didn't have enough bullets for all of them.

Kass took another couple of steps forward. "We speak English."

The German soldiers looked at each other and spoke quickly amongst themselves in their own language.

The first officer stepped forward. "You have our surrender," he offered and it was clear these men would not be causing them any problems.

"Look what you did," Bailey spat. "You evil bastards!" She walked forward ready to gun them all down but Kass reached out and stopped her.

"Wait," he said calmly.

The officer looked broken. "It is true as you say," his German accent obvious. "The crimes we have witnessed and been a part of are the hell we have had to endure." He looked at all of the group as he spoke. "For an eternity we have been guarding these prisoners with no escape for us and no place to hide from what we did."

"They are not prisoners," Bailey called again. "They are dead!" The last word carried all her passion at the cruelty inflicted on so many whose bodies lay everywhere.

"That may be so," the officer was looking at his battered boots, "but still we had to guard them."

"Why?" Kass remained passive and calm and only wanted to get all the facts.

The officer faced him once more. "The dogs of course. They were once ours and worked with us but the smell and the decay drove them mad. We ran out of bullets long ago and had no way to fight back. The dogs guarded us as we guarded the dead around us."

"Then why do you now remain?" Tom called over. "If you know you are dead why do you wait here?"

The German officer looked behind him at his men, all of them looking on without expression. He turned back to face Tom. "We wondered the same thing for more time than I can remember. Maybe now you have come to kill us and perhaps we can be at peace at last?"

"Why should you have peace?" Bailey blasted. Ashley had moved to her side and gently put a hand on her shoulder.

"Easy now," she said softly to her friend. "Seventy years in this hell is a high price for anyone to pay."

The officer sank to his knees and implored the group once again. "Do you think there is anything we wouldn't do to change what happened?" His eyes were full of remorse and sorrow. "Do you think we wanted these things? Most of us had no choice. We would have been shot for deserting and shot for not obeying."

"Better to be shot and die without this blood on your hands though," Ryan added.

"Yes, my young friend," the officer returned. "So much easier to understand things looking back. How I wish I could go back and put things right."

Kass was watching the reactions of the other officers and soldiers but saw only resignation and misery.

"Why is it I wonder," the officer began again. "Such crimes we have committed and yet we have to endure here. If any are deserving of a place in Hell, then surely here we stand."

The thought troubled Kass. He also didn't understand why they were still here. They should have been gone long ago instead of this limbo existence; unless of course the Void was actually Hell itself?

Once again the officer on his knees looked up, his face now desperate. "Please, my friends. Kill us so that we can escape this place, even if it means we burn for eternity in the fires of Hell. This place is beyond torture for us."

"I hear you," Kass called back, "But we cannot kill you."

The German soldiers looked back in shock. "Why?" the officer called back. "Surely you can put this wrong right and put an end to us."

"It is not our place to judge," Kass called back.

"True," Squire Fox said as he walked between the team of Runners. "That is my bit." He walked to the front and moved ahead of his brother. Shine moved up and stood right next to him carrying his coat.

Everyone saw that his bandages were gone and the bite wounds had gone also. His arm and hand were covered in blood still but he was otherwise unhurt. Shine stood at his side with a dreamy faraway look on her face. Moving up with them was Elle who looked equally at peace with everything.

Squire turned and rummaged in his coat. "You guys step back a bit," he said softly to the team who were spread out facing the Germans.

When he turned back to the officer he was holding the Catching. "Please stand to face your judgement," he said quietly. Doing as he was told the SS Commander stood and pulled what was left of his uniform straight. "The rest of you," he called to the other Germans, "Spread out into single file." He waved his arms to both sides to signal where the rest should go and stand.

The officer at the front called out instructions in German and immediately there was shuffling movement as the other guards and soldiers fanned out.

Squire threw a glance behind him at his brother before turning once again. He held the Catching at arms length and pressed the button. The four sections opened slowly and Squire watched and waited. As soon as they were flat the crystal burst into light and a shrill whistle filled the air.

The intensity of the light in the crystal grew and grew but it stayed where it was within the Catching. The high pitched sound slowly turned into a scream that hurt Squire's ears and the handle of the Catching vibrated in his hand.

The Germans and the Runners behind him were wincing at the noise coming from the madly vibrating light source at the end of Squire's arm.

Still the noise grew and the vibration and tremors from the Catching were so bad that Squire didn't know if he could hold on to it. He dropped to one knee and immediately Shine grabbed his hand with both of hers to try and steady it.

The light was so bright now that everyone had closed their eyes against the argent flare. At the centre of it Squire and Shine knelt in the dirt with their heads bent forward and their eyes squeezed tightly shut.

"Do it now!" Shine screamed as loudly as she could but even then Squire barely heard her.

He did do it then; he thought the words in his mind and the power within the Catching was released. White light burst from the gem with more power than he could have imagined. Instead of the usual single target it enveloped thirty-nine Germans all at once in a beam of light to match the brilliance of the sun. They were all ablaze in white brilliance that shimmered and there seemed to be two dimensions going on at once. Squire lifted his head and looked past the quivering Catching he struggled so hard to hold. The ring of soldiers were all aflame in white fire. Slowly they dissipated and floated away and the high pitched scream also started to die down.

Eventually the light went out and the arms of the Catching returned to their closed position. Squire's hand was numb from holding it and as soon as it was closed Shine let go of his hand and let out a big sigh.

Slowly the Runners got to their feet and looked around. The soldiers were all gone and as they watched the dead also started to fade.

Within a minute the whole camp lay empty around them. All traces that the dead had ever been there had gone and the Runners were all that remained.

Squire was sitting in the dry dirt with his coat in a heap beside him. At his side was Shine. Her new clothes now christened in dirt, blood and sick, but she looked so happy.

"Three times Shine," Squire said quietly to her. "Three times in less than an hour you came to help me. I'm so pleased you made it this time." He gave her a smile that was full of relief.

Shine stood up and brushed the dirt from her backside and then offered Squire a hand to pull him up. He took it and she leant backwards to help haul him up. "I told you before," she said with a smile, "Anytime."

The others also dusted themselves down now that all the excitement seemed to be over. "I don't get it," Bailey said walking over to the others. "Why didn't they burn?"

The others already knew the answer but Elle said it for them. "The Bible says that God can forgive anything, as a parent forgives a child. I expect that in the time they were trapped here they learned regret and remorse and maybe they did enough to be at peace."

Before Bailey could cut in again Kass cut her off gently. "It is not our job to judge. We leave that to the only one that can."

Squire bent down and picked up his filthy coat and put it back on. Even as he did the concentration camp started to fade away and very quickly the team were falling once again. Looking at his watch he saw that they still had nearly ten minutes of time left and cautioned the team. "Nobody listen to anything now. We've had enough excitement for one visit."

Everyone agreed and the ten-minute fall to the barn would give them all a chance to think.

They arrived in an untidy heap in the barn. Now there were more of them and only had the same amount of space they bumped into each other and pretty much all landed up on the floor.

There was some light hearted laughing as the stress of the last hour ended with an unglamorous landing. No one had remained clean on the jump and no one cared that they were left sitting on a dusty barn floor.

"So, do you wanna get off me?" Squire had been pinned down by Tom, who was struggling to untangle himself from

Ashley's coat. There was more laughing and eventually everyone was up and busy sorting themselves out.

"Amber?" Kass looked at this brother who was emptying his coat pockets and stashing everything away.

"Nah," he called back. "Let's go green tonight."

Raising an eyebrow Kass went to the bench and did as requested. He wasn't sure it was the right choice after the adventure they had just been on, but he was pretty worn out and didn't fancy another Amber meeting. He suspected Squire felt the same. The signal went out to the whole team that everything was all clear.

Both Ashley and Shine were at the big metal sink in the corner of the barn and were washing their blood stained hands and bracelets before putting them away. They were soon joined by Squire who first dumped his coat in the big plastic bin next to the sink and then waited in line to get washed up a bit.

"You've got sick down you," he mentioned to Shine, who looked down at herself and just shrugged.

"Sick, blood, dirt, straw. Beyond caring really." Her face was the picture of peace and the smile in her eyes held a dreamlike quality. She dried her hands and went to remove her gun holsters and refill the magazines from the fresh box of ammo Tinker had left.

When everything had been put away Squire sat on the bench and addressed the waiting Void Runners. "It's been another full on evening everyone and you have been incredible once again." He looked out at the faces and was amazed at them. They had faced such

355

dangers and challenges and yet none of them appeared to have been put off; if anything they were eager to get back to the Void for more.

"I made a choice to call a green run tonight as we are meeting tomorrow for the full debrief with the whole team and I think everything can wait until then. For now, you are free to go or hang around it you so wish."

Tom approached the front and asked if it would be alright if he and Ryan headed off to the pub for a game of pool and a beer or two.

"Sounds like an excellent idea," Squire smiled. "Any chance you could drop Elle home on the way?"

Tom, who now had Ryan with him agreed at once. "Sure we can," he said eager to be useful. "We'll see you tomorrow for the meeting."

As it was they wouldn't. The Saturday night Void run would be the last time they were all together.

The sky was still light half an hour later and a cluster of the remaining Runners sat on the grass in the garden outside. Anna had brought out jugs of cider for those that remained and they sat and enjoyed the warmth of the evening sun.

Ashley and Paige had headed off earlier to find the boys and challenge them to a game of pool. They had picked up Daisy on the way and Paige had got changed into social gear and then stopped off once more for Ashley to put on something clean.

"So tell us how you fixed Squire's arm," Anna called over to Shine. She was sitting cross legged on the grass with a half full glass of cider at her feet and odd bits of straw still hanging on to her.

"Well," she started in her chirpy high voice. "It wasn't me is the first thing; it was Elle. One minute she was there all sicky and weak and then she just said 'pray' so I did." She looked around at the others hoping it made some sense.

"Was it the same as Ashley the night before?" Bailey was laying on her front pitched up on her elbows and sipping orange juice.

Kass popped the metal top off his second bottle of beer with a satisfying hiss.

"I don't know what Ashley felt really, although we did talk about it at our house afterwards. She put her hand on me and, well I dunno. Everything went really fuzzy and warm and it felt like my hands were burning with something." She looked at Squire sitting next to her with a beer and a cigarette. "It was like a massive goose bump party and I just put my hands on his arm and it got better." Looking at the others all listening with avid interest she wished she could explain it better. She tried to make up for it by downing her cider and then pouring herself another.

Squire was feeling quite mellow already as the beer dulled his senses and allowed him to relax. "What do you think then Brains?" he asked his brother.

357

Kass didn't really know although he had given it a great deal of thought. "I think we are being protected." His statement had the attention of everyone. "I have no idea by who or even why but I think they can access Elle somehow."

No one knew how to respond. It was possible of course and was as good as any other explanation they had come up with.

"That kind of power though," Bailey mused almost to herself. "That can only come from one place surely." She looked at the others and they all seemed to agree.

"It makes sense," Anna said, "But why Elle? Couldn't they just pick anyone?"

"I'm not so sure," Squire replied. "She has got something about her." He tried to think of the right words. "She's very high in Spirit like her parents. Perhaps that makes her the obvious choice." He looked at the others for approval. "I don't know. I leave the clever stuff for others to figure out."

They talked quietly in the garden until the stars were bright in the heavens above them. It was still warm outside and the moon lit them up with a blue cast.

"We should be going," Bailey said at last and began putting her boots back on, having taken them off to let her feet cool down.

"It's early still," Anna protested. "Well, almost early then."

Bailey was finishing her laces but looked up to calmly nod her head in the direction of Shine. When they followed the direction of her nod they could see her swaying around and looking very pleased with the world.

"Oh, I see," Squire said trying to get himself to his feet. Once he was up he moved a step toward her and reached down and gently shook her shoulder. "Shine," he called quietly, "Time to go."

She slowly opened her eyes and tried to find the source of the noise. Even with the world gently swaying as it was she saw the shadow of Squire next to her. "Hi," she called back too loudly and her whole face grinned back and her eyes rolled around.

"Oh dear," Kass said while trying not to laugh. "This is going to be entertaining." They had all got to their feet now and he and Anna collected the glasses and bottles from the lawn.

Bailey was on the other side of Shine now and reached out and took hold of the top of her arm. "Shine," she called from inches away. "We're going to get up at the count of three." Squire had also taken hold of her other arm and was chuckling quietly.

"Here we go," Bailey went on, "One, two, three." They both pulled and the tiny figure of Shine came upright with a bit of a wobble and a stagger. "There we go," Bailey encouraged. She was also laughing now. "Are you okay Shine? Do you want me to steer you?"

"No," came the reply. "I'm fine." Squire and Bailey slowly let go only to see her pitch over sideways and back onto the lawn with a thump.

The laughter in the garden of the farmhouse was now in full flow.

Shine sang quietly to herself with her face resting up against the back door window of Bailey's car. In the passenger seat Squire was still finding it funny having had a couple of beers too many himself.

When they arrived at the new house Bailey and Squire helped the quietly singing Shine out of the car and up the stairs. They laid her on the bed and Bailey took off her trainers for her. "Goodnight Shine," she called and they left her to it.

Ashley had appeared from her bedroom with bleary eyes to see what all the noise was about but didn't stay long. The sounds from behind the door of Shine's room were clue enough that someone was having a happy evening.

Squire declined the coffee and the lift home he was offered and had left shortly afterwards to find his own way. The fresh air and the laughter had made him feel quite tired and he headed off down the road quite content with the world. As he lit a cigarette and looked up at the stars he had to admit to himself it had been a day to remember.

XVI.

Sunday morning arrived too early for some. Shine would awake on the bathroom floor with no recollection of how she got there. She took her fragile head back to bed and didn't surface until after lunchtime.

When Daisy went to check on her dad at 10.00am she found him out for the count and left him to it. She and Paige got themselves ready without him and then left him a note on the fridge before heading out.

Gone to church. Where you should be! P&D x

Both Justin and George would ask questions after the service was over as to his whereabouts and if he was okay. They would both give the same answer and assure them he would be at the meeting later.

George had been given brief details about Friday's run and seemed desperate to hear all about it as well as the Saturday green run. Justin was also chomping at the bit for all the news as there seemed to have been a massive jump in the team's success in lots of areas.

He was looking forward to an evening of revelation with the team and he would not be disappointed.

At a little after 11.00am a groggy looking Squire padded around the house in his jeans and a T shirt. The kettle had already done its duty and he was enjoying his first tea of the day when the doorbell chimed.

He changed direction and headed for the door but paused to look in the mirror on the way to make sure he didn't look too scary. He was pleased to see that his hair was a bit lopsided and he needed a shave but apart from that everything appeared to be in order.

He opened the front door and a burst of warm air rushed over him as the heat of the day poured in to his house to find some shade. Standing in front of him was a young lady with slightly glowing skin from the heat and a very large black canvas case over her shoulder.

"Oh, hello," she said with half a smile. "I'm sorry to bother you on a Sunday morning, but I am an art student and wondered if you would have a minute to look at my work?"

Squire took it all in within a matter of seconds. "Have you been carrying that case around for very long today?"

She looked briefly at it then answered, "Probably a couple of hours."

He gave her a small smile and he understood the flushed face now. "Have many people looked at your work today?" He suspected he already knew the answer from the slightly desperate look in her eyes.

"Well no," she said with a little sigh, "Not yet anyway."

"Well, in that case," he went on, "I would be delighted to look at your work."

The smallest hint of a smile bloomed on her face and she lifted the case from her shoulder and carefully set it down. Her actions were a little wary but he warmed to her for making the effort to at least try and get out there and make some money.

"While you get ready," he added, "It's really hot out here. Can I get you a cold drink?"

Now the smile was broader. "Oh yes please," she said, "I'm absolutely baking."

"Coming right up then," he turned and headed back down the hall to the kitchen. He returned a minute later with a tall glass of orange juice from the fridge and had added a few ice cubes for good measure. They chinked about as he offered it to her and then he sat down on the front step and lit a cigarette.

She took the glass and took a long drink that bit into the back of her throat. "Ah, thank you," she said with a sigh. Feeling a little more at ease she sat herself down on the front path and began hauling canvas boards out of the case.

She was a pretty girl of perhaps nineteen or twenty years old with luxurious long brown hair and the most amazing green and hazel eyes.

Squire looked at her paintings one at a time and tried his best to ask educated questions about the motivation or concept of the art. A lot of the pieces were very modern and had objects placed in unusual settings or from strange angles but all had a unique look. It was clear she had a great eye and imagination and had spent many hours putting the details into the work. He was impressed.

He took his time with each one and waited for the art magic to strike him and for him to see something he would like to have on his wall, but although they were good they were not really his thing.

She finished her drink quickly and he offered her a refill. "Oh yes please," she said, now much more relaxed and happy.

"Same again or something different," he asked as he got back to his feet.

"Oh I don't mind," she smiled.

He returned once again with a glass of cold Coke which was eagerly taken and started on. "I'm Lydia by the way," she said and he had the feeling this was the nearest she had come to anyone other than her parents taking an interest in her paintings.

"I am very pleased you called today Lydia," he returned. "I'm Squire Fox."

Her already large oval eyes opened wider for a moment and a strange look flickered on her face. "I know that name," she said but looked confused. "Do you know my family maybe? My name's Lydia Barnes."

Squire thought for a moment but couldn't recollect knowing any Barnes at all.

"How strange," she went on. "Maybe déjà vu." She gave him a 'don't worry about it' smile and handed him the next canvas.

Now it was his turn to look confused. "What is this?" The painting was quite large and quite detailed. The majority of the board was filled with the face of a clock from a steep angle looking up to the top from below where the number 6 would be.

Squire Fox was looking at a painting of Doris. The clock was right in every detail and even the swirling hands were correct. The wooden case was missing but the face was painted against the Void. The swirling greys made the brass face stand out in almost 3D perspective.

"I wasn't really sure about this one," she started. "I wanted to represent time and the way it is endless and flowing. This is what I ended up with."

Squire continued to stare totally transfixed. His heart was hammering in his chest and his eyes scanned the face of the clock he knew so well over and over again.

"Do you like it?" she asked tentatively.

Very slowly he broke from his stare and looked back at her. He took in every detail and made sure he would remember her face if he saw it again. "How much do you want for this?"

Her slender 5'1" frame seemed to flinch slightly and surprise arrived on her face. "Erm, I don't know really." She hadn't expected to actually sell anything. "Would forty pounds be okay?" She said the last bit with a hint of fear as she was desperate not to be too expensive.

Squire got back to his feet and headed inside only to return a moment later with his wallet. Lydia's eyes grew again and she had that elation moment of her first ever sale.

She watched him rummage around and withdraw some notes and offer them to her. Even as her hand reached out to take them she could see it was more than forty pounds. She took the notes and looked up at him. He was looking intently at her. "This is all I have on me."

She slowly fanned out the notes. "This is way too much," she said. "I can't take this."

"Lydia Barnes," he began. "It is worth every penny of that and more but that is all I have on me. I don't know how you have heard my name before but this painting is special to me."

She quickly counted through the money and her eyes kept getting bigger. "Two hundred and twenty pounds," she said looking amazed and didn't seem to want to accept it.

"Please take it," Squire insisted, "and if I'm not being too forward I wonder if I could have your phone number? I would like to meet up and pay the rest of what I owe you."

Now she looked even more surprised. "You don't owe me anything," she pleaded. "Of course you can have my number but you don't need to give me any more money."

"Let me just grab a pen and paper for you," he said as he got up and went to the table in the hallway and started looking through the drawer.

"You got time Mister," she called from the front path.

Squire Fox froze on the spot and felt the hairs stand up on the back of his neck. A sudden pit in his stomach opened up and he felt immediately sick. He slowly picked up a pen and a pad of paper and walked stiffly back to the door. Lydia was still sitting on the path and was packing away her paintings in her case. She looked up and smiled.

"What did you just say?" He asked the question but was sure he didn't want to hear the answer.

"Oh, sorry," she replied happily. "I was just saying that you've got time. That's the name of the painting."

Squire relaxed just a little. "Ah yes of course," he responded. "Did you just call me Mister?"

Lydia had finished packing and was getting to her feet and brushing the dust from her backside. "Erm, no I don't think so."

She took the pad and wrote her number down for him and thanked him time and time again for being her first customer and for being so generous.

"You've made my whole day," she called to him as she backed down the path with a big smile on her face. As she walked off she waved and would always remember the one who took some time and set her on her path as an artist.

Paige and Daisy arrived home around lunchtime and the three of them headed off to find lunch somewhere. Squire rarely cooked Sunday dinner in favour of spending the time doing something with the family.

They found a quiet country pub that served amazing food and sat in the garden afterwards listening to the birds and the sounds of summer as mowers filled the air with the scent of freshly cut grass.

After that they headed for a walk along the Beacon; a giant hill that overlooked the countryside for miles around in every direction and formed part of the Chiltern Hills.

No matter when they visited it always seemed windy on the Beacon and always blew the cobwebs away. They played Titanic on the edge of the steepest section and stood one behind the other with their arms out wide and hummed 'My Heart Will Go On' from the film before collapsing in giggles as Paige called out "Iceburg!"

It was quiet up there and only the sounds of the wind disturbed the peace. They sat and let the sun kiss their faces and watched the hang gliders sail past effortlessly defying gravity on their silent canvas wings. The Void was forgotten and the perils it brought as well as the moments of amazement. That's why Squire did it; for those few memories that couldn't be explained easily, but brought so much of life in to a place full of death.

They returned home late in the afternoon refreshed and tired from the fresh air and watched cartoons until evening. There was a folder full of notes and thoughts Squire had put together for the meeting and Daisy was full of curiosity.

"So, what are you going to change then," she asked as the suns light turned a warm tone on the walls inside the house.

"Well," he said from his chair where he sat slouched with his legs over one of the arms. "For a start I want two teams running instead of one big one."

Paige was laying on the couch and asked without opening her eyes, "Why?"

"When I used to go in with just Kass we rarely had much action that was really dangerous, but as the team has got bigger that has changed," he replied. "It was the same before, when there were more of us. It cost us a lot of people but settled down again when we were a small group."

"I guess that makes sense but it will be hard to make smaller teams," Daisy put in.

"Not really," he responded. "Kass will lead a team with Ryan as Guardian, Ashley as Healer and Elle as the Spirit. I will take the other with Bailey as Guardian, Shine as Healer and Tom as Spirit. Both teams balance."

"What does the spirit role do?" Paige looked up. "I understood the others but not that one."

Squire considered the easiest way to explain. "They both have something special about them that I can't quite put my finger on. Tom hears the voices in the Void faster and clearer than anyone I have seen before and Elle, well how do I even start to try and explain what she can do."

The girls listened and thought carefully. They had heard in great detail how, on two recent occasions Elle had been able to transmit incredible energy to another member of the team. On both occasions there had been a healing miracle that even those that saw it happen found hard to understand.

Daisy's brow had furrows as she tried to concentrate. "How is she doing it though? She doesn't remember any of it."

"I don't think she is 'doing' anything," Squire answered. "Something happens to her that we can't explain. The most exciting thing is that whatever 'it' is she is open to it." He looked back at them both, his eyebrows rising. "Imagine what this world could be like if we were all open to whatever power is working through her."

"That is kinda mad," Paige responded in agreement. "So what else is planned?"

"Well, I won't be doing many more Void runs for starters." Squire swung his legs down and stretched out. There was silence from both girls but he was almost sure it was out of relief as much as anything. "I'm too old for this now and so is Kass. The new team are brilliant and they don't need us holding them back." Daisy and Paige listened but had no reply. "Tom will lead one team and Bailey the other, and the rest will be shared out," he finished and got to his feet. "I don't know about you two but I'm going to hit the bathroom in a bit and see if I can make myself look less old and knackered."

He headed out of the lounge and into the kitchen for a tea and smoking session before he would need to start getting ready for the meeting at the Farmhouse. Both Paige and Daisy headed to their rooms to get changed and would soon be back down again looking casual but tidy.

"Bailey wants us to head over to her place," Paige explained to her dad. "She's ordered enough Indian for all of us. Wanna come?"

Squire had just finished his tea and was trying to find the cup a space in the dishwasher. "No, you two go ahead. I'm going for an extreme make-over in the bathroom." He rubbed his spiky chin and offered them a smile. "Wish me luck."

"I would rather wish you could arrive on time for a change," Daisy offered in her best sarcastic tone.

"Ha, I doubt even Elle could manage that one," Paige put in as they started heading for the front door.

Squire leant against the kitchen worktop and smiled to himself. "Well it's good to excel at something I suppose," he said quietly to himself.

"Starts at 7.00," Daisy called from the open front door. "See you about quarter past." Chuckling to himself Squire headed upstairs. The bathroom door closed behind him.

The best part of an hour later Squire emerged from the bathroom followed by a cloud of steam. The super hot bath had eased his tired and complaining body and cleaned his skin to a pink shine.

Freshly shaved and groomed he was sure he was in good shape for the meeting and would win points on smelling amazing if nothing else.

Now wrapped in a towel tied around his waist he headed for his room to get dressed in something typical and uninteresting. He picked out a pair of faded blue jeans and a white T shirt and trainers. Looking at himself in the mirror he was pleased with the result. Scruffy but clean – his favourite kind of fashion.

XVII.

Once downstairs and armed with fresh tea Squire sat in the lounge with a file on his lap and was checking his notes one more time. He hoped he had covered enough to go forward with and had a leadership plan laid out, as well as the positions and timings for the rest of the two teams.

As he sat in his chair his eyes fell on the back of the painting leaning against the wall. He had meant to do something with it earlier but the girls had come home and he had forgotten all about it.

Putting his notes on the arm of the chair he went over and picked up the painting and took another look at it at arm's length. The face of the clock he knew so well on a background of swirling grey. How Lydia had been able to paint such an accurate copy of Doris he had no idea but she had managed it in almost 3D realism.

"Time in the Void," he said to himself quietly and in his mind he heard Lydia say again "You got time Mister."

As he stared at the painting he saw for the first time that the swirling of the Void in the background was on the left side of the border and the face of the clock would be falling that way. Looking from his position that would have meant time was going?

"You got time Mister."

The old lady's voice rang in his head too loud and clear for any memory. Instinctively he looked around the room to find her but he was still alone.

"The foolish man can find a path the wisest of men can never see."

The voice sounded again in his head. He laid the painting down carefully on the seat of the couch and slowly looked around him. He knew he hadn't just remembered the last memory from the old lady; she was close and watching him. "I am a foolish man," he called to the air around him, "but I can't see a path."

"No one can tell you the way; you have to find it."

Squire looked at the ceiling and closed his eyes. He was tired of this game already but his mind raced to try and put something together from the fragments he knew. Each time he had met her there had been a chance he was asleep. This time he couldn't see her but knew he was wide awake. He thought of each time she had visited him and the things she had said tumbled through his mind. At last something seemed to jump out at him and he opened his eyes. "Bailey. She is the key."

"You must find the Dreamer."

"Yes," he said to himself. "Bailey is the Dreamer, but how do I find her?" There was no reply to his question so he continued to talk aloud. "She found me. Walking up to me outside the house and calling my name even though I didn't know her. She said she had a dream a couple of years ago and that is where we met. If I need to

374

find her," his mind struggled to make the next part sound sensible, "I need to look for her in the Void two years ago?"

As he waited for an answer his eyes once more fell on the painting laying on the couch and at the clock that looked like it was falling backwards in the Void. His heart lurched and pounded in his chest. "I have to go back in time?"

"You got time Mister."

"I don't know how to change the time in the Void," he said again, his mind still struggling to make any connections that would help. "You say I've got time but I have no control over it." He started pacing the room now knowing he was getting closer. The old lady's responses seemed to confirm he was on the right track. "Somehow," he started again, "I have to go back in time two years to find Bailey. Two years," he continued to pace. "That would have been about the time," he broke off suddenly. His voice died in mid-sentence. The colour drained from his face and his eyes stared. Slowly he sank to his knees.

"No." His voice sounded haunted. A racing mind full of ideas suddenly shocked in to silence.

"You are going to see the things right under your nose soon enough."

"No," he said again in disbelief. Shocked into silence he stayed on his knees and waited for his suddenly spinning head to steady. For now, he couldn't think; the room was spinning and he struggled to stay in control. The pieces of the puzzle that had eluded him for so long came crashing into place.

"You already know all the answers"

Very slowly he stood. He walked like a zombie, his mind overloading with so many thoughts that his body had to go on to auto-pilot. He walked to the hallway with thoughts pouring through his head faster than he could cope with. He picked up his spare black coat and put it on almost in a trance and then he picked up his car keys from the table and opened the front door. Just before he stepped outside he stopped as some small idea nagged at his mind. Closing the door again he turned for the stairs and rushed up them and into his room.

"Not always the fool," he said as he picked up his new watch and put it on. Now he headed once again for the front door and this time he made it outside.

Once in his car he strapped on his seat belt and drove away with wide eyes. He didn't allow himself to plan now, he just acted on instinct. He drove as quickly as he could but not to the meeting; he headed the other way. The roads were as quiet as always for early evening on a Sunday as most people settled down with their families. Taking advantage of the empty roads Squire pushed on hard and was in Highgate fifteen minutes later.

As the first members of the team started arriving at the farmhouse Squire Fox was pulling into the car park of Highgate Hospital. He parked as close as he could to the main entrance and left his car unlocked as he walked up the steps and in through the main door. He tried hard to look as calm and casual as possible as it was past visiting time and not that many people came to visit the 'prisoners' here very often.

The reception desk nurse looked up and seeing who it was gave him a smile and pressed the door release button. She didn't seem unduly concerned with the lateness of the visit. Everyone knew Mr Fox was a little random with his visits but seemed a kindly soul.

Squire walked through the security doors and went straight upstairs. His heart pounded as he walked up the empty upper corridor towards room 220 and wondered how easy it was going to be to steal someone. He didn't encounter anyone on his way and was soon stood outside the room and was staring at the door number. "I gave her £220 for the painting," he whispered to himself. He entered slowly and quietly in case any staff were in the room but he was in luck. Sasha was alone and lay on her bed already in pyjamas and a warm dressing gown. Squire went straight over and sat on the edge of the bed and looked into the vacant eyes of his small friend and the voice once again returned to his head.

"Some things that cannot be broken can be repaired."

Her eyes rolled around in their blind searching of places and things she couldn't see. "Hello little one," he said quietly.

377

Her eyes stopped rolling and her mouth twisted into the shape of a smile. Squire's heart was lifted at the sight but he didn't have time to wait though and searched the room with his eyes. He found what he was looking for almost at once; the wheelchair in the corner used for Sasha's bathroom visits. He got up and pulled it up to the bedside and flicked down the panels for her feet to rest on, and then he leaned over and gently lifted her off the bed and sat her in the chair.

He checked to make sure she was sitting upright enough so that she wouldn't slide out and once he was happy that all was well they both left the room.

The next part he was unsure of but went ahead anyway. If anyone spotted them he was going to be in for some serious trouble. The elevator took them down to the ground floor and as soon as the doors opened he headed out with the wheelchair in front of him. So far he had been lucky enough not to run in to any staff but his luck was about to get tested even more.

Ahead of him down the corridor were the double security doors leading to the front foyer. No way was he going to be able to sneak past reception. He looked through the window ahead and saw her sitting at the desk typing up notes and looking busy.

"Doors will be opened for you."

"I hope so," he mumbled to himself and kept moving up to the doors. He looked down at Sasha who was oblivious to everything and was dribbling on to her shoulder. He prayed he was doing the right thing for her.

Ahead of him movement caught his eye in the main reception area. The reception nurse had got up with a pile of folders and was taking them to the office area behind her and then disappeared from sight.

Automatically he reached out to press the door release button but before he touched it they swished into motion to allow them through. Looking back, he was glad he hadn't touched it. The buzzer would have sounded at the front desk and his journey would have been over.

He pushed the wheelchair through the doors but kept his eyes on the office and hoped the nurse would not reappear. Muttering thanks to the air above him he pushed the wheelchair out of the main doors and down the wheelchair ramp to the car park.

He was at his car a few moments later and after opening the passenger door of the Mercedes he carefully lifted Sasha in and settled her down before closing the door. He abandoned the wheelchair where it was and then ran around the car and jumped in to his seat. Reaching over and around Sasha he put on her seatbelt and checked one more time that she was as settled and comfortable as possible. He fired up the engine and switched the headlights on for his journey into the unknown.

George Brooker arrived first that evening and was greeted by Kass at the door. "Kass," George almost boomed, "good to see you my boy." He bustled in and was full of smiles and had a slight bounce in his step.

Anna was not surprised at the change. The team had grown very quickly and was now full of energetic young people who could move things along at a faster pace. The proof was already pretty convincing; the last two runs had been extraordinary.

They were joined minutes later by Justin and Elle who both looked jubilant. Even before the meeting was underway George was full of praise. "Elle," he called when they had sat down, "I could not be more delighted. Our youngest ever member of the Runners and already I am hearing the most amazing things."

"Thanks," Elle said with a shy smile. She was too modest to say anything else and got back up again to escape the conversation and went to see Anna in the kitchen.

Kass noted the reaction in his mind but remained quiet. "She's a good girl that one," George added to Justin. "A great to credit to you and Sarah."

Justin was thumbing through his notes from the last meeting but looked up to accept the comment. "Thanks George," he responded and pushed his glasses back up with his index finger. "I don't think either of us can take praise for her being in the team though. That was all her own work."

A knock at the door stopped the conversation and Kass got up to let in the next arrivals. He returned a moment later and was followed by the girls who greeted those already there before heading to their normal positions.

George had not fully put down his position as Chairman and was friendly but formal. "Good evening ladies," he started, "Bailey, Ashley and Emily." He gave them a smile which was still stiff and more for show than anything else.

The smallest member of the Runners stopped in front of him and gave him a hard look before announcing, "My name is Shine."

George's smile faltered for just a moment but he regained his composure within a second. "Of course my dear, of course. My memory is not what it once was." He tried to smile but his eyes were hard and cold. He was not used to being answered back and he didn't like it.

Paige and Daisy appeared from the dining room having gone to the kitchen first to say hello to Anna and Elle. They noisily chatted to each other as they took their seats and were so at home with the meetings they barely noticed who else had arrived.

It wasn't long before they were joined by Tinker, Ted and the boys and the volume in the room raised another notch as more voices were added.

Anna and Elle soon arrived with the first of the many cups of tea and coffee that they would get through in the meeting and everyone was in good spirits. It was already well past 7.00pm but no one really noticed in their rush to catch up on news and the odd funny story. The curtains were closed for the evening and the room was cosy and warm and almost full to capacity.

The gravel courtyard had more cars in it than normal as Squire pulled in and parked up. He moved quietly now knowing there were many people about and he didn't have time for explanations.

He opened the passenger door and carefully lifted Sasha out and carried her to the barn. She was so light he had no trouble with her, but opening the door at the same time caused some issues. With a bit of nimble sidestepping he managed it and pulled the door shut behind them.

The lights were on as always and the monitors were doing their constant scrolling of information on magnetic fields. Squire took Sasha over to the cross in the centre of the floor and carefully laid her down. He had no doubt that her mind was already slow enough to enter the Void; now he tried to calm himself for his own jump.

He studied the monitors and saw a peak that he thought would be big enough in six minutes. Just enough time but he would need to work fast. He set the system for its first phase and then set the return phase for fifteen minutes after that.

Having watched Kass set the machine so many times over the years he felt confident he had done it right. Next he checked Doris and his watch and set them both the same. "Fifteen minutes Sasha," he said to himself. "I hope that's going to be enough for what I have in mind."

He headed for his box and started to remove his gear and fill his coat pockets. His mind was still working overtime as he strapped on his gun holster and filled it with a fully loaded Banisher. There were still parts of the puzzle missing and he searched his memory for the answers with his time now quickly running out.

"You got time Mister."

The voice of the old lady in his head startled him for a moment. "Time," he said to the room. "Yes, time is the key to this, but I don't know how to change time." He felt the first stirrings of panic and used all his willpower to push the feelings back down. "What the hell am I doing? I have to go back in time in the Void but I don't know how."

"Memory can be a powerful thing."

Squire paused as the words rolled through his mind. "My memories," he said aloud as another part of the puzzle slipped into place. He went over to the bench and took out two bracelets from their box and scanned them in.

"Target one, black locked in."

"Target two, red locked in."

383

Without slowing he went and knelt at Sasha's side. She lay there motionless except for the occasional tripping. Picking up her right arm he clipped a bracelet onto her wrist before laying it back down again.

"The foolish man can find a path the wisest of men can never see."

"Is that right," he said to the room. "Well I'm feeling like a fool right now." He gently picked up Sasha and knelt himself in the middle of the cross with her resting on his knee and wrapped in his arms. He looked at her one more time and thought he saw a smile appear. "Let's go and find your sister," he said to her, then turned to watch the clock.

He stared as he had done a thousand times or more before and as he did an image flashed in his mind of the party at the Manor House. "Of course," he whispered. He concentrated his mind on his memories of that party; the sunny day, the sounds of joy in the air and the garden full of activity and people. As the picture got bigger and started to feel real he focused on what he had been doing. People were getting out of the pool to go and get food. Steph never got out though, so what had he been doing?

His memory worked backwards from the food. He had been listening and laughing with Kass doing impressions of Sméagol and then he had gone to queue up. He had been standing in the line with Paul McCoy and they had been talking about the Catching.

With all his concentration he pictured that conversation and the scene around him. He tried to live in that moment with as much of himself as possible.

"Nobody told you the answer; you already knew it, deep down where your mind didn't bother to look."

On the bench the monitor changed its display but Squire didn't see it. He was already miles away.

Magnetic Field: Alternating

Initiating Grab

There was a white flash in his mind and the barn disappeared in an instant.

The conversation in the farmhouse was cheery and lively as small groups of people talked to those closest to them. Squire was now really late and Paige had wanted to ring him to make sure he was on his way.

The talking suddenly stopped when all the lights in the farmhouse flickered for a few seconds. Everyone looked up and around the room and then at each other.

"What the bloody hell." Kass was on his feet and heading for the door and was closely followed by everyone else. Someone had Void jumped and there was only one person missing.

They all piled in to the barn and looked around. The magnets were almost at the end of their cycle and then fell silent. The clock ticked out the time loudly on the bench.

Kass headed straight over to it and studied the monitors. Everyone waited and watched but no one spoke. "Fifteen minutes," Kass said turning to them. "That's when we'll get some answers." His shoulders slumped and he looked suddenly older. "There is nothing else for it but to wait."

People started talking again in rushed whispers. Bailey stood silently by though, "What are you up to," she said in a blank tone. She was worried and it was written all over her face.

"Why has he gone without us," Shine called to no one in particular as she wandered toward the Fox Box and sat down.

"That's not all of it," Paige said gloomily as eyes turned to her. "Why has he gone at all? He's supposed to be at the meeting."

No one had answers to any of the questions, but the level of talking in the barn grew steadily as the team came up with theories and more questions.

A few minutes later the conversation was muted as George asked for some quiet; his phone was ringing. He took the call and all those standing there would remember how his face drained of colour and his eyes glazed over.

When the call was over he returned the phone to his pocket and looked from Kass to Justin, and then to Ted and everyone else.

"It was the hospital," he said with a voice that had the slightest tremble in it. "They can't find Sasha."

Everyone reached the same conclusion at once and Kass turned back to the bench and opened the wooden box stood there. A few moments later, and with everyone watching him he turned back to them. "There's two missing."

The silence in the room was full of shock. Wide eyes stared back at him from all of those in front of him.

"Oh my good God," George Brooker spoke for them all. "What have you done?"

XVIII.

Squire Fox fell into the Void and immediately struggled to get his bearings. He looked and found to his amazement that Sasha was still in his arms, her head bowed just as before.

"Sasha," he called at the top of her head. The head in his arm lifted and he was looking into a familiar face he hadn't seen like that in two years. Her eyes focused on his and they were clear and alert although he had no idea if she realised where she was. Her long brown hair billowed around her as they travelled the Void.

He spoke on, urgently and as clearly as he could. "Sasha, think of your sister. Take me to her."

She nodded twice, two brief movements and then closed her eyes. She understood. The corners of her mouth formed a smile.

Squire added for good measure, "Sasha, right now."

She felt him, knew he was here again. She couldn't see him or hear him but still she sensed him there; falling. There was something else this time, her sister was with him and she knew her as well as anyone.

She reached out with all her emotions and stretched out her hand to the unseen presence. They were coming. Her heart ached in desperate relief.

She knew she had to hang on longer but her lungs were screaming for air. Her temples throbbed with every slowing heartbeat and her chest convulsed trying to force her to breathe the air she didn't have.

Things were going dark and she knew she would pass out soon. Her chest convulsed so hard she blew out bubbles of exhausted air from her lungs. She saw the bubbles rising above her but still she refused to let herself breathe in the liquid death that surrounded her.

She couldn't hold on any longer; she reached her hand up in her final moments of consciousness.

The dreary garden of George Brooker's Manor House materialised around Squire and Sasha. The colours were all washed out and wrong. The lawn was a miserable grey-green and the sky was a dismal imitation of the glorious summer day it should have been. The whole place was deserted and silent. The barbeques and tables were laid out but there was no one in sight. As soon as his feet were on the ground Squire put Sasha down on her feet and he ran.

The pool was in sight and he was in full flow in seconds. He was out of shape and his legs soon started to complain and his clogged up lungs ran out of steam all too quickly. He didn't let up and pressed on with legs that rapidly grew wooden and numb.

389

He could hear Sasha's bare feet padding on the grass behind him and he prayed they would be in time. She also struggled on legs that hadn't walked for two years, legs that were running from memory alone.

She looked up through the water at her outstretched hand but her vision was going dark. Wracking convulsions shook her body as it battled with her mind to make her breathe.

Suddenly a strong hand had her by the wrist and was hauling her up. Seconds later she broke the surface and her screaming lungs gulped in air in a noisy groan as it rushed past her throat.

Her olive skin was grey and her lips had a blue tinge and the air filled her aching chest making her head spin.

She gasped air repeatedly as her dying body refilled with oxygen. She was aware of hands hauling her out of the pool and laying her down at the side.

Her chest howled in pain from the burst of exertion but gradually she came to her senses and looked up to see her sister and Squire crouched next to her.

Their concerned faces were gazing at her and waiting for her to recover; then he was speaking. "Easy Steph, relax and breathe slow and deep."

The colour was coming back to her and her eyes were losing the panic stare they had a minute before. She was still panting; her shoulders pumping up and down, but she was feeling better with every breath. Her throat called out for a drink as it was dry and painful from the sudden force of air her body demanded.

"You found me," she panted and suddenly she burst into tears. Sasha joined in a second later and the sisters hugged in the miracle of being together again.

As he watched them he was filled with the most amazing of emotions. He had done something he never could have believed possible. A rare chance to speak to someone who had been lost to him forever. Now, as he watched the two sisters pour out their emotions on each other's shoulders he also noticed the difference in them; they were now both the same age. Steph had not changed at all but Sasha had aged another two years. This was going to take some explaining when they got back.

Knowing he was on limited time he looked at his watch; only a few minutes left.

"Steph, it's going to be okay now. You're going to be safe," Sasha was saying into her shoulder. "We can go home soon."

Concern suddenly appeared on Squire's face. "Oh crap," he said slowly.

The girls looked at him anxiously through tear streaked faces and puffy eyes. "What is it?" Sasha asked without letting go of her sister.

"The greatest prize requires the greatest sacrifice."

Squire let his troubled face relax and softened his tone. "It's nothing," he said. He reached for his bracelet and popped it open and then reaching forward he clipped it on to Steph's wrist.

Steph and Sasha watched his movements and realised immediately what the problem was. "You didn't bring a spare," Sasha said with eyes suddenly full of concern.

Steph also understood, "How are you going to get back?"

Squire offered them both a simple smile, "It's okay, it doesn't matter." Nodding almost just to himself he added, "I am the fool after all."

"What!" they said in unison. Steph couldn't believe the sudden twist of fate. She had waited all this time to be saved only to now lose her rescuer. The girls started crying again and reached out for him knowing he would soon be gone.

"Take it back," Steph pleaded and started to pull at the bracelet he had put on her only moments before.

Squire grabbed her hands and stopped her struggle. "No," he whispered calmly. "This is the way it was meant to be."

Once more he looked at his watch; the fifteen minutes were almost up. There was time for a brief hug with each of his sobbing friends and for his parting words. "Tell my girls I love them, and they are not to worry about me."

Two sobbing faces looked back at him. The joy of being re-united now mixed with the new sadness of loss.

Squire gave them a smile and they vanished before his eyes. He looked at the spot where they had been for several minutes unable to fully take in his situation. Now a watery patch of patio was the only sign that they had been there. He looked slowly at the dreary and empty garden of the Manor House for the last time and even as he did it started to fade. In less than a minute he was floating again in the swirling grey of the Void.

George Brooker paced around the barn, his face flushed with worry. So many times in the past Squire Fox had skirted around procedures and rules and this time was going to be the last. He had caused embarrassment for him in front of all the new members and he had no doubt the police would be involved and potentially the whole secrecy of the project blown apart.

Everyone else had gathered at the entrance side of the barn except for Kass, who was over at the bench looking at the monitors. "Couple more minutes," he called to the others, and he turned and walked back to them to await the return of his brother. As he got back to Anna he whispered, "Why do I have such a bad feeling about this?"

Paige also heard the whisper and she and Anna were both at full attention. She scanned the room again although she already knew that everyone else connected with the team were there and waiting for answers too.

"What's he doing this time?" Anna's whisper was a little too loud and attracted attention from some of the others. There was no time for further questions though as the electro-magnets started to cycle up like two tiny jet engines.

Everyone turned to the centre cross and waited. Justin was already trying to come up with a peaceful way to calm George down from the torrent of words he knew would be arriving shortly.

The female computer voice then spoke into the barn.

Target red: Acquired

Target black: Acquired

Withdrawing Targets

The two magnets peaked momentarily in a high pitched hum that reverberated around the barn; followed by a 'popping' sound.

As the magnets started to slow down everyone stared with wide eyed shock at the scene before them. Steph sat on the floor in a wet black swimsuit and was in the arms of her sister in her pyjamas and dressing gown. Both were sobbing loudly.

The silence in the room was only interrupted by the ticking of the clock. Finally, Ted exclaimed "What in the name of God?"

George stood where he was with his eyebrows high and his eyes wide in shock. "Impossible," he mumbled to no one in particular.

Movement broke out very slowly; no one really knew what to do. Anna approached the girls slowly with concern all over her face. She moved like she didn't believe what she was actually seeing, but when she reached the girls she slowly put her hand on Steph's shoulder.

The shock all around the room was starting to turn to emotion. Paige and Daisy were starting to realise something amazing had happened that had a terrible twist to it. They and everyone else saw a dead girl come back to life in front of their eyes.

The room was suddenly full of commotion as people started to respond out of their shocked state and try desperately to understand what had happened. Gently everything turned to chaos around them. Tom and Ryan ran back to the farmhouse on Anna's instructions to fetch blankets for the girls while Ashley and Shine tried in vain to comfort them.

Justin, Tinker and Kass were debating loudly and had been joined by Ted and a very pale George.

The quietest members of the team were Paige, Daisy and Bailey. The others' main focus was on the miracle that had landed in the barn; theirs was on the one who was missing. Finally, Paige could wait no longer and headed over to Steph and Sasha. Squatting down next to Anna she spoke to them gently, but firmly, "Where is my dad?"

Even though the question was not said loudly everyone in the room heard it. All eyes and ears were suddenly focused on the centre of the room.

"He only had two bracelets," Sasha cried. "He's still in there."

There were groans and despair now as the attention shifted away from the girls and to their missing friend. People turned to face each other and all the expressions were of confusion and hopelessness. It was Bailey who turned and acted first.

Immediately she started strapping on her guns and called to Kass, "Send me in."

Kass tried to think but everything was happening too fast. "We don't know where he is," he responded with a look of resignation on his face.

Bailey was taking two bracelets and scanning them in. "Send me in, now!" The last word was shouted and she looked fiercely at Kass, and then looked away.

"Target blue: Locked in."

"Target orange: Locked in."

He followed her eyes to where they settled on Paige and Daisy. Their eyes were looking back at Bailey imploring her to do something and suddenly Kass felt terrible. There he was giving reasons why they couldn't go searching the Void when they had lost their father. He broke into action and headed for the monitors.

"I want a team ready to follow when we get back," he called as he tapped away on the keyboard.

He set the clock and his watch for thirty minutes and pulled another bracelet from the box. Bailey was already standing in the centre of the room and people were helping Steph and Sasha to their feet and out of the way.

"Target yellow: Locked in."

Kass went to join Bailey and they both turned to the clock. "Only three minutes," he said to her. "Try and relax quickly so we don't miss this peak."

She nodded back and allowed her eyes to stare ahead and tried to blank everything else out.

"I'm going to need some silence please," Kass called out and the room fell quiet at once as everyone else virtually held their breath. All eyes were now on the two motionless figures in the middle of the room. The electro-magnets started up once more and grew steadily louder.

Magnetic Field: Alternating

Initiating Grab

The broken voice of Daisy called out an instant before they vanished from the room. "Please bring him back."

He drifted for an age, or maybe it was only minutes. He had no idea how much time had passed.

Pain and sorrow filled him as he thought of Paige and Daisy back home. He didn't think he had ever felt a loss so great and his mind could not take the suffering his choices would cause them. He tumbled through the Void like a dead leaf falling from a tree in autumn, spinning his way down into nothing.

He also thought of Steph and Sasha arriving safely in the barn and hoped they would be okay. Surely one of them would be able to raise the alarm and they would get the help and support they were going to need.

His eyes were closed and he allowed his mind to go still and quiet; he wasn't really ready to take it all in.

As he fell through the emptiness he was suddenly aware that he wasn't alone. There was no one else around but he could feel it as surely as he felt the wind of the Void tearing at his hair and coat.

"Well, you sure showed me some moves today." The soothing sound of the old lady seemed to come from everywhere and nowhere and he relaxed. He was pleased she had come to him.

"So you are here as well as back there," he said with almost a little joy in his voice. "I suspect you are also somewhere else as well?"

The warmth and the friendliness in the old lady's voice grew, "Now what have I told you Mister?"

Squire Fox smiled, "I already know all the answers."

"Yes," she spoke softly, "I said exactly that. You have done well."

He thought for a minute about what he had actually achieved. "One life for two," he replied to the emptiness rushing past him. "I suppose I should be pleased with myself."

There was silence for a while, but then the voice returned. "I wasn't sure you had it in you, but you played your part well. You found the path that the wise will never find and you repaired that which could not be broken."

"So what happens now?" he called. "Do I get to find out who you really are? Do I get to finally see what lies beyond the Void?"

"Yes you do. Are you ready to see those things Mister?"

Squire thought for some time before answering again. "If you show me those things, I can't come back, can I?"

"You wouldn't want to," the voice in his head responded. "No one can return from where you go next. It is forbidden."

There was silence once again as the miles of Void unravelled before him but he was at peace as he fell. He was glad not to be alone for a while and he was in no rush for it to end.

"Mister, you must find the Dreamer."

"Oh yes," he replied softy. "I had almost forgotten about that bit." He still hadn't had time to come to terms with his situation but he also wanted to complete his work. "Which was my task? To find the Dreamer or mend what can't be broken?

"Both," she replied. "The Dreamer is an essential part of the puzzle and it was the sisters that got you here.

Squire was rather enjoying the conversation for a change and was pleased to get answers rather than riddles. "Got me here?" he asked.

"You know the answer to that too Mister, you just need to work it out. Without your devotion to them and your memories you would not have time jumped and you would not have had the weapons and tools to enable you to get this far."

He heard the truth in her words and expected there was far more to it than she had explained. "Elle," he began again, "was that you helping to control her when she went into a trance?"

"No Mister that was not me, but one far greater than I." The old lady's tone now changed. "There will be time for answers later. Now you must go to the Dreamer before she wakes."

Squire Fox knew the conversation was over and turned his mind to his next task. He closed his eyes.

Anna had taken Steph and Sasha to the farmhouse and was heating them some soup. They sat in the living room still wrapped in their blankets looking shell shocked. Their lives had changed very quickly and they were numb trying to put it all together.

Tinker had driven Ashley back to her house and she had collected enough clothes for the two girls to keep them going for the next day or so.

George Brooker had headed over to Highgate Hospital with Ted to explain the disappearance of Sasha. They had concocted a story on the way. Sasha had suddenly recovered and had left with Squire and was perfectly safe. They both knew it sounded terrible but it was going to have to do for now. If the police came to investigate they would indeed find Sasha safe and well; case closed.

Justin sat with Paige and Daisy in the kitchen and tried to comfort them. Their grief was difficult to fathom, like a parent of a missing child. They seemed to have hope but were still coming to terms with the chance that they would not see him again.

The lights in the farmhouse flickered announcing the return of Kass and Bailey. Everyone waited for news. The remainder of the team had all drawn lots to see who would go next and having lost the draw Ryan was acting as news runner.

Ten minutes later the lights dimmed and flickered again and the next team were away. Ryan was now in the living room and everyone who was around had gathered there to get an update.

"Well, no luck so far," Ryan began. "Kass has gone back in with Bailey again, and Tom and Shine have gone too." He let this sink in before continuing. "Bailey has been quite badly hurt though; they were attacked by a Fargle and it got her before she got it."

"Is she okay?" Paige asked, speaking for everyone.

"I think she will be alright," Ryan went on. "She got bitten on the shoulder pretty bad. She had blood down her front and back but Shine went in with her kit and was going to patch her up after they jumped out."

Anna was shaking her head slowly. "I think this is going to be a long night." She turned to Steph and Sasha. "Right you two, up to bed with you."

Ryan added, "If we get any news we will come and wake you. Don't worry."

"I'll stay with them," Daisy volunteered and got to her feet to show them upstairs.

"So will I," Ashley also got to her feet and waited for the others.

Anna cleared the soup bowls away and said "Take them to my room. I won't be needing it tonight."

Daisy led them away and up the stairs in convoy. Once they reached the main bedroom Ashley dug into the bag she had hastily packed and pulled out a couple of long nightshirts. "These will do you for tonight," she said and the four of them went about settling down.

Steph and Sasha were soon wrapped up in bed and Ashley and Daisy sat on each side. There was no way they were going to be able to sleep; too much had happened so they talked quietly and the night wore slowly on.

The bedside lamp flickered for a few seconds marking the return of the second trip and fifteen minutes later it did it again. The girls waited for their turn with the news knowing those downstairs would be catching up first.

A few minutes later Shine came in quietly and seeing they were all awake went and sat on the bed next to Ashley. Her shirt, arms and hands were blood stained and she looked tired.

The second trip also had no success but the third crew had gone in with grim determination.

"What happened to you?" Ashley asked looking at her battered appearance.

"Oh," Shine said, lifting her hands to look at them. "It's not me, this is from Bailey. She's going to need stitches for that bite she got. I couldn't stop it bleeding but she's patched up well enough for now."

"Who went back in this time?" Daisy asked.

"Oh, well, Kass was exhausted and handed leadership to Bailey, but he's going to look after things from the barn. So it's Bailey, Ryan, Elle and Paige."

"What!" Daisy exclaimed. "My sister's gone in?"

Shine tried to pacify her shocked friends. "George wasn't happy about it, but Justin and Kass said she stood a better chance of being able to locate her father with her mind, or maybe he will come to her. It's been a strange night so I think almost anything goes from now on."

After another fifteen minutes of chatting about their last trip, Ashley said she needed to go and get ready for her turn. She told Daisy she would do her best and left them together on the bed. Sasha had fallen asleep at last and the others talked now only in hushed whispers.

All Squire Fox needed to do was to find Bailey with his mind. He had found it easy to locate her in the Void from the very first jump they had made together. With his eyes closed he just thought of her and pictured her like he had done before. It wasn't long before he picked up her presence and allowed himself to be taken to her.

The supermarket aisle Squire found himself in was not very busy. In fact, it was almost deserted. At one end there was a boy band singing a song he didn't know. They were all dressed in black suits and clicking their fingers to the beat. There was no band in sight but music came from somewhere.

Walking the other way and around the corner Squire found who he was looking for, although the sight was a little strange.

Bailey Moreton stood gazing at the shelves and rubbing her chin trying to decide what to pick. She had a shopping trolley with her and in the child seat was a big white rabbit on a red lead and who was marking off items on a shopping list.

Squire wandered over and stood next to her and noticed the faraway look in her eyes. She was wearing a lavish red ball gown and white gloves and holding a pack of fish fingers.

"Hello Dreamer," he said calmly.

She turned to look at him with eyes that went straight through him. "Have you come to help me with the shopping," she asked. "I don't know what to pick and I've got the Queen coming for dinner."

Squire was overjoyed to see her again and also wondered if it would be the last time. "No, I'm sorry I haven't come to do shopping today," he replied, "although I would give the fish fingers a miss to be honest."

She looked at the packet in her hand and then slowly put it back on the shelf. "Bouncy thought she would like fish fingers."

Squire looked at the rabbit in the trolley and realised who Bouncy was. Turning back to her he asked, "Do you know me?"

She looked at him again, then at the rabbit who simply shrugged his shoulders at her.

"I'm Squire Fox," he said. There was no recognition on her face at all and her eyes stayed fixed in a dreamy, far away stare. "Some things that cannot be broken can be repaired," he said in clear, slow words. There was no reaction again but Squire already knew she would remember and tell him those same words in another two years. "I have to say goodbye now Bailey," he smiled at her one last time. "Now it's time for you to wake up."

Looking down she noticed a chrome tube like device in his hand. It opened slowly and she stared at it, transfixed. Suddenly everything went white. Within five seconds everything had faded away as Bailey's dream came to an abrupt end.

A very long way away 22-year-old Bailey Moreton woke up with a start. Something about the Queen and her rabbit and Squire Fox saying "Some things that cannot be broken can be repaired." She lay in her bed wondering what that meant, repeating it to herself over and over. Finally, she tried to get back to sleep; and who the hell was Squire Fox anyway?

The lights in the farmhouse would flicker on and off for the remainder of the night until Paige finally asked everyone to stop.

"I know you are all trying your best to help but there is no use killing ourselves trying to do it," she told them.

Bailey had needed help getting to the kitchen and into a chair having gone on every jump throughout the night. She had been up over twenty-four hours and was also bleeding badly.

Ashley and Shine had removed her blood soaked jacket and were cleaning the wound on her shoulder and trying to stop the bleeding. Ted had looked in to supervise and was happy that everything looked clean and that no stitches would be needed. Shine applied butterfly tape over the bite cuts and they carefully bandaged her up.

Her vest top was soaked in blood down one side, but Bailey was falling asleep where she sat so they guided her to a chair in the living room and settled her down and wrapped her in a blanket. She mumbled to herself as sleep finally came to her bring her rest, "Where are you?"

When the sun came up not long after Bailey went to sleep most of the team had gathered in the lounge looking weary and downcast. They all needed sleep badly but didn't want to close the door on the previous day just yet.

Steph had come downstairs leaving her sister sleeping. She felt horribly responsible and wanted to be able to help. "When I was in the Void," she started, "I could feel when Squire was there." All eyes had turned to her and even though the others were exhausted they listened carefully. "I want to join the team and see if I can help find him."

Justin looked up from his coffee, "We don't need to rush into any quick decisions," he said quietly, "but thank you for your offer."

Daisy's eyes were red and puffy and she was too emotional from the events of last night to do anything except stare ahead in a silent trance. "We'll be okay," Paige assured her and rubbed her shoulder. "We are going to find him."

George Brooker was still pale and looked in shock. "For now Kass will run the Void Runners." He looked up and found him silently sitting in his chair with Anna at his side. "May I suggest though," George added hesitantly, "that every team from now on take an extra bracelet with them. When we find him we can bring him home."

Kass nodded his agreement and massaged his tired forehead with his fingers. "Somehow he found a way to do the impossible last night," he looked at the tired faces around him, "but we don't know how." He paused to let his words sink in. "We have to learn to do the same."

"We lost the Catching," Elle said quietly from where she lay on the floor. Tinker shifted awkwardly in his chair and a hope sprung up in his mind only to be dashed a second later. "I can't make another one," he said. All eyes turned to him then. "We don't have anyone on the other side like we did before."

It was true and the news was an additional shock to a team already rocked by bad news.

"We'll find another way then," Tom added trying to be positive. "So many amazing things have happened this week; nothing is impossible." Those gathered would take comfort with that thought.

"My brother did say he thought there was another way," Kass added. "Unfortunately he is not here to tell us what he was thinking."

From the chair where she slept Bailey murmured "Some things that can't be broken," before falling silent again.

The Void rushed past silently and endlessly and Squire Fox tumbled without purpose or direction. He had no idea how long he had been falling and didn't care. He heard flashes of voices in his head but deliberately ignored them all. For now, he didn't have the energy for anything.

He became aware at some point that he was not alone as the miles flew past him and he roused himself once more. "Do you have more for me to do?"

There was no reply to his question for a long time and he wondered if he had been mistaken, but finally he did get one. "No Mister, you have done everything." The old West Indian lady's voice had found him once again and he was pleased.

"Then you have come to take me," he replied. He felt he was ready. He was tired beyond belief and had no regrets.

"Yes Mister," the smooth voice came back to him as unhurried as always. "You have earned your rest."

The giant expanse of the Void lay before him and waves of tiredness washed over him. "Come with me now Edward Fox."

At the sound of that name he smiled and a lightness filled his heart. Squire Fox closed his eyes and drifted away.

The Void Runners continues in The Journey

Epilogue

The weeks and months following that evening were intense for everyone involved with the Void Runners.

Kass Fox was offered the position of chairman, but declined in order to continue his work and research at the barn. The position then fell to Justin. He would also decline, feeling that it would be wrong for the humble church pastor to be living in mansion like comfort.

Finally, Ted Dawes stepped forward to be caretaker chairman until such time as someone better able was found. He moved into the Manor House soon after and would soon be finding his evenings occupied playing chess with George Brooker.

There was indeed quite an inquest into the sudden awakening of Sasha Gentry which led to exhaustive tests. The hospital could not explain how her mind had suddenly awakened and professionals were called in from London. Sasha kept the truth out of all the questioning and finally the case was closed. Whilst there was a mention of it in a medical journal the event was considered 'not newsworthy' by the media. The doctor who had dismissed Squire Fox's claim that Sasha had spoken was severely reprimanded and Mr Fox vindicated.

Steph was good to her word and joined the Void Runners. After some time rehabilitating she ran the testing and passed with flying colours. Both she and Sasha moved into the Manor House but did not learn to play chess. Their parents had left the area a year after Sasha had been admitted to Highgate Mental Hospital finding the memories too painful to be around. They had not visited since then and were not told that both their daughters had returned at the request of the girls.

Tom Stonley took a senior role within the team and would soon be leading groups entering the Void. His relationship with Ryan flourished and they became almost like brothers.

Ashley and Shine continued to live in Orchard Close and worked hard at their medical studies alongside Ted's team at Mendip Hospital. They also continued their roles within the team but were not called on often for emergency assistance.

Bailey Moreton struggled for many months to recover from the events of that evening. She lost her dominance for a time but would regain her confidence and determination after the initial shock had passed. She alternated living between Orchard Close and The Lair in Shillyford to support and comfort Paige and Daisy Fox.

It was no surprise that Paige joined the Void Runners straight after losing her father and it was no time at all before it was clear she had the same traits. Almost at once she began a long lasting habit of failing to follow procedures. Daisy continued as researcher but turned rather reclusive and quiet. Even with the combined efforts of her sister and Bailey to encourage her she continued to mourn the loss of her father.

Paul McCoy continued his efforts to create gadgets for the team but everything became more difficult without the input of Sasha and Steph. His creations were taken into the Void by Steph but not with the same success as before.

The teams carried out more runs than ever before in the hope of finding their lost friend. They adapted their visits to the task in hand and closed their minds to all other voices and sounds except the one they searched for. As suggested, an extra bracelet was always taken with them just in case contact was made with Squire Fox, but after months of searching no trace was found.

INDEX

- Anna Fox (33) Wife to Kass. Lives at The Farmhouse, Shillyford

- Ashley Lord (19) Void Runner. Special – Healer. Lives in Orchard Close, Shillyford.

- Bailey Moreton (24) *Dreamer*: Void Runner. Special – Guardian. Lives in Orchard Close, Shillyford.

- Daisy Fox (16) Researcher for the Void Runner Team. Daughter of Squire. Lives at The Lair, Shillyford.

- *Dreamer* (24) Bailey Moreton

- Elle Naylor (15) Void Runner. Special – Spirit. Daughter of Justin and Sarah. Studies at Highgate Upper School.

- Emily Watts (18) *Shine*: Void Runner. Special – Healer. Lives in Orchard Close, Shillyford

- George Brooker (72) Chairman of the Void Runner team. Lives at The Manor House, Shillyford

- Jennifer Fox (d) Wife of Squire. Mother of Paige and Daisy. Lost in the Void.

- Justin Naylor (34) Religious head of the Void Runner team. Pastor of New Hope Church, Shillyford. Husband to Sarah. Father to Elle.

- Kassidy Fox (35) *Kass*: Void Runner. Special – Genius. Husband of Anna. Lives at The Farmhouse, Shillyford.
- Lydia Barnes (19) Art student. Lives in Shillyford
- *Master* (d) Founder of the Void. Lost in the Void
- Paige Fox (18) Security: Void Runner team. Daughter of Squire. Lives at The Lair, Shillyford.
- Paul McCoy (52) *Tinker*: Special equipment maker and provider for the Void Runner team.
- Ryan Grey (26) Void Runner. Special - Guardian
- Sarah Naylor (32) Wife of Justin
- Sasha Gentry (16) Cared for by Highgate Mental Institution
- *Shine* (18) Emily Watts
- Steph Gentry (d) Student. Died at George Brooker's 70th Birthday Party
- Squire Fox (48) *Squire*: Void Runner. Special – Leader. Father of Paige and Daisy Fox. Lives at The Lair, Shillyford.
- Ted Dawes (53) Medical Director for the Void Runners and of Mendip Private Hospital
- *Tinker* (52) Paul McCoy
- Tom Stonley (21) Void Runner. Special - Spirit

Lightning Source UK Ltd.
Milton Keynes UK
UKOW05n1339211016

285857UK00001B/6/P